Covariances in Computer Vision and Machine Learning

Synthesis Lectures on Computer Vision

Editors
Gérard Medioni, *University of Southern California*
Sven Dickinson, *University of Toronto*

Synthesis Lectures on Computer Vision is edited by Gérard Medioni of the University of Southern California and Sven Dickinson of the University of Toronto. The series publishes 50–150 page publications on topics pertaining to computer vision and pattern recognition. The scope will largely follow the purview of premier computer science conferences, such as ICCV, CVPR, and ECCV. Potential topics include, but not are limited to:

- Applications and Case Studies for Computer Vision

- Color, Illumination, and Texture

- Computational Photography and Video

- Early and Biologically-inspired Vision

- Face and Gesture Analysis

- Illumination and Reflectance Modeling

- Image-Based Modeling

- Image and Video Retrieval

- Medical Image Analysis

- Motion and Tracking

- Object Detection, Recognition, and Categorization

- Segmentation and Grouping

- Sensors

- Shape-from-X

- Stereo and Structure from Motion

- Shape Representation and Matching

- Statistical Methods and Learning

- Performance Evaluation

- Video Analysis and Event Recognition

Covariances in Computer Vision and Machine Learning

Hà Quang Minh and Vittorio Murino

ISBN: 978-3-031-00692-0   paperback
ISBN: 978-3-031-01820-6   ebook

DOI 10.1007/978-3-031-01820-6

A Publication in the Springer series
SYNTHESIS LECTURES ON COMPUTER VISION

Lecture #13
Series Editors: Gérard Medioni, *University of Southern California*
                 Sven Dickinson, *University of Toronto*
Series ISSN
Print 2153-1056   Electronic 2153-1064

Covariances in Computer Vision and Machine Learning

Hà Quang Minh
Istituto Italiano di Tecnologia

Vittorio Murino
Istituto Italiano di Tecnologia
and
University of Verona

SYNTHESIS LECTURES ON COMPUTER VISION #13

ABSTRACT

Covariance matrices play important roles in many areas of mathematics, statistics, and machine learning, as well as their applications. In computer vision and image processing, they give rise to a powerful data representation, namely the covariance descriptor, with numerous practical applications.

In this book, we begin by presenting an overview of the *finite-dimensional covariance matrix* representation approach of images, along with its statistical interpretation. In particular, we discuss the various distances and divergences that arise from the intrinsic geometrical structures of the set of Symmetric Positive Definite (SPD) matrices, namely Riemannian manifold and convex cone structures. Computationally, we focus on kernel methods on covariance matrices, especially using the Log-Euclidean distance.

We then show some of the latest developments in the generalization of the finite-dimensional covariance matrix representation to the *infinite-dimensional covariance operator* representation via positive definite kernels. We present the generalization of the affine-invariant Riemannian metric and the Log-Hilbert-Schmidt metric, which generalizes the Log-Euclidean distance. Computationally, we focus on kernel methods on covariance operators, especially using the Log-Hilbert-Schmidt distance. Specifically, we present a two-layer kernel machine, using the Log-Hilbert-Schmidt distance and its finite-dimensional approximation, which reduces the computational complexity of the exact formulation while largely preserving its capability. Theoretical analysis shows that, mathematically, the approximate Log-Hilbert-Schmidt distance should be preferred over the approximate Log-Hilbert-Schmidt inner product and, computationally, it should be preferred over the approximate affine-invariant Riemannian distance.

Numerical experiments on image classification demonstrate significant improvements of the infinite-dimensional formulation over the finite-dimensional counterpart. Given the numerous applications of covariance matrices in many areas of mathematics, statistics, and machine learning, just to name a few, we expect that the infinite-dimensional covariance operator formulation presented here will have many more applications beyond those in computer vision.

KEYWORDS

covariance descriptors in computer vision, positive definite matrices, infinite-dimensional covariance operators, positive definite operators, Hilbert-Schmidt operators, Riemannian manifolds, affine-invariant Riemannian distance, Log-Euclidean distance, Log-Hilbert-Schmidt distance, convex cone, Bregman divergences, kernel methods on Riemannian manifolds, visual object recognition, image classification

Contents

Acknowledgments

In preparing this book, the authors are indebted to the work carried out over the years by many other researchers from various different fields, whose contributions have all helped make the current topic an active research area. We also wish to thank the anonymous reviewers for their many valuable comments and suggestions which helped us improve the book. Last but not least, we wish to thank the series editors Gérald Medioni and Sven Dickinson, as well as the team at Morgan & Claypool, in particular Diane Cerra and Christine Kiilerich, for helping us bring this book to fruition.

Hà Quang Minh and Vittorio Murino
October 2017

Introduction

Symmetric Positive Definite (SPD) matrices, in particular covariance matrices, play an important role in many areas of mathematics, statistics, and their applications in many disciplines in science and engineering. The practical applications of SPD matrices are numerous, including Diffusion Tensor Imaging (DTI) in brain imaging [5, 29, 66, 95], kernel learning [2, 60] in machine learning, radar signal processing [3, 9, 40], and Brain Computer Interface (BCI) applications [7, 8, 24, 100].

In the field of computer vision and image processing, covariance matrices have recently emerged as a powerful approach for data representation. In the simplest setting in this approach, a 2D image is represented by a covariance matrix, called its *covariance descriptor*, encoding correlations between different, typically low-level, features extracted from that image. This representation is compact, robust to noise, and is flexible in its ability to combine various different image features together. Practically, the covariance matrix representation of images has been demonstrated to work very well and as a consequence, it has been generalized for representing videos, 3D shapes, and 3D point clouds. The successful applications of the covariance matrix representation are many, including tracking [50, 94], object detection and classification [120, 122, 123], face recognition [20, 46, 72, 73, 90, 108, 125, 127], emotion recognition [134], texture classification [19, 20, 72, 108], image retrieval [21], image set classification [34, 51, 52, 127], video surveillance [119, 120], action recognition [41, 46, 101, 133], activity recognition [125], person re-identification [19, 20, 46, 73], and 3D vision [20, 23, 35, 36, 48, 115, 116]. Recently, apart from low-level features, covariance matrices of convolutional features have also been employed, both directly [126], and as parts of deep networks with end-to-end-learning [53, 131].

Finite-dimensional covariance matrices. Mathematically, covariance matrices, properly regularized if necessary, are SPD matrices, whose properties must be considered for optimal design of numerical algorithms. Our focus here is on the geometrical structures of SPD matrices and how to exploit them algorithmically. The set $\mathrm{Sym}^{++}(n)$ of all $n \times n$ SPD matrices is not a vector subspace of Euclidean space under the standard matrix addition and scalar multiplication operations. Instead, it is an open convex cone, since it is only closed under positive scalar multiplication. At the same time, it also admits a smooth manifold structure and can be endowed with a Riemannian metric. Consequently, in general, the optimal measure of similarity between covariance matrices is not the Euclidean distance, but a distance/similarity measure that captures the intrinsic geometrical structures of $\mathrm{Sym}^{++}(n)$. Among the most widely used Riemannian metrics for $\mathrm{Sym}^{++}(n)$ is the classical *affine-invariant Riemannian metric* [10, 11, 65, 86, 92, 123], under which $\mathrm{Sym}^{++}(n)$ becomes a Riemannian manifold with nonpositive sectional curvature. Another commonly used Riemannian metric for $\mathrm{Sym}^{++}(n)$ is the recently introduced *bi-invariant* Log-Euclidean metric [5, 6], under which the manifold is flat, that is having zero sectional curvature. Compared to the affine-invariant Riemaian metric, the Log-Euclidean metric is faster to compute, especially on large datasets. Furthermore, the Log-Euclidean metric endows $\mathrm{Sym}^{++}(n)$ with a vector space and inner product structure, turning it into an inner product space. Thus, it can be used to define many positive definite kernels, such as the Gaussian kernel, allowing kernel methods to be applied directly on the manifold [55, 72, 120]. Another approach that is different from the Riemannian metric approach utilizes the Bregman divergences, e.g., Alpha Log-Det divergences [18], with the symmetric Stein divergence [110] as a special case, which exploit the convex cone structure of $\mathrm{Sym}^{++}(n)$. These divergences are not Riemannian metrics but also possess desirable theoretical properties, are efficient to compute, and have been shown to work well on various applications, see, e.g., [21, 60, 128].

From finite-dimensional covariance matrices to infinite-dimensional covariance operators. Despite their effectiveness in many applications, one major limitation of covariance matrices is that they only encode *linear* correlations between the original input features. The desire to encode *nonlinear* input correlations motivated the generalization of the covariance matrix representation framework to the infinite-dimensional setting by the use of positive definite kernels, as follows.

As is widely known in kernel-based machine learning [103, 104], each positive definite kernel on the original input features of an image, such as the Gaussian kernel, induces a feature map that nonlinearly maps each input point into a high- (generally infinite) dimensional feature space. The covariance matrix of the infinite-dimensional and highly nonlinear features in the feature space, which is an *infinite-dimensional covariance operator*, then encodes the nonlinear correlations between the original input features. This infinite-dimensional covariance operator is then used as the representation for the image. In the exact formulation, this representation is *implicit* and all necessary computations are carried out via the Gram matrices corresponding with the given kernels.

As in the finite-dimensional setting, the geometrical structures of infinite-dimensional covariance operators play a crucial role in the design of numerical algorithms. Regularized infinite-dimensional covariance operators are positive definite operators, which form a convex cone and an *infinite-dimensional smooth manifold*. The generalizations of the affine-invariant Riemannian metric, Log-Euclidean metric, and Bregman divergences to the infinite-dimensional setting have all been mathematically developed recently, with the first due to [64] in the general Hilbert space setting and [78] in the RKHS setting, and the latter two due to [75, 76, 79, 80] (see also related work in [44, 135]). In particular, in [76], we introduced the Log-Hilbert-Schmidt metric, which generalizes the Log-Euclidean metric in [6] and allows kernel methods to be applied directly on the manifold of positive definite operators.

Numerical experiments to date have indicated that the results obtained by kernel methods using the Log-Hilbert-Schmidt metric and infinite-dimensional covariance operators substantially outperform those obtained using Log-Euclidean metric and finite-dimensional covariance matrices. However, this comes with a considerably higher computational cost, especially on large data sets. To overcome this issue, recently we introduced an approximate version of the Log-Hilbert-Schmidt metric [84], which is more efficient computationally while at the same time maintaining an effective discriminative capability.

Aims of the book.   The following are the two principal aims of the current book.

1. We aim to provide a methodical overview of the finite-dimensional matrix representation approach along with the geometry of SPD matrices. Computationally, we focus on kernel methods on covariance matrices.

2. We aim to present some of the latest developments, both mathematically and computationally, on the infinite-dimensional covariance operator representation and the geometry of positive definite operators. Computationally, we focus on kernel methods on covariance operators. A large portion of the material in this part of the book has been developed by the authors and collaborators.

   It is worth pointing out that, compared to the finite-dimensional case, the mathematical theory in the infinite-dimensional setting dated from very recently and is still undergoing active development at the time of writing.

Organization of the book.   This book consists of two parts, arranged as follows.

Part I: Covariance Matrices and Applications.

- In Chapter 1, "Data Representation by Covariance Matrices," we present an overview of the finite-dimensional covariance matrix representation, along with its connection to the estimation of covariance matrices of multivariate Gaussian probability density functions.

- In Chapter 2, "Geometry of SPD Matrices," we present an overview of the various distances and divergences between SPD matrices, including Euclidean distance, affine-invariant Riemannian distance, Log-Euclidean distance, and Alpha Log-Determinant divergences (which include the symmetric Stein divergence as a special case). We discuss their different invariance properties, along with the corresponding interpretations, and their connections to different distances/divergences between multivariate Gaussian probability density functions. Also briefly discussed are the highly general Alpha-Beta Log-Det divergences, which include both the affine-invariant Riemannian distance and Alpha Log-Determinant divergences as special cases, and the power Euclidean distance, which includes the Log-Euclidean distance as a special case.

- In Chapter 3, "Kernel Methods on Covariance Matrices," we describe kernel methods on covariance matrices using the Euclidean distance/inner product, and more importantly, the Log-Euclidean distance/inner product. Numerical experiments in image classification are presented.

Part II: Covariance Operators and Applications.

- In Chapter 4, "Data Representation by Covariance Operators," we generalize the covariance matrix representation in Part I to the infinite-dimensional setting, via infinite-dimensional feature maps associated with positive definite kernels.

- In Chapter 5, "Geometry of Covariance Operators," we present several geometrical structures of positive Hilbert-Schmidt operators and positive trace class operators, along with the corresponding distances, divergences, and inner products, namely (i) Hilbert-Schmidt distance and inner product; (ii) Affine-invariant Riemannian distance; (iii) Log-Hilbert-Schmidt distance and inner product; and (iv) Alpha Log-Determinant divergences. We show in particular how they can be evaluated, via closed form expressions of Gram matrices, in the case of RKHS covariance operators.

- In Chapter 6, "Kernel Methods on Covariance Operators," we present the following concepts.

  - A two-layer kernel machine using the Hilbert-Schmidt distance/inner product and, more importantly, the Log-Hilbert-Schmidt distance/inner product.

  - A two-layer kernel machine with the finite-dimensional approximate Log-Hilbert-Schmidt distance.

  - Convergence analysis of the approximate Log-Hilbert-Schmidt distance, the approximate Log-Hilbert-Schmidt inner product, and the approximate affine-invariant Riemannian distance. These convergences are all non-trivial and, in particular, we show why, mathematically, we prefer the approximate Log-Hilbert-Schmidt distance over the approximate Log-Hilbert-Schmidt inner product.

  - Numerical experiments in image classification.

Finally, Appendix A contains further technical material and mathematical proofs.

PART I

Covariance Matrices and Applications

CHAPTER 1

Data Representation by Covariance Matrices

We begin by describing the covariance matrix framework for image representation and its generalization to the representation of videos and 3D objects. We then present a statistical interpretation of this framework, which shows that assuming that an image can be represented by a covariance matrix is essentially equivalent to assuming that its features are random variables generated by a multivariate Gaussian probability distribution with mean zero. We discuss two different empirical estimates of the covariance matrix of this distribution which are commonly used in practice, namely the maximum likelihood estimate (MLE) and the unbiased estimate, along with their theoretical properties. By representing images as covariance matrices, similarity measures between images can then be chosen to be distances/divergences between the corresponding covariance matrices, or equivalently, distances/divergences between the corresponding multivariate Gaussian probability distributions, which will be presented in Chapter 2.

1.1 COVARIANCE MATRICES FOR DATA REPRESENTATION

Covariance matrix representation of images.   Covariance matrices were first proposed as region descriptors for images in [122], with application in object detection and texture classification, and [94], with application in tracking. The covariance matrix framework for image representation proceeds as follows. For each image F, at every pixel (or a subset of the pixels), we extract a feature vector consisting of n features, for example intensity, gradient, colors, and filter responses. Suppose that we perform feature extraction at m pixels, with each pixel giving a feature vector $x_i \in \mathbb{R}^n$, $i = 1, \ldots, m$, we then obtain a data matrix of size $n \times m$, given by

$$\mathbf{X} = [x_1, \ldots, x_m], \tag{1.1}$$

with each column consisting of features extracted at the ith pixel.

We define the *empirical mean* of the data matrix $\mathbf{X}$ to be the $n \times 1$ vector

$$\mu_{\mathbf{X}} = \frac{1}{m} \sum_{i=1}^{m} x_i. \tag{1.2}$$

We define the *empirical covariance matrix* associated with the data matrix $\mathbf{X}$ to be the $n \times n$ matrix

$$C_{\mathbf{X}} = \frac{1}{m} \sum_{j=1}^{m} (x_j - \mu_{\mathbf{X}})(x_j - \mu_{\mathbf{X}})^T = \frac{1}{m} \mathbf{X} J_m \mathbf{X}^T. \tag{1.3}$$

The covariance matrix $C_{\mathbf{X}}$ is then used as the representation for the image F and we call $C_{\mathbf{X}}$ the *covariance descriptor* of F.

In Eq. (1.3), the $m \times m$ matrix J_m is the column centering matrix, defined by

$$J_m = I_m - \frac{1}{m} \mathbf{1}_m \mathbf{1}_m^T, \quad \text{where} \quad \mathbf{1}_m = (1, \dots, 1)^T \in \mathbb{R}^m.$$

It is a symmetric, positive semi-definite matrix, with the property that $J_m^2 = J_m$. Given any matrix $A \in \mathbb{R}^{n \times m}$, the right multiplication with J_m gives the matrix $A J_m$, which is obtained by subtracting from A its mean column. It is straightforward to see from Eq. (1.3) that $C_{\mathbf{X}}$ is a symmetric, positive *semi-definite* matrix. Furthermore, it can be readily verified that 0 is an eigenvalue of J_m, with corresponding eigenvector $\mathbf{1}_m$, and 1 is an eigenvalue of J_m of multiplicity $m - 1$, with the corresponding eigenspace being the subspace of $\mathbb{R}^m$ orthogonal to $\mathbf{1}_m$, hence $\text{rank}(J_m) = m - 1$. Consequently, $C_{\mathbf{X}}$ has rank at most $m - 1$.

Features for constructing covariance descriptors.   The following is an example of the features used for constructing covariance descriptors. Suppose that we are given a color image F. At the pixel at location (x, y) in the image F, we extract the following feature vector

$$\mathbf{f}(x, y) = \left[I(x, y), R(x, y), G(x, y), B(x, y), \left| \frac{\partial R}{\partial x} \right|, \left| \frac{\partial R}{\partial y} \right|, \left| \frac{\partial G}{\partial x} \right|, \left| \frac{\partial G}{\partial y} \right|, \left| \frac{\partial B}{\partial x} \right|, \left| \frac{\partial B}{\partial y} \right| \right], \tag{1.4}$$

where $I(x, y)$ denotes the intensity at pixel (x, y), R, G, and B denote the color channels red, green, blue, respectively, and the remaining terms denote the magnitudes of the partial derivatives of the three color channels. The feature vectors at all the pixels then form the data matrix $\mathbf{X}$, with each column of $\mathbf{X}$ corresponding to one feature vector, which, in this particular example, has dimension 10. One then forms the covariance matrix $C_{\mathbf{X}}$ by Eq. (1.3). For an example of the covariance matrix constructed by the features given in Eq. (1.4), see Figure 1.1.

A key property of covariance descriptors is the flexibility in choosing the features and hence in designing the descriptors themselves. Many other features have been utilized, including the location (x, y), the Gabor filters, SIFT, and, recently, convolutional features from deep learning.

Motivations for the covariance descriptor.   Before providing a statistical interpretation of the covariance descriptor $C_{\mathbf{X}}$ in Section 1.2, we list some of its motivations from the perspectives of computer vision, as follows.

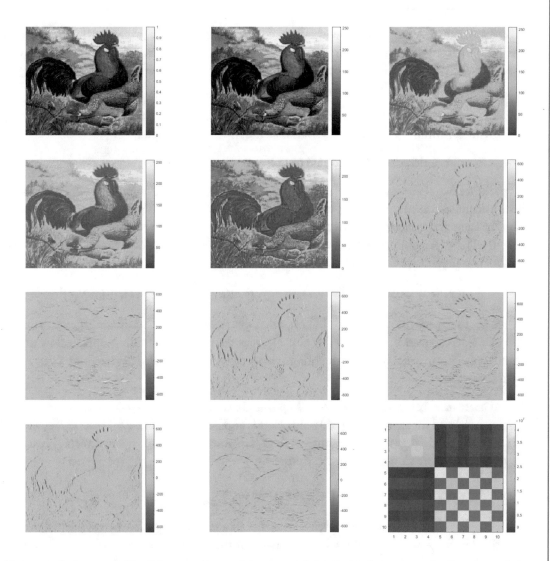

Figure 1.1: An example of the covariance descriptor. At each pixel (x, y), a 10-dimensional feature vector $\mathbf{f}(x, y) = [I(x, y), R(x, y), G(x, y), B(x, y), |\frac{\partial R}{\partial x}|, |\frac{\partial R}{\partial y}|, |\frac{\partial R}{\partial x}|, |\frac{\partial R}{\partial y}|, |\frac{\partial R}{\partial x}|, |\frac{\partial R}{\partial y}|]$ is extracted. From top to bottom, left to right: the original color image; the grayscale image I; the three color channels R (red), G (green), and (blue); the magnitudes of the partial derivatives $|\frac{\partial R}{\partial x}|, |\frac{\partial R}{\partial y}|, |\frac{\partial G}{\partial x}|, |\frac{\partial G}{\partial y}|, |\frac{\partial B}{\partial x}|, |\frac{\partial B}{\partial y}|$; and, finally, the 10×10 covariance matrix of these features.

1. Covariance descriptors encode *linear correlations (second-order statistics)* between all the different extracted features.

2. Covariance descriptors allow the flexibility in using multiple, different features and the ability to fuse them together. The features can be either the traditional handcrafted ones, such as colors or SIFT, or convolutional features that have emerged recently from deep learning.

3. The image representation by covariance matrices is compact (this, however, is not the case with the infinite-dimensional covariance descriptors in Chapter 4).

4. Covariance descriptors are robust to noise.

Covariance matrix representation for videos.   The covariance descriptors for 2D images have been generalized for representing videos, see e.g., [41, 101], which include a temporal dimension. In this case, it is necessary to employ features that capture the temporal information, such as optical flow. An example of a feature vector in this setting is the following (see, e.g., [41] for a more comprehensive feature vector)

$$\mathbf{f}(x, y, t) = [x, y, t, I_t(x, y, t), u(x, y, t), v(x, y, t), u_t(x, y, t), v_t(x, y, t)], \qquad (1.5)$$

where (x, y) denote the spatial coordinates, t denotes the temporal coordinate, $I(x, y, t)$ denotes the raw video sequence, $(u(x, y, t), v(x, y, t))$ denotes the corresponding optical flow at pixel position (x, y, t), with I_t, u_t, v_t denoting, respectively, the partial derivatives of I, u, and v, with respect to t.

Covariance matrix representation for 3D point clouds.   The covariance descriptors have also been generalized for representing 3D point clouds and 3D shapes, see, e.g., [23, 35, 36, 48, 115, 116]. In this setting, geometric features such as curvature and surface normal vectors have been employed to construct covariance descriptors.

1.2   STATISTICAL INTERPRETATION

We now provide a statistical interpretation of the image representation by covariance matrices described in Section 1.1. We show in particular that this representation is essentially equivalent to representing each image by a multivariate Gaussian distribution ρ with zero mean, with the empirical covariance matrix $C_{\mathbf{X}}$ being the maximum likelihood estimate of the covariance matrix C of ρ, given the data matrix $\mathbf{X}$. In this viewpoint, the feature vectors extracted from the image are random observations of an n-dimensional random vector with probability distribution ρ.

Let ρ be a Borel probability distribution on $\mathbb{R}^n$ with finite second moment, that is

$$\int_{\mathbb{R}^n} ||x||^2 d\rho(x) < \infty. \qquad (1.6)$$

Then its first moment is also finite and hence the mean vector

$$\mu = \int_{\mathbb{R}^n} x d\rho(x) \in \mathbb{R}^n \tag{1.7}$$

is well-defined. Moreover, ρ defines a unique $n \times n$ matrix C such that the following bilinear form from $\mathbb{R}^n \times \mathbb{R}^n \rightarrow \mathbb{R}$ is well-defined

$$\langle y, Cz \rangle = \int_{\mathbb{R}^n} \langle x - \mu, y \rangle \langle x - \mu, z \rangle d\rho(x), \quad y, z \in \mathbb{R}^n. \tag{1.8}$$

The matrix C is called the covariance matrix of ρ and is given by

$$C = \int_{\mathbb{R}^n} (x - \mu)(x - \mu)^T d\rho(x). \tag{1.9}$$

It is straightforward to see that C is a symmetric, positive semi-definite matrix.

Equivalently, let $X = (X_1, \ldots, X_n)$ be an n-dimensional random vector with probability distribution ρ, with each X_i, $1 \leq n$, being a real-valued random variable. Then μ is the expected value of X, that is

$$\mu = \mathbb{E}(X), \tag{1.10}$$

and C is its covariance matrix, with

$$C = \mathbb{E}[(X - \mu)(X - \mu)^T]. \tag{1.11}$$

The (i, i)th diagonal element of C, $1 \leq i \leq n$, given by

$$C_{ii} = \mathbb{E}[(X_i - \mu_i)^2] \tag{1.12}$$

is the *variance* of the random variable X_i, and the (i, j)th entry of C, $1 \leq i, j \leq n, i \neq j$, which is given by

$$C_{ij} = \text{cov}(X_i, X_j) = \mathbb{E}[(X_i - \mu_i)(X_j - \mu_j)] \tag{1.13}$$

is the *covariance* between the two random variables X_i and X_j. The *correlation* between X_i and X_j is then given by

$$\text{corr}(X_i, X_j) = \begin{cases} \dfrac{C_{ij}}{\sqrt{C_{ii} C_{jj}}}, & i \neq j, \\ 1, & i = j. \end{cases} \tag{1.14}$$

Given the data matrix $\mathbf{X} = [x_1, \ldots, x_m]$, if the columns $x_i \in \mathbb{R}^n$, $1 \leq i \leq m$, are random observations of the random vector X, then $\mu_{\mathbf{X}}$, as defined in Eq. (1.2), and $C_{\mathbf{X}}$, as defined in Eq. (1.3), are the empirical versions of the true mean μ and the true covariance matrix C, respectively. Furthermore, $C_\mathbf{X}$ encodes, empirically, the correlations between the different pairs of real-valued random variables X_i and X_j.

Consider the case $\rho \sim \mathcal{N}(\mu, C)$, the multivariate Gaussian distribution in $\mathbb{R}^n$ with mean $\mu \in \mathbb{R}^n$ and covariance matrix C. Furthermore, we assume throughout the book that in the Gaussian distribution $\rho \sim \mathcal{N}(\mu, C)$, the covariance matrix C is also non-singular, so that it is positive definite. Then ρ possesses a density function, which we denote by the same symbol and which is defined explicitly and completely in terms of μ and C, namely

$$\rho(x) = \frac{1}{\sqrt{(2\pi)^n \det(C)}} \exp\left(-\frac{1}{2}(x - \mu)^T C^{-1}(x - \mu)\right). \tag{1.15}$$

If the mean $\mu = 0$, then $\mathcal{N}(0, C)$ is determined completely by its covariance matrix C.

Thus, if the feature vectors of an image F are random observations of a random vector with a multivariate Gaussian distribution $\rho \sim \mathcal{N}(0, C)$, with mean zero and covariance matrix C, then the representation of the image F by C is equivalent to representing F by the probability distribution ρ itself. The representation of F by the empirical covariance matrix $C_\mathbf{X}$, which approximates C, can then be considered an approximation of the exact probability representation.

Maximum likelihood estimate (MLE) interpretation of the empirical mean and empirical covariance matrix. Assume that the columns x_i, $1 \leq i \leq m$, in the data matrix $\mathbf{X} = [x_1, \ldots, x_m]$ are IID (independent, identically distributed) samples drawn from a Gaussian distribution $\mathcal{N}(\mu, C)$. The *likelihood function* of the parameters μ and C given the data matrix $\mathbf{X}$ has the form

$$\mathcal{L}(\mu, C | \mathbf{X}) = (2\pi)^{-mn/2} \det(C)^{-m/2} \exp\left(-\frac{1}{2} \sum_{i=1}^{m} (x_i - \mu)^T C^{-1}(x_i - \mu)\right), \tag{1.16}$$

with the log-likelihood function given by

$$\log \mathcal{L}(\mu, C | \mathbf{X}) = -\frac{mn}{2} \log(2\pi) - \frac{m}{2} \log \det(C) - \frac{1}{2} \sum_{i=1}^{m} (x_i - \mu)^T C^{-1}(x_i - \mu). \tag{1.17}$$

It can be shown (see e.g., [54] for the derivation) that the global maximizer of the log-likelihood function is precisely $(\mu_\mathbf{X}, C_\mathbf{X})$.

Thus, in the Gaussian setting, $\mu_\mathbf{X}$ and $C_\mathbf{X}$ are the maximum likelihood estimates of the true mean μ and the true covariance matrix C, respectively.

Unbiased estimate of the covariance matrix. The empirical mean $\mu_\mathbf{X}$, as defined in Eq. (1.2), is an *unbiased* estimate of the true mean μ, in the sense that its expectation is precisely the true mean, that is

$$\mathbb{E}(\mu_\mathbf{X}) = \mu.$$

On the other hand, the empirical covariance matrix C_X, as defined in Eq. (1.3), is a *biased* estimate of the true covariance matrix C, since

$$\mathbb{E}(C_X) = \frac{m-1}{m} C \neq C. \tag{1.18}$$

It is common in the literature to multiply C_X by a factor of $\frac{m}{m-1}$ to obtain

$$\tilde{C}_X = \frac{1}{m-1} \sum_{i=1}^{m} (x_i - \mu_X)(x_i - \mu_X)^T = \frac{1}{m-1} X J_m X^T, \tag{1.19}$$

which is an unbiased estimate of C, since now

$$\mathbb{E}(\tilde{C}_X) = C. \tag{1.20}$$

Comparison of the two estimates via the mean squared error (MSE).   In practical applications, both estimates, the MLE estimate C_X and the unbiased estimate $\tilde{C}_X$, have been employed. In computer vision applications with covariance descriptors, the unbiased estimate $\tilde{C}_X$ was employed in, e.g., [35, 122, 123], while the MLE estimate was employed in, e.g., [19, 48, 94, 116]. It is thus instructive to have a comparison between them. An important measure between the different empirical estimates with respect to the true covariance matrix is the mean squared error (MSE). For an estimate $\hat{C}$ of C, its MSE with respect to C is defined to be (see Appendix A.1 for further detail)

$$\mathrm{MSE}(\hat{C}) = \mathbb{E}(||\hat{C} - C||_F^2), \tag{1.21}$$

where $|| \ ||_F$ denotes the Frobenius norm, which, for an $n \times m$ matrix $A = (a_{ij})$, $1 \leq i \leq n, 1 \leq j \leq m$, is defined by

$$||A||_F^2 = \mathrm{tr}(A^T A) = \sum_{i=1}^{n} \sum_{j=1}^{m} a_{ij}^2. \tag{1.22}$$

Consider the case where the columns x_i, $1 \leq i \leq m$, in the data matrix $\mathbf{X} = [x_1, \ldots, x_m]$ are IID (independent, identically distributed) random samples drawn from a multivariate Gaussian distribution $\mathcal{N}(\mu, C)$. The univariate case has been discussed thoroughly in the statistics literature, see e.g., [15, Examples 7.3.3 and 7.3.4] (together with the accompanying discussion). In this case, the columns x_i, $1 \leq i \leq m$, are IID samples drawn from the distribution $\rho \sim \mathcal{N}(\mu, \sigma^2)$, $\sigma \neq 0$, and the corresponding estimates are

$$C_X = \sigma_X^2 = \frac{1}{m} \sum_{i=1}^{m} (x_i - \mu_X)^2, \quad \tilde{C}_X = \tilde{\sigma}_X^2 = \frac{1}{m-1} \sum_{i=1}^{m} (x_i - \mu_X)^2, \tag{1.23}$$

with the MSEs given by

$$\mathbb{E}(\sigma_{\mathbf{X}}^2 - \sigma^2)^2 = \frac{2m-1}{m^2}\sigma^4 < \mathbb{E}(\tilde{\sigma}_{\mathbf{X}}^2 - \sigma^2)^2 = \frac{2}{m-1}\sigma^4. \tag{1.24}$$

In the multivariate case, the MSEs are given by (Lemma A.1 in Appendix A.1)

$$\mathbb{E}||C_{\mathbf{X}} - C||_F^2 = \frac{m-1}{m^2}[\mathrm{tr}(C)]^2 + \frac{1}{m}\mathrm{tr}(C^2) < \mathbb{E}||\tilde{C}_{\mathbf{X}} - C||_F^2 = \frac{1}{m-1}\left\{[\mathrm{tr}(C)]^2 + \mathrm{tr}(C^2)\right\}, \tag{1.25}$$

with the biases and variances given by

$$\mathrm{bias}(C_{\mathbf{X}}) = \frac{1}{m}||C||_F, \quad \mathrm{bias}(\tilde{C}_{\mathbf{X}}) = 0, \tag{1.26}$$

$$\mathrm{var}(C_{\mathbf{X}}) = \frac{(m-1)}{m^2}\left\{[\mathrm{tr}(C)]^2 + \mathrm{tr}(C^2)\right\} < \mathrm{var}(\tilde{C}_{\mathbf{X}}) = \frac{1}{m-1}\left\{[\mathrm{tr}(C)]^2 + \mathrm{tr}(C^2)\right\}. \tag{1.27}$$

Thus, in the Gaussian setting, the biased MLE $C_{\mathbf{X}}$ has smaller MSE than the unbiased estimate $\tilde{C}_{\mathbf{X}}$, since it has smaller variance. Furthermore, the bias of $C_{\mathbf{X}}$ is $\frac{1}{m}||C||_F$, which goes to zero as $m \to \infty$. Thus the MLE estimate is *asymptotically unbiased*.

More importantly, however, is the fact that both estimates are *consistent*, in the sense that the MSE approaches zero as the sample size $m \to \infty$, that is

$$\lim_{m\to\infty} \mathbb{E}||C_{\mathbf{X}} - C||_F^2 = \lim_{m\to\infty} \mathbb{E}||\tilde{C}_{\mathbf{X}} - C||_F^2 = 0. \tag{1.28}$$

In general, as discussed in [15], without further information, there is no strong case to favor one estimate over the other. While they are different, especially when the sample size m is small, this difference, via the factor $\frac{m-1}{m}$, diminishes as m becomes large. In the current work, following our own previous work [75, 76, 84], we employ the MLE estimate $C_{\mathbf{X}}$, as defined in Eq. (1.3), which leads to more elegant formulations in the infinite-dimensional setting in Chapter 4. Readers who wish to employ the unbiased estimate $\tilde{C}_{\mathbf{X}}$ in Eq. (1.19) can simply replace the factor $\frac{1}{m}$ by $\frac{1}{m-1}$.

Regularization.   Both estimates $C_{\mathbf{X}}$ and $\tilde{C}_{\mathbf{X}}$ are simple to implement and are straightforward to generalize to the covariance operator setting in Chapter 4. However, they may not necessarily be good estimates of the true covariance matrix C when the number of observations m is smaller than the dimension n. This is particularly true when C is strictly positive definite. As we noted in Section 1.1, the $n \times n$ matrix $C_{\mathbf{X}}$ has $\mathrm{rank}(C_{\mathbf{X}}) \le m-1$ and thus for $n \ge m$, $C_{\mathbf{X}}$ is rank-deficient and hence not positive definite. Even when $C_{\mathbf{X}}$ is positive definite, it might not necessarily be well-conditioned.

To overcome these limitations, in the current book, we employ the following regularized covariance matrix

$$\hat{C}_{\mathbf{X},\gamma} = C_{\mathbf{X}} + \gamma I, \tag{1.29}$$

for some regularization parameter $\gamma > 0$. The regularized covariance matrix $\hat{C}_{\mathbf{X},\gamma}$ is guaranteed to be always well-conditioned and positive definite. This also allows us to apply to $\hat{C}_{\mathbf{X},\gamma}$ the mathematical theory and algorithms for SPD matrices, which we describe in Chapter 2. Furthermore, this regularization approach is straightforward to implement and is readily generalizable to the infinite-dimensional setting in Chapter 4.

Also related to the above regularization approach is the line of work on *shrinkage estimators*, see e.g., [39, 67, 121]. In [67], the authors proposed an estimator of the form

$$\hat{C}_{\mathbf{X}} = (1 - \rho)C_{\mathbf{X}} + \rho v I, \tag{1.30}$$

with $0 \leq \rho \leq 1$ and $v > 0$ chosen so as to minimize the mean squared error $\mathbb{E}||\hat{C}_{\mathbf{X}} - C||_F^2$. The idea in this approach is to shrink the eigenvalues of $C_{\mathbf{X}}$ toward the eigenvalues of the matrix vI (or in general, a well-conditioned, positive definite target matrix T). Since the true covariance matrix C is unknown, both ρ and v need to be estimated from the given data. Currently, this approach has been proposed for high-dimensional covariance matrices but, at the time of writing, we are not aware of any work on shrinkage estimators for infinite-dimensional covariance operators.

CHAPTER 2

Geometry of SPD Matrices

In practical applications, such as image classification and clustering, it is necessary to have a similarity measure between images. Having represented images by covariance matrices, this means that we need to have a similarity measure between covariance matrices. Since covariance matrices, properly regularized if necessary, are symmetric, positive definite (SPD matrices), a natural approach to measuring their similarity is via a distance (or distance-like) function between SPD matrices.

Let $\mathrm{Sym}^{++}(n)$ denote the set of SPD matrices of size $n \times n$. In this chapter, we present several distance and distance-like functions on $\mathrm{Sym}^{++}(n)$ that are the most commonly used in the literature. They are the following:

1. Euclidean distance;

2. affine-invariant Riemannian distance;

3. Log-Euclidean distance; and

4. Bregman divergences, in particular Log-Determinant divergences.

These functions arise from three different viewpoints of $\mathrm{Sym}^{++}(n)$. In the first viewpoint, $\mathrm{Sym}^{++}(n)$ is considered simply as a subset of the Euclidean space $\mathbb{R}^{n^2}$ and thus automatically inherits the Euclidean distance on this space. In the second viewpoint, $\mathrm{Sym}^{++}(n)$ is considered as a smooth manifold and the affine-invariant Riemannian distance and Log-Euclidean distance are geodesic distances corresponding to two different Riemannian metrics on this manifold. Finally, in the third viewpoint, $\mathrm{Sym}^{++}(n)$ is considered as an open convex cone, with this convex structure giving rise to the Bregman divergences.

Each of these viewpoints has its own theoretical and computational advantages and disadvantages, as we now discuss in detail.

2.1 EUCLIDEAN DISTANCE

Let $\mathbb{R}^{n \times n}$ denote the set of all $n \times n$ real matrices, which is a vector space of dimension n^2 under the standard matrix addition and scalar multiplication operations $(+, \cdot)$. Let $\mathrm{Sym}(n)$ denote the set of all symmetric $n \times n$ real matrices, then $(\mathrm{Sym}(n), +, \cdot)$ is a vector subspace of $(\mathbb{R}^{n \times n}, +, \cdot)$ of dimension $\frac{n(n+1)}{2}$, since by symmetry, each matrix in $\mathrm{Sym}(n)$ can be represented by its upper triangular entries. Then the set of all $n \times n$ real SPD matrices $\mathrm{Sym}^{++}(n)$ is an open subset of $\mathrm{Sym}(n)$.

For $A, B \in \mathbb{R}^{n \times n}$, a straightforward and commonly used distance between A and B is the Euclidean distance, which is also called the Frobenius distance, defined by

$$d_E(A, B) = ||A - B||_F. \tag{2.1}$$

Here $|| \;\; ||_F$ denotes the Frobenius norm, which is defined by

$$||A||_F = \sqrt{\mathrm{tr}(A^T A)} = \sqrt{\sum_{i,j=1}^{n} a_{ij}^2}, \quad A = (a_{ij})_{i,j=1}^{n}. \tag{2.2}$$

The Frobenius norm is associated with the Frobenius inner product

$$\langle A, B \rangle_F = \mathrm{tr}(A^T B) = \sum_{i,j=1}^{n} a_{ij} b_{ij}, \quad A = (a_{ij})_{i,j=1}^{n}, B = (b_{ij})_{i,j=1}^{n}. \tag{2.3}$$

One immediately sees that the Frobenius inner product $\langle A, B \rangle_F$ and Frobenius norm $||A||_F$ are obtained by essentially converting A and B into vectors[1] in $\mathbb{R}^{n^2}$ and taking the standard Euclidean inner product and norm, respectively, of the corresponding $\mathbb{R}^{n^2}$ vectors.

Unitary invariance. An important property of the Frobenius distance is the following. Let $C \in \mathbb{R}^{n \times n}$ be an invertible matrix, with $C^T C = I$, that is C is a unitary matrix.[2] Then by property of the trace operation

$$\langle CAC^T, CBC^T \rangle_F = \mathrm{tr}(CA^T C^T CBC^T) = \mathrm{tr}(C^T CA^T C^T CB) = \mathrm{tr}(A^T B) = \langle A, B \rangle_F.$$

Thus, the Frobenius inner product is invariant under the transformation $A \to CAC^T$, $B \to CBC^T$, where $C^T C = I$. It then follows that

$$d_E(CAC^T, CBC^T) = d_E(A, B), \quad C^T C = I. \tag{2.4}$$

We call this property *unitary invariance*.

Computational complexity. For two matrices A, B in $\mathbb{R}^{n \times n}$, the computational complexity for computing $d_E(A, B)$ is $O(n^2)$. Thus for a set $\{A_i\}_{i=1}^{N}$ of N matrices in $\mathbb{R}^{n \times n}$, the computational complexity required for computing the matrix of all pairwise distances $\{d_E(A_i, A_j)\}_{i,j=1}^{N}$ is $O(N^2 n^2)$.

Advantages and disadvantages of the Euclidean distance. Among all the distance/distance-like functions considered in this chapter, the Euclidean distance $||A - B||_F$ is the simplest and the fastest to compute, since it only involves the pointwise multiplication and addition of matrix entries. However, it has its disadvantages compared to the other distances and divergences on $\mathrm{Sym}^{++}(n)$, namely the following.

---

[1]In MATLAB, the operation $A(:)$ converts A into a vector by stacking its columns on top of each other.
[2]Here we use the terminology *unitary*, which is also standard in the infinite-dimensional setting. A real, finite-dimensional unitary matrix is also commonly called an *orthogonal matrix*.

- By treating each matrix simply as a vector, it disregards any structure inherent in the matrices A and B. On the set $\mathrm{Sym}^{++}(n)$, $||A - B||_F$ captures neither the fact that A, B are SPD matrices, nor the manifold and convex cone structures of $\mathrm{Sym}^{++}(n)$.

- The metric space $(\mathrm{Sym}^{++}(n), ||\ ||_F)$ is *incomplete*. This means that a Cauchy sequence $\{A_k\}_{k \in \mathbb{N}}$ of SPD matrices, that is a sequence such that $||A_k - A_l||_F$ becomes arbitrarily small for k, l large enough, e.g., as resulting from an iterative algorithm, might not converge to an SPD matrix. This is in contrast to *complete metric spaces*, where Cauchy sequences are always guaranteed to converge to an element in the space.

- The Euclidean metric might lead to a *swelling effect*, that is when computing the mean of a set of SPD matrices, the determinant of the Euclidean matrix mean can be strictly larger than the determinants of the original matrices (see [6] for a discussion of this phenomenon and its undesirability in the context of brain imaging).

- The suboptimality of the Euclidean distance has also been demonstrated in many practical applications.

In the following sections, we present the affine-invariant Riemannian and Log-Euclidean distances, which are defined based on the manifold structure of $\mathrm{Sym}^{++}(n)$, and the Bregman divergences, which are defined based on the convex cone structure of $\mathrm{Sym}^{++}(n)$. A summary of the distances and divergences considered in this chapter is given in Table 2.1. Apart from unitary invariance, they satisfy the following properties:

- scale invariance;

- affine invariance (for d_{aiE} and $d_{\mathrm{logdet}}^{\alpha}$), that is the matrix C in Eq. (2.4) can be any invertible matrix in $\mathbb{R}^{n \times n}$;

- invariance under inversion; and

- the metric spaces $(\mathrm{Sym}^{++}(n), d_{\mathrm{aiE}})$, $(\mathrm{Sym}^{++}(n), d_{\mathrm{logE}})$, and $(\mathrm{Sym}^{++}(n), d_{\mathrm{stein}})$ are complete.

A summary of these properties is given in Table 2.2.

2.2 INTERPRETATIONS AND MOTIVATIONS FOR THE DIFFERENT INVARIANCES

Before describing the non-Euclidean distances and divergences on $\mathrm{Sym}^{++}(n)$, let us discuss the interpretations and motivations for the invariances satisfied by them, as listed in Table 2.2, especially in our current context of covariance descriptors. As we see later on, these invariances also illuminate the crucial differences between the extrinsic Euclidean distance and the intrinsic Log-Euclidean distance on $\mathrm{Sym}^{++}(n)$, both of which arise from Riemannian metrics with curvature zero.

Table 2.1: Several commonly used distances and divergences on $\text{Sym}^{++}(n)$. Here $||\ ||_F$ denotes the matrix Frobenius norm.

Euclidean distance	$d_E(A, B) = ||A - B||_F$
Affine-invariant Riemannian distance	$d_{\text{aiE}}(A, B) = ||\log(A^{-1/2}BA^{-1/2})||_F$
Log-Euclidean distance	$d_{\text{logE}}(A, B) = ||\log(A) - \log(B)||_F$
Log-Determinant divergences	$d_{\text{logdet}}^{\alpha}(A, B) = \frac{4}{1-\alpha^2}\log\left[\frac{\det(\frac{1-\alpha}{2}A + \frac{1+\alpha}{2}B)}{\det(A)^{\frac{1-\alpha}{2}}\det(B)^{\frac{1+\alpha}{2}}}\right]$
	$-1 < \alpha < 1$
	$d_{\text{logdet}}^{1}(A, B) = \text{tr}(B^{-1}A - I) - \log\det(B^{-1}A)$
	$d_{\text{logdet}}^{-1}(A, B) = \text{tr}(A^{-1}B - I) - \log\det(A^{-1}B)$
Symmetric Stein divergence ($\alpha = 0$) $(d_{\text{stein}}^2(A, B) = \frac{1}{4}d_{\text{logdet}}^0(A, B))$	$d_{\text{stein}}^2(A, B) = \log\det(\frac{A+B}{2}) - \frac{1}{2}\log\det(AB)$

Table 2.2: Properties of four commonly used distances on $\text{Sym}^{++}(n)$: (i) Euclidean distance $d_E(A, B) = ||A - B||_F$; (ii) affine-invariant Riemannian distance $d_{\text{aiE}}(A, B) = ||\log(A^{-1/2}BA^{-1/2})||_F$; (iii) Log-Euclidean distance $d_{\text{logE}}(A, B) = ||\log(A) - \log(B)||_F$; (iv) square-root of the symmetric Stein divergence $d_{\text{stein}}(A, B) = \sqrt{\log\det(\frac{A+B}{2}) - \frac{1}{2}\log\det(AB)}$. Here $||\ ||_F$ denotes the matrix Frobenius norm.

	Euclidean	Log-Euclidean	Affine-Invariant	Stein
Geodesic distance	Yes	Yes	Yes	No
Affine invariance	No	No	Yes	Yes
Scale invariance	No	Yes	Yes	Yes
Unitary invariance	Yes	Yes	Yes	Yes
Inversion invariance	No	Yes	Yes	Yes
Inner product distance	Yes	Yes	No	No
Complete metric	No	Yes	Yes	Yes

Affine invariance. Let $GL(n)$ denote the set of all $n \times n$ invertible matrices. A distance/divergence function $d : \text{Sym}^{++}(n) \times \text{Sym}^{++}(n) \to \mathbb{R}^+$ is said to be *affine-invariant* if for any invertible matrix $A \in GL(n)$, we have

$$d(AC_1 A^T, AC_2 A^T) = d(C_1, C_2) \quad \forall C_1, C_2 \in \text{Sym}^{++}(n). \tag{2.5}$$

To see the meaning and significance of this property in our context, let us recall the statistical interpretations of the covariance descriptors as described in Section 1.2 (see also the discussion in [92]).

Let X be a random n-vector with probability distribution ρ. Let $A \in GL(n)$ be any $n \times n$ invertible matrix and $b \in \mathbb{R}^n$ be an arbitrary vector. Then we have the following *affine transformation*

$$\Gamma_{A,b} : \mathbb{R}^n \to \mathbb{R}^n, \quad \Gamma_{A,b}(X) = AX + b. \tag{2.6}$$

The expected value of the transformed random vector $\Gamma_{A,b}(X)$ is then given by

$$\mu_{\Gamma_{A,b}(X)} = \mathbb{E}[\Gamma_{A,b}(X)] = A\mathbb{E}(X) + b = A\mu_X + b. \tag{2.7}$$

The corresponding covariance matrix is given by

$$C_{\Gamma_{A,b}(X)} = \mathbb{E}[(\Gamma_{A,b}(X) - \mu_{\Gamma_{A,b}(X)})(\Gamma_{A,b}(X) - \mu_{\Gamma_{A,b}(X)})^T] = AC_X A^T. \tag{2.8}$$

Thus if the random vector X undergoes the affine transformation $X \to AX + b$, then its covariance matrix undergoes the transformation $C_X \to AC_X A^T$, independent of the translation factor b.

For two random vectors X, Y, an affine-invariant distance/divergence function d on $\text{Sym}^{++}(n)$ then gives

$$d(C_{\Gamma_{A,b}(X)}, C_{\Gamma_{A,b}(Y)}) = d(AC_X A^T, AC_Y A^T) = d(C_X, C_Y),$$

that is this distance/divergence is invariant if X and Y undergo the same, but *arbitrary*, affine transformation on $\mathbb{R}^n$.

This invariance property remains true when we transition from the theoretical covariance matrices to the empirical covariance matrices. Let $\mathbf{X} = [x_1, \ldots, x_m]$ be a data matrix of size $n \times m$, where the vectors $x_i \in \mathbb{R}^n$, $1 \le i \le n$, are random, independent observations of the random vector X. Then under the affine transformation $\Gamma_{A,b}$, the empirical expected value becomes

$$\mu_{\Gamma_{A,b}(\mathbf{X})} = \frac{1}{m} \sum_{i=1}^{m} (Ax_i + b) = A\mu_{\mathbf{X}} + b, \tag{2.9}$$

and the empirical covariance matrix becomes

$$C_{\Gamma_{A,b}(\mathbf{X})} = \frac{1}{m} \sum_{i=1}^{m} (Ax_i + b - \mu_{\Gamma_{A,b}(\mathbf{X})})(Ax_i + b - \mu_{\Gamma_{A,b}(\mathbf{X})})^T = AC_{\mathbf{X}} A^T. \tag{2.10}$$

Thus, the empirical covariance matrix also undergoes the same transformation $C_{\mathbf{X}} \rightarrow A C_{\mathbf{X}} A^T$. Hence, if two data matrices $\mathbf{X}$ and $\mathbf{Y}$ undergo the same, but arbitrary, affine transformation $\Gamma_{A,b}$, then an affine-invariance distance/divergence between their corresponding empirical matrices remains the same, that is

$$d(C_{\Gamma_{A,b}(\mathbf{X})}, C_{\Gamma_{A,b}(\mathbf{Y})}) = d(A C_{\mathbf{X}} A^T, A C_{\mathbf{Y}} A^T) = d(C_{\mathbf{X}}, C_{\mathbf{Y}}).$$

Affine invariance is satisfied by the affine-invariant Riemannian distance and the Log-Determinant divergences.

Scale invariance. This is a special case of the affine-invariance property, with $b = 0$ and $A = \sqrt{s} I_n$, for some scalar $s > 0$, in the affine transformation $\Gamma_{A,b}$ in Eq. (2.6). This property states that if we scale the random vectors X and Y (or the corresponding data matrices $\mathbf{X}$ and $\mathbf{Y}$) by the same factor $\sqrt{s}$, then the distance/divergence between their corresponding covariance matrices, which are scaled by the factor s, remains the same, that is

$$d(s C_X, s C_Y) = d(C_X, C_Y). \tag{2.11}$$

Scale invariance is satisfied by the Log-Euclidean distance, which does not satisfy the full affine invariance property. It is not satisfied by the Euclidean distance.

Unitary invariance. This is another special case of the affine invariance property, with $b = 0$ and $A^T = A^{-1}$ in Eq. (2.6), that is A is an $n \times n$ unitary matrix. This property states that if the random vectors X and Y undergo the same, but arbitrary *unitary* transformation A in $\mathbb{R}^n$, such as a rotation, then the distance/divergence between the corresponding covariance matrices remains the same, that is

$$d(C_{\Gamma_A(X)}, C_{\Gamma_A(Y)}) = d(A C_X A^{-1}, A C_Y A^{-1}) = d(C_X, C_Y). \tag{2.12}$$

Unitary invariance is satisfied by all four distances/divergences listed in Table 2.1, namely Euclidean distance, Log-Euclidean distance, affine-invariant Riemannian distance, and Log-Determinant divergences.

Invariance under inversion. A distance/divergence function $d : \mathrm{Sym}^{++}(n) \times \mathrm{Sym}^{++}(n) \rightarrow \mathbb{R}^+$ is said to be *invariant under inversion* if

$$d(C_1, C_2) = d(C_1^{-1}, C_2^{-1}), \quad \forall C_1, C_2, \in \mathrm{Sym}^{++}(n). \tag{2.13}$$

To see the significance of this property, consider the correspondence between $\mathrm{Sym}^{++}(n)$ and the set of multivariate Gaussian density functions on $\mathbb{R}^n$ with mean zero. We recall that each Gaussian density function $\mathcal{N}(0, C)$, $C \in \mathrm{Sym}^{++}(n)$, is completely determined by its covariance matrix C, or equivalently, its precision matrix C^{-1}. Hence, we can take as the distance/divergence between two multivariate Gaussian density functions $\mathcal{N}(0, C_1), \mathcal{N}(0, C_2)$ the distance/divergence between the corresponding covariance matrices C_1 and C_2. The invariance property in Eq. (2.13) states that one obtains the exact same measure by taking the same distance/divergence between the corresponding precision matrices C_1^{-1} and C_2^{-1}.

Invariance under inversion is satisfied by all the *symmetric* non-Euclidean distances/divergences listed in Table 2.1, namely the Log-Euclidean distance, affine-invariant Riemannian distance, and symmetric Stein divergence, but not the Euclidean distance.

2.3   BASIC RIEMANNIAN GEOMETRY

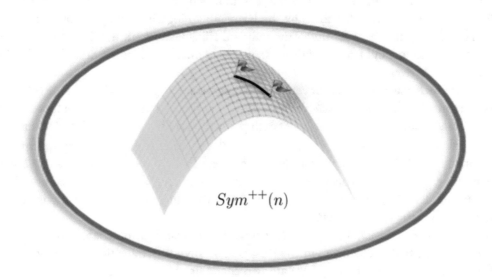

Figure 2.1: The set $\text{Sym}^{++}(n)$ of $n \times n$ SPD matrices viewed as a Riemannian manifold.

Let us consider the viewpoint of $\text{Sym}^{++}(n)$ as a Riemannian manifold. We first provide a brief overview of Riemannian geometry and refer to, e.g., [28, 58] for a comprehensive treatment. In general, Riemannian manifolds are generalizations of two-dimensional regular surfaces in 3D space, with one of the simplest examples being the two-dimensional sphere, on which many of the abstract concepts involved assume a much more concrete form (see, e.g., [27] for a comprehensive treatment).

The following are some of the key concepts from Riemannian geometry which are necessary for our current purposes.

- Riemannian metric and the associated Riemannian distance (i.e., the shortest distance between two points on the manifold).

• Geodesics, Riemannian exponential map, and Riemannian logarithm map.

We are particularly interested in *geodesically complete manifolds*, on which there always *exists* a geodesic connecting any two points, whose length is equal to their Riemannian distance. Among geodesically complete manifolds, we are interested in those which are simply connected and have nonpositive curvature, the so-called *Cartan-Hadamard* manifolds. On these manifolds, the geodesic connecting two points is *unique* and its length, which is equal to their Riemannian distance, is completely determined by the Riemannian logarithm map. Examples of this class of manifolds are the space $\mathbb{R}^n$ under the standard Euclidean metric and $\text{Sym}^{++}(n)$ under both the affine-invariant and Log-Euclidean Riemannian metrics, which we describe in Sections 2.4 and 2.5, respectively.

Smooth manifold, tangent vector, and tangent space. Informally speaking (see, e.g., [68] for the formal definition), a *topological manifold* $\mathcal{M}$ of dimension n, $n \in \mathbb{N}$, is a topological space that is *locally Euclidean*, in the sense that each point P on $\mathcal{M}$ has a neighborhood $\mathcal{U}$ that is homeomorphic to an open subset $\hat{\mathcal{U}} = \varphi(\mathcal{U}) \subset \mathbb{R}^n$, where $\varphi : \mathcal{U} \to \hat{\mathcal{U}}$ is a homeomorphism, that is a continuous bijective map with a continuous inverse.[3] The pair $(\mathcal{U}, \varphi)$ is called a *coordinate chart*, or simply *chart* on $\mathcal{M}$. A collection of charts whose domains cover $\mathcal{M}$ is called an *atlas* of $\mathcal{M}$. For $P \in \mathcal{U}$, let $\varphi(P) = (x_1(P), \dots, x_n(P)) \in \mathbb{R}^n$, then the component functions $(x_1, \dots, x_n)$ of φ are called the *local coordinates* on $\mathcal{U}$.

A *smooth manifold*, also called *differentiable manifold*, is a topological manifold $\mathcal{M}$ with a *smooth atlas*, that is any chart in the atlas can be smoothly transitioned to any other chart. This means that if $(\mathcal{U}, \varphi)$ and $(\mathcal{V}, \psi)$ are two charts on $\mathcal{M}$ belonging to this atlas, then either $\mathcal{U} \cap \mathcal{V} = \emptyset$, or the transition map $\psi \circ \varphi^{-1} : \varphi(\mathcal{U} \cap \mathcal{V}) \to \psi(\mathcal{U} \cap \mathcal{V})$, as a map between two open subsets $\varphi(\mathcal{U} \cap \mathcal{V})$ and $\psi(\mathcal{U} \cap \mathcal{V})$ in $\mathbb{R}^n$, is C^∞, that is having continuous partial derivatives of all orders.

Two key concepts for working on a smooth manifold $\mathcal{M}$ are *tangent vector* and *tangent space*. These are the generalizations of the corresponding concepts on a regular surface $\mathcal{S}$ in $\mathbb{R}^3$. We recall that (see, e.g., [27]), for a parametrized smooth curve $\gamma : I = (a, b) \to \mathbb{R}^3$, where $I = (a, b) \subset \mathbb{R}$ is some interval on the real line, with $\gamma'(t) \neq 0 \; \forall t \in I$, the tangent vector to the curve at the point $\gamma(t_0)$, $t_0 \in I$, is the vector $\gamma'(t_0)$. On a regular surface $\mathcal{S} \subset \mathbb{R}^3$, a tangent vector to $\mathcal{S}$ at a point $P \in \mathcal{S}$ is the tangent vector at P of a smooth curve on $\mathcal{S}$ passing through P. More specifically, it is the tangent vector $\gamma'(0)$ of a smooth curve $\gamma : (-\epsilon, \epsilon) \to \mathcal{S}$, for some $\epsilon > 0$, with $\gamma(0) = P$. It can then be shown that the set of all tangent vectors to $\mathcal{S}$ at P forms a two-dimensional vector space, called the *tangent plane* of $\mathcal{S}$ at P, denoted by $T_P(\mathcal{S})$.

The generalization of the concept of tangent vectors to an abstract smooth manifold $\mathcal{M}$ is based on the above definition of tangent vectors of curves as their derivatives, as follows (see [28] and [68] for further detail). First consider the case $\mathcal{M} = \mathbb{R}^n$. Let $\gamma : (-\epsilon, \epsilon) \to \mathbb{R}^n$ be a smooth curve in $\mathbb{R}^n$, $\gamma(0) = P$, with coordinates $\gamma(t) = (x_1(t), \dots, x_n(t))$. The tangent vector

---

[3]Formally, $\mathcal{M}$ is also required to be a *Hausdorff* space, that is any two distinct points in $\mathcal{M}$ are contained in two disjoint open sets, and *second countable*, that is there exists a countable basis for the topology of $\mathcal{M}$ (see, e.g., [68] for further detail).

to γ at $t = 0$ is

$$V = \gamma'(0) = (x_1'(0), \ldots, x_n'(0)).$$

Let $\mathcal{D}_P$ be the set of all functions $f : \mathbb{R}^n \to \mathbb{R}$ that are differentiable at P, then $\mathcal{D}_P$ is a vector space under function addition and scalar multiplication. By the chain rule, the *directional derivative* of a function $f \in \mathcal{D}_P$ along the vector V at the point P is given by

$$\frac{d(f \circ \gamma)}{dt}\Big|_{t=0} = \sum_{j=1}^{n} \frac{\partial f}{\partial x_j}\Big|_{t=0} \frac{\partial x_j}{\partial t}\Big|_{t=0} = \left(\sum_{j=1}^{n} x_j'(0) \frac{\partial}{\partial x_j}\Big|_P \right) f. \tag{2.14}$$

Thus, the tangent vector V of the curve γ at the point P defines a linear map from $\mathcal{D}_P \to \mathbb{R}$, namely the directional derivative along V. This viewpoint leads to the following definition of the concept of tangent vectors on a general smooth manifold $\mathcal{M}$.

Let $\mathcal{M}$ be a smooth manifold and $\gamma : (-\epsilon, \epsilon) \to \mathcal{M}$ be a smooth curve on $\mathcal{M}$, with $\gamma(0) = P$. Let $\mathcal{D}_P$ be the set of all functions $f : \mathcal{M} \to \mathbb{R}$ that are differentiable at P. The *tangent vector to the curve* γ at P is defined to be the *linear map* $\gamma'(0) : \mathcal{D}_P \to \mathbb{R}$ given by

$$\gamma'(0) f = \frac{d(f \circ \gamma)}{dt}\Big|_{t=0}, \quad f \in \mathcal{D}_P. \tag{2.15}$$

A *tangent vector at* P is then defined to be the tangent vector at $t = 0$ for a smooth curve $\gamma : (-\epsilon, \epsilon) \to \mathcal{M}$ with $\gamma(0) = P$. The set of all tangent vectors at a point $P \in \mathcal{M}$ forms the *tangent space* of $\mathcal{M}$ at P, denoted by $T_P(\mathcal{M})$.

Assume the local coordinate representation $\varphi(\gamma(t)) = (x_1(t), \ldots, x_n(t)) \in \mathbb{R}^n$, with $\varphi(P) = \varphi(\gamma(0)) = (x_1(0), \ldots, x_n(0))$. Then

$$(f \circ \gamma)(t) = ((f \circ \varphi^{-1}) \circ (\varphi \circ \gamma))(t) = (f \circ \varphi^{-1})(x_1(t), \ldots, x_n(t)),$$

with the function $f \circ \varphi^{-1} : \mathbb{R}^n \to \mathbb{R}$. By the chain rule

$$\gamma'(0) f = \frac{d(f \circ \gamma)}{dt}\Big|_{t=0} = \sum_{j=1}^{n} x_j'(0) \frac{\partial(f \circ \varphi^{-1})}{\partial x_j}\Big|_{\varphi(P)} = \left(\sum_{j=1}^{n} x_j'(0) \frac{\partial}{\partial x_j}\Big|_P \right) f, \tag{2.16}$$

where we define $\frac{\partial}{\partial x_j}\Big|_P f = \frac{\partial(f \circ \varphi^{-1})}{\partial x_j}\Big|_{\varphi(P)}$. Note that in the case $\mathcal{M} = \mathbb{R}^n$, we have $\varphi = \mathrm{id}_{\mathbb{R}^n}$, the identity map, and the expansion in Eq. (2.16) reduces to the expansion in Eq. (2.14). From this expansion, it can be shown that the tangent space $T_P(\mathcal{M})$ is an n-dimensional vector space. Furthermore, for a smooth chart $(\mathcal{U}, \varphi)$ containing P, with $\varphi(P) = (x_1(P), \ldots, x_n(P))$, a basis for the tangent space $T_P(\mathcal{M})$ is the set $\{ \frac{\partial}{\partial x_j}\Big|_P \}_{j=1}^n$.

Riemannian manifold and Riemannian metric. A *Riemannian manifold* $\mathcal{M}$ is a smooth manifold equipped with a *Riemannian metric*. Informally speaking, a Riemannian metric on $\mathcal{M}$

is a formulation for defining distances on the manifold. Formally, for each point P on $\mathcal{M}$, let $T_P(\mathcal{M})$ denote the tangent space to $\mathcal{M}$ at P. A Riemannian metric on $\mathcal{M}$ (see, e.g., [28, 58, 68]) is a family of inner products $\langle\,,\,\rangle_P$ defined on each tangent space $T_P(\mathcal{M})$ that varies smoothly with the base point P. Let $(\mathcal{U}, \varphi = (x_1, \ldots, x_n))$ be a local coordinate chart containing P, so that the tangent space $T_P(\mathcal{M})$ admits the basis $\{\frac{\partial}{\partial x_j}\big|_P\}_{j=1}^n$, then the Riemannian metric can be represented as an $n \times n$ SPD matrix $(g_{ij}(P))_{i,j=1}^n$, defined by

$$g_{ij}(P) = \left\langle \frac{\partial}{\partial x_i}\Big|_P, \frac{\partial}{\partial x_j}\Big|_P \right\rangle_P, \quad 1 \le i, j \le n. \tag{2.17}$$

Given a smooth manifold $\mathcal{M}$, a Riemannian metric $\langle\,,\,\rangle_P$, $P \in \mathcal{M}$, induces the norm $||V||_P = \sqrt{\langle V, V\rangle_P}$, $V \in T_P(\mathcal{M})$, which induces a distance on the tangent space $T_P(\mathcal{M})$. We thus have a family of distances on the tangent spaces $T_P(\mathcal{M})$, $P \in \mathcal{M}$, which varies smoothly with P and which in turn induces a distance function on the manifold $\mathcal{M}$, as follows.

Riemannian distance. Let $I \subset \mathbb{R}$ be an open interval and $\gamma : I \to \mathcal{M}$ be a smooth, i.e., C^∞, curve on $\mathcal{M}$. Let $\dot{\gamma}(t)$ denote the tangent vector to the curve at the point $\gamma(t)$. Let $[a, b] \subset I$ be a closed interval. Then at any point $t \in [a, b]$, the tangent vector $\dot{\gamma}(t)$, in the tangent space $T_{\gamma(t)}(\mathcal{M})$, has length $||\dot{\gamma}(t)||_{\gamma(t)}$. The length of the curve segment γ, with t ranging from a to b, can then be defined to be the integration of the lengths of these tangent vectors over the entire segment, i.e.,

$$L(\gamma) = \int_a^b ||\dot{\gamma}(t)||_{\gamma(t)} dt. \tag{2.18}$$

If γ is a piecewise smooth curve, then its length is defined to be the summation of the lengths of all its smooth pieces.

Definition 2.1   The Riemannian distance between two points $A, B \in \mathcal{M}$, induced by the Riemannian metric $\langle\,,\,\rangle_P$, is defined to be

$$d(A, B) = \inf\{L(\gamma) : \gamma : [a, b] \to \mathcal{M} \text{ piecewise smooth}, \gamma(a) = A, \gamma(b) = B\}. \tag{2.19}$$

The following result is fundamental and can be found in [28, 58, 68].

Theorem 2.2   *The function $d : \mathcal{M} \times \mathcal{M} \to \mathbb{R}^+$ as defined in Eq. (2.19) satisfies all the axioms of a metric, namely*

1. *Positivity: $d(A, B) \ge 0$, with $d(A, B) = 0 \iff A = B$,*

2. *Symmetry: $d(A, B) = d(B, A)$,*

3. *Triangle inequality: $d(A, B) \le d(A, C) + d(C, B)$,*

∀$A, B, C \in \mathcal{M}$, so that $(\mathcal{M}, d)$ is a metric space.

The Riemannian distance $d(A, B)$ is closely connected with the lengths of geodesic curves on $\mathcal{M}$, as we explain next.

Geodesics. A geodesic curve γ on a Riemannian manifold $\mathcal{M}$ is a generalization of a straight line in $\mathbb{R}^n$, in the sense that it is a curve with zero acceleration. Specifically, a smooth curve $\gamma : [a, b] \to \mathcal{M}$ is called a *geodesic* if it is a critical point of the energy functional

$$E(\gamma) = \frac{1}{2} \int_a^b ||\dot{\gamma}(t)||^2_{\gamma(t)} dt.$$

An important property of geodesics is that they have constant speed, that is

$$\frac{d}{dt} ||\dot{\gamma}(t)||_{\gamma(t)} = 0.$$

Riemannian exponential map. For a given point $P \in \mathcal{M}$ and a given tangent vector $V \in T_P(\mathcal{M})$, the theory of ordinary differential equations guarantees that there exists $\epsilon > 0$ and a unique geodesic curve $\gamma_V : [0, \epsilon] \to \mathcal{M}$, starting at the point P and moving along $\mathcal{M}$ in the direction V, that is with $\gamma_V(0) = P$ and $\dot{\gamma}_V(0) = V$. Furthermore, there is always a neighborhood $\mathcal{U}_P \subset T_P(\mathcal{M})$ of $0 \in T_P(\mathcal{M})$ such that γ_V is defined on $[0, 1]$ ∀$V \in \mathcal{U}_P$. The *Riemannian exponential map* Exp_P is then defined by

$$\mathrm{Exp}_P : \mathcal{U}_P \subset T_P(\mathcal{M}) \to \mathcal{M}, \quad \mathrm{Exp}_P(V) = \gamma_V(1), \tag{2.20}$$

that is $\mathrm{Exp}_P(V)$ is the point on $\mathcal{M}$ reached at unit time ($t = 1$) by the geodesic curve γ_V. Since γ_V is a geodesic, its speed $||\dot{\gamma}(t)||_{\gamma_V(t)}$ is constant and thus the length of γ_V, with $\gamma_V(0) = P$, $\gamma_V(1) = \mathrm{Exp}_P(V)$, is given by

$$L(\gamma_V) = \int_0^1 ||\dot{\gamma}_V(t)||_{\gamma_V(t)} dt = ||\dot{\gamma}_V(0)||_{\gamma_V(0)} = ||V||_P. \tag{2.21}$$

Example 2.3   For $\mathcal{M} = \mathbb{R}^n$ under the standard Euclidean metric, $T_P(\mathcal{M}) \cong \mathbb{R}^n$ ∀$P \in \mathbb{R}^n$ and

$$\gamma_V(t) = P + Vt, \quad \forall t \in \mathbb{R}, \text{ with } \mathrm{Exp}_P(V) = P + V \ \ \forall P, V \in \mathbb{R}^n. \tag{2.22}$$

Thus, in general, $\mathrm{Exp}_P(V)$ can be viewed as a generalization of the operation of vector addition in $\mathbb{R}^n$, with the base point $P \in \mathcal{M}$ being the initial point and $\mathrm{Exp}_P(V) \in \mathcal{M}$ being the end point, respectively, of a geodesic curve with initial direction $V \in T_P(\mathcal{M})$ and length $||V||_P$. A geometrical interpretation of the exponential map Exp_P is given in Figure 2.2; see also the discussion in [92].

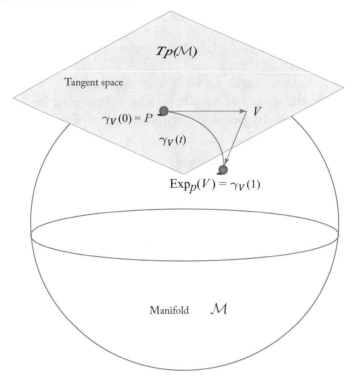

Figure 2.2: Geometrical interpretation of the Riemannian exponential map. At a point P on the manifold $\mathcal{M}$, given a tangent vector V in the tangent space $T_P(\mathcal{M})$ at P, there is a unique geodesic γ_V, starting at P and moves along the manifold in the direction V, that is $\gamma_V(0) = P$, $\dot{\gamma}_V(0) = V$. The Riemannian exponential map Exp_P maps V to the point $\gamma_V(1)$ on the manifold, that is $\mathrm{Exp}_P(V) = \gamma_V(1)$. The length of the curve γ_V joining P and $\mathrm{Exp}_P(V)$ on the manifold $\mathcal{M}$ is precisely the length of the vector V in the tangent space $T_P(\mathcal{M})$, that is $L(\gamma_V) = ||V||_P$. If $\mathcal{M}$ is a Cartan-Hadamard manifold, such as $\mathrm{Sym}^{++}(n)$, then the geodesic connecting any two points on $\mathcal{M}$ is unique, with length equal to their Riemannian distance, so that $d(P, \mathrm{Exp}_P(V)) = L(\gamma_V) = ||V||_P$. If $\mathcal{M} = \mathbb{R}^n$, then $\mathrm{Exp}_P(V) = P + V$ and, in general, $\mathrm{Exp}_P(V)$ can be considered as a generalization of this vector addition operation.

Geodesically complete manifolds. A Riemannian manifold $\mathcal{M}$ is said to be *geodesically complete* if $\forall P \in \mathcal{M}$, the exponential map Exp_P is defined on all of $T_P(\mathcal{M})$, in which case we can write $\mathrm{Exp}_P : T_P(\mathcal{M}) \to \mathcal{M}$. For a geodesically complete manifold $\mathcal{M}$, there exists a geodesic connecting any two points, whose length is equal to their Riemannian distance (such a geodesic is called *minimizing*), due to the following fundamental result (see e.g., [28, 58] for the full statement).

Theorem 2.4 (Hopf-Rinow). *For a Riemannian manifold $\mathcal{M}$, the following statements are equivalent.*

1. *$(\mathcal{M}, d)$ is a complete metric space.*

2. *$\mathcal{M}$ is geodesically complete, that is the exponential map Exp_P is defined on all of $T_P(\mathcal{M}) \;\forall P \in \mathcal{M}$.*

Either of these two statements implies that any two points $A, B \in \mathcal{M}$ can be joined by a geodesic of length $d(A, B)$, that is by a geodesic of shortest length.

Riemannian logarithm map. Let us consider now the inverse of the Riemannian exponential map. A map $f : \mathcal{M} \to \mathcal{N}$ between two smooth manifolds $\mathcal{M}$ and $\mathcal{N}$ is said to be a *diffeomorphism* if it is a smooth bijection with a smooth inverse. One important property of the exponential map Exp_P is that there exists a neighborhood $\mathcal{V}_0$ of $0 \in T_P(\mathcal{M})$ so that Exp_P maps $\mathcal{V}_0$ diffeomorphically onto a neighborhood of $\mathcal{W}_P$ of P in $\mathcal{M}$. This implies that there exists an inverse function for Exp_P, which we denote by

$$\begin{aligned}
\mathrm{Log}_P : \mathcal{W}_P \subset \mathcal{M} &\to \mathcal{V}_0 \subset T_P(\mathcal{M}), \\
\mathrm{Log}_P(Q) = V &\Longleftrightarrow \mathrm{Exp}_P(V) = Q,
\end{aligned} \tag{2.23}$$

that maps $\mathcal{W}_P \subset \mathcal{M}$ diffeomorphically onto $\mathcal{V}_0 \subset T_P(\mathcal{M})$.

Example 2.5   For $\mathcal{M} = \mathbb{R}^n$ under the standard Euclidean metric,

$$\mathrm{Exp}_P(V) = P + V, \quad \text{so that} \quad \mathrm{Log}_P(Q) = Q - P, \quad P, Q, V \in \mathbb{R}^n. \tag{2.24}$$

Thus, in general, Log_P can be viewed as a generalization of the vector subtraction operation in $\mathbb{R}^n$, with base point P. A geometrical interpretation of the logarithm map Log_P is given in Figure 2.3, see also the discussion in [92].

Curvature. A fundamental concept of Riemannian geometry is that of curvature, which essentially measures how much a Riemannian manifold deviates from Euclidean space. We briefly discuss this concept here and refer the readers to [28], for example, a comprehensive treatment. The concept of curvature on Riemannian manifold generalizes the much more concrete concept of *Gaussian curvature* for regular surfaces in $\mathbb{R}^3$, which is treated thoroughly in e.g., [27]. In brief, let $\mathcal{S}$ be a regular, oriented surface in $\mathbb{R}^3$ and P be a point on $\mathcal{S}$. Let V be a unit vector in the tangent plane $T_P(\mathcal{S})$ and $N(P)$ be the unit normal vector to $\mathcal{S}$ at P, then the intersection of the plane containing $V, N(P)$ with $\mathcal{S}$ is called a *normal section* of $\mathcal{S}$. Each normal section is thus a curve on $\mathcal{S}$ passing through P and possessing a curvature, called *normal curvature*. The maximum and minimum of the normal curvatures at P are called the *principal*

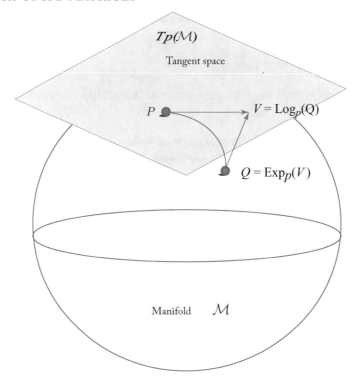

Figure 2.3: Geometrical interpretation of the Riemannian logarithm map. At a point P on the manifold $\mathcal{M}$, the logarithm map Log_P is the inverse of the exponential map Exp_P and maps a neighborhood of P in $\mathcal{M}$ onto a neighborhood of the vector 0 in the tangent space $T_P(\mathcal{M})$. If $\mathcal{M}$ is a Cartan-Hadamard manifold, such as $\mathrm{Sym}^{++}(n)$, then $\forall P \in \mathcal{M}$, $\mathrm{Log}_P :$ $\mathcal{M} \to T_P(\mathcal{M})$ diffeomorphically, that is it is bijective, smooth, and the inverse Exp_P is also smooth. In that case, the Riemannian distance between P and Q is precisely the length of V in $T_P(\mathcal{M})$, that is $d(P, Q) = \|V\|_P = \|\mathrm{Log}_P(Q)\|_P$. If $\mathcal{M} = \mathbb{R}^n$, then $\mathrm{Log}_P(Q) = Q - P$ and in general, $\mathrm{Log}_P(Q)$ can be considered as a generalization of this vector subtraction operation.

curvatures of the surface $\mathcal{S}$ at P. The product of the principal curvatures is called the *Gaussian curvature* of $\mathcal{S}$ at P, which is a quantity intrinsic to $\mathcal{S}$.

Let now $\mathcal{M}$ be a Riemannian manifold. For a fixed point $P \in \mathcal{M}$, consider a *two-dimensional* subspace Σ_P of the tangent space $T_P(\mathcal{M})$ at P. Let R denote the *Riemannian curvature tensor* (see, e.g., [28], Chapter 4, for the definition and Section 2.4 below for an example in the $\mathrm{Sym}^{++}(n)$ setting). Then for any basis vectors $\{X, Y\} \in \Sigma_P$, the quantity

$$K(\Sigma_P) = K_P(X, Y) = \frac{\langle R(X, Y)X, Y \rangle_P}{\|X\|_P^2 \|Y\|_P^2 - \langle X, Y \rangle_P^2} \tag{2.25}$$

is well-defined and is *independent* of the choice of the basis vectors $X, Y \in \Sigma_P$. This quantity is called the *sectional curvature* of Σ_P at P. In particular, for a regular surface $S \subset \mathbb{R}^3$, there is precisely one two-dimensional subspace of $T_P(S)$, namely $T_P(S)$ itself. In this case, the sectional curvature $K(T_P(S))$ coincides with the Gaussian curvature of S at P. In general, the sectional curvature $K(\Sigma_P)$ is the Gaussian curvature at P of a small surface formed by geodesics on $\mathcal{M}$ starting at P, with directions lying on the two-dimensional subspace Σ_P of $T_P(\mathcal{M})$.

Some common examples of manifolds with constant sectional curvature are

- Euclidean space $\mathbb{R}^n$, with $K = 0$ (flat manifold).

- n-dimensional unit sphere $\mathbb{S}^{n-1} = \{(x_1, \ldots, x_n) \in \mathbb{R}^n : x_1^2 + \cdots + x_n^2 = 1\}$, with $K = 1$ (positive curvature).

- n-dimensional hyperbolic space $\mathbb{H}^n = \{x = (x_1, \ldots, x_n) \in \mathbb{R}^n : x_n > 0\}$, under the Riemannian metric $g_{ij}(x_1, \ldots, x_n) = \frac{\delta_{ij}}{x_n^2}$, with $K = -1$ (negative curvature).

Of particular interest for our current purposes are manifolds with *nonpositive sectional curvature*, which we turn to next.

Manifolds with nonpositive curvature and uniqueness of geodesics. On a geodesically complete manifold, there is always a minimizing geodesic joining any two points. Such a minimizing geodesic is not necessarily unique, however. An obvious example is the two-dimensional sphere, where any two antipodal points are joined by infinitely many minimizing geodesics of equal length. We now consider a class of Riemannian manifolds in which uniqueness of minimizing geodesics is guaranteed, namely simply connected manifolds with nonpositive (or seminegative) sectional curvature. The space $\mathbb{R}^n$ under the standard Euclidean metric and the manifold $\mathrm{Sym}^{++}(n)$ of SPD matrices, under both the affine-invariant and Log-Euclidean Riemannian metrics, belong to this class. The following theorem is a fundamental result for this class of manifolds, see, e.g., [28, 58, 62].

Theorem 2.6 (Cartan-Hadamard). *Assume that $\mathcal{M}$ is a geodesically complete Riemannian manifold with nonpositive sectional curvature. If $\mathcal{M}$ is simply connected, then the exponential map $\mathrm{Exp}_P : T_P(\mathcal{M}) \to \mathcal{M}$ is a diffeomorphism $\forall P \in \mathcal{M}$.*

A Riemannian manifold satisfying the hypothesis of Theorem 2.6 is called a *Cartan-Hadamard manifold*. On such a manifold, since $\mathrm{Exp}_P : T_P(\mathcal{M}) \to \mathcal{M}$ is a diffeomorphism, the Riemannian logarithm map $\mathrm{Log}_P : \mathcal{M} \to T_P(\mathcal{M})$ is well-defined on all of $\mathcal{M}$ and is a diffeomorphism from $\mathcal{M}$ onto $T_P(\mathcal{M})$.

Riemannian distance and Riemannian exponential and log maps. An important consequence of Theorem 2.6 is that on a Cartan-Hadamard manifold $\mathcal{M}$, any two points $P, Q \in \mathcal{M}$ are joined by a *unique geodesic* whose length is equal to their geodesic distance. In fact, let $V \in$

$T_P(\mathcal{M})$ be the unique tangent vector in $T_P(\mathcal{M})$ such that $Q = \mathrm{Exp}_P(V)$, then this geodesic curve has the form

$$\gamma_V(t) = \mathrm{Exp}_P(tV), \quad V = \mathrm{Log}_P(Q).$$

The Riemannian distance between P and Q is then given by

$$d(P, Q) = L(\gamma_V) = ||V||_P = ||\mathrm{Log}_P(Q)||_P. \tag{2.26}$$

Equivalently,

$$d(P, \mathrm{Exp}_P(V)) = ||V||_P. \tag{2.27}$$

Thus, on Cartan-Hadamard manifolds, the geodesic connecting two points P, Q is unique and the Riemannian distance $d(P, Q)$ is determined completely via knowledge of the Riemannian logarithm map. We apply this fact on the manifold $\mathrm{Sym}^{++}(n)$ of SPD matrices, which is described next.

2.4   AFFINE-INVARIANT RIEMANNIAN METRIC ON SPD MATRICES

We start with one of the most widely studied and well-understood Riemannian metrics on $\mathrm{Sym}^{++}(n)$, namely the *affine-invariant Riemannian metric*. In the mathematics literature, the study of this Riemannian metric goes as far back as [105] and [86]. For more recent treatment, we refer to [10, 11, 65, 92, 117], for example.

For $\mathcal{M} = \mathrm{Sym}^{++}(n)$, for each $P \in \mathrm{Sym}^{++}(n)$, the tangent space at P is given by

$$T_P(\mathrm{Sym}^{++}(n)) \cong \mathrm{Sym}(n), \tag{2.28}$$

where $\mathrm{Sym}(n)$ is the vector space of symmetric $n \times n$ matrices.

Riemannian metric. The affine-invariant Riemannian metric is defined by the following inner product on the tangent space at $P \in \mathrm{Sym}^{++}(n)$,

$$\langle A, B \rangle_P = \langle P^{-1/2}AP^{-1/2}, P^{-1/2}BP^{-1/2} \rangle_F, \quad \forall A, B \in \mathrm{Sym}(n). \tag{2.29}$$

Equivalently, since $\langle A, B \rangle_F = \mathrm{tr}(A^T B)$, we have

$$\langle A, B \rangle_P = \mathrm{tr}(P^{-1}AP^{-1}B). \tag{2.30}$$

The inner product $\langle \, , \, \rangle_P$ defines a notion of length, namely the corresponding norm $|| \, ||_P$, on the tangent space $T_P(\mathrm{Sym}^{++}(n))$, with

$$||A||_P = ||P^{-1/2}AP^{-1/2}||_F = \sqrt{\mathrm{tr}(P^{-1}AP^{-1}A)}, \quad A \in \mathrm{Sym}(n). \tag{2.31}$$

In particular, at the identity matrix I,

$$||A||_I = \sqrt{\text{tr}(A^2)} = ||A||_F. \tag{2.32}$$

Affine-invariance. The terminology *affine-invariant* is motivated by the following. Let $GL(n)$ denote the set of invertible $n \times n$ matrices. Each matrix $C \in GL(n)$ gives rise to the following linear transformation

$$\Gamma_C : \mathbb{R}^{n \times n} \to \mathbb{R}^{n \times n}, \Gamma_C : A \to \Gamma_C(A) = CAC^T,$$

which is called an affine or congruent transformation (the two matrices A and CAC^T are said to be congruent to each other, see, e.g., [87]). Clearly, if $A \in \text{Sym}(n)$, then $CAC^T \in \text{Sym}(n)$ and if $P \in \text{Sym}^{++}(n)$, then $CPC^T \in \text{Sym}^{++}(n)$, so that $\Gamma_C : \text{Sym}(n) \to \text{Sym}(n)$ and $\Gamma_C : \text{Sym}^{++}(n) \to \text{Sym}^{++}(n)$.

As can be readily verified, the inner product $\langle \, , \, \rangle_P$ is invariant under all affine transformations; that is,

$$\langle CAC^T, CBC^T \rangle_{CPC^T} = \langle A, B \rangle_P = \text{tr}(P^{-1}AP^{-1}B), \quad \forall C \in GL(n), \tag{2.33}$$

hence the name *affine-invariant Riemannian metric*.

Sectional curvature. Under the affine-invariant metric, $\text{Sym}^{++}(n)$ becomes a Riemannian manifold with *nonpositive sectional curvature*, as confirmed by the following result, whose proof can be found in [62] (we note that [62] uses a different sign convention for the Riemannian curvature tensor, opposite that of [28], which we follow here).

Theorem 2.7   *Under the affine-invariant Riemannian metric, $\text{Sym}^{++}(n)$ is a Cartan-Hadamard manifold, that is it is geodesically complete, simply connected, and with nonpositive sectional curvature.*

In fact, in this setting, the sectional curvature of $\text{Sym}^{++}(n)$ can be computed explicitly. For simplicity, we illustrate this on the tangent space at the identity matrix I (see [62], [120] for the derivation). On $T_I(\text{Sym}^{++}(n)) \cong \text{Sym}(n)$, the Riemannian curvature tensor R assumes a particularly simple form

$$R(X, Y)Z = [[X, Y], Z], \quad X, Y, Z \in \text{Sym}(n), \tag{2.34}$$

where $[X, Y] = XY - YX$ denotes the matrix commutator between X and Y. Thus by definition, for any two linearly independent matrices $X, Y \in \text{Sym}(n)$, the sectional curvature of the two-dimesional subspace of $\text{Sym}(n)$ spanned by X and Y is given by

$$K_I(X, Y) = 2\frac{\text{tr}[(XY)^2 - X^2Y^2]}{\text{tr}(X^2)\text{tr}(Y^2) - (\text{tr}(XY))^2} \leq 0, \tag{2.35}$$

where the inequality on the right-hand side follows from the Cauchy-Schwarz inequality, with zero equality if and only if $XY = YX$, that is if and only if X and Y commute.

Geodesic curve. Since the sectional curvature is nonpositive, by the Cartan-Hadamard Theorem (Theorem 2.6) and the subsequent discussion in Section 2.3, there is a unique geodesic connecting any two points $A, B \in \mathrm{Sym}^{++}(n)$ whose length is the Riemannian distance between A and B. This distance is completely determined by the Riemannian exponential and log maps, which are diffeomorphisms between $\mathrm{Sym}^{++}(n)$ and the tangent space $T_P(\mathrm{Sym}^{++}(n)) \cong \mathrm{Sym}(n)$.

For any fixed $P \in \mathrm{Sym}^{++}(n)$ and any $V \in \mathrm{Sym}(n) \cong T_P(\mathrm{Sym}^{++}(n))$, the geodesic curve $\gamma_V(t)$, with $\gamma_V(0) = P$ and $\dot{\gamma}_V(0) = V$ is given by (for a derivation, see, e.g., [85])

$$\gamma_V(t) = P^{1/2} \exp(tP^{-1/2}VP^{-1/2})P^{1/2}, \quad t \in \mathbb{R}. \tag{2.36}$$

For any two points $A, B \in \mathrm{Sym}^{++}(n)$, the unique geodesic curve $\gamma_{AB} : [0, 1] \to \mathrm{Sym}^{++}(n)$ joining them, with $\gamma_{AB}(0) = A, \gamma_{AB}(1) = B$, is given by

$$\gamma_{AB}(t) = A^{1/2} \exp[t \log(A^{-1/2}BA^{-1/2})]A^{1/2}, \quad t \in [0, 1]. \tag{2.37}$$

Riemannian exponential and logarithm maps. It follows that the Riemannian exponential map $\mathrm{Exp}_P : T_P(\mathrm{Sym}^{++}(n)) \to \mathrm{Sym}^{++}(n)$ is well-defined on all of the tangent space $T_P(\mathrm{Sym}^{++}(n))$, with

$$\mathrm{Exp}_P(V) = \gamma_V(1) = P^{1/2} \exp(P^{-1/2}VP^{-1/2})P^{1/2}, \quad V \in \mathrm{Sym}(n). \tag{2.38}$$

Its inverse, the Riemannian logarithm map $\mathrm{Log}_P : \mathrm{Sym}^{++}(n) \to T_P(\mathrm{Sym}^{++}(n))$ is well-defined on all of $\mathrm{Sym}^{++}(n)$ and is given by

$$\mathrm{Log}_P(A) = P^{1/2} \log(P^{-1/2}AP^{-1/2})P^{1/2}, \quad A \in \mathrm{Sym}^{++}(n). \tag{2.39}$$

In particular, at the identity matrix I,

$$\mathrm{Exp}_I(V) = \exp(V), \quad \mathrm{Log}_I(A) = \log(A), \quad V \in \mathrm{Sym}(n), \ A \in \mathrm{Sym}^{++}(n). \tag{2.40}$$

In Eqs. (2.36), (2.37), (2.38), and subsequently, $\exp(A)$ refers to the matrix exponential map. In Eq. (2.39) and subsequently in all the mathematical expressions in the rest of the chapter, $\log(A)$ refers to the *principal matrix logarithm* of A, which is an inverse function of $\exp$. For more detail on the matrix exponential and principal logarithm maps, we refer to Appendix A.2.

Affine-invariant Riemannian distance. By Eqs. (2.26), (2.39), and (2.31), the affine-invariant Riemannian distance between two matrices $A, B \in \mathrm{Sym}^{++}(n)$ is given by

$$d_{\mathrm{aiE}}(A, B) = ||\mathrm{Log}_A(B)||_A = || \log(A^{-1/2}BA^{-1/2})||_F, \tag{2.41}$$

where $\log$ denotes the principal matrix logarithm as defined in Eq. (A.13).

Equivalently, since the geodesic joining A and B is unique, with length equal to the Riemannian distance between A and B, by Eqs. (2.18) and (2.37),

$$d_{\mathrm{aiE}}(A, B) = L(\gamma_{AB}) = \int_0^1 \|\dot{\gamma}_{AB}(t)\|_{\gamma_{AB}(t)} dt = \|\log(A^{-1/2} B A^{-1/2})\|_F.$$

Let $\{\lambda_k\}_{k=1}^n$ denote the eigenvalues of $A^{-1/2} B A^{-1/2}$, which are the same as the eigenvalues of $A^{-1} B$, then we have the equivalent expression

$$d_{\mathrm{aiE}}(A, B) = \sum_{k=1}^n \log^2(\lambda_k). \tag{2.42}$$

This is the expression that is used to compute $d_{\mathrm{aiE}}(A, B)$ in an actual implementation.

Remark 2.8   We use the notation $d_{\mathrm{aiE}}(A, B)$ to denote the *finite-dimensional* affine-invariant Riemannian distance between the SPD matrices A and B to emphasize that the norm of the function $\log(A^{-1/2} B A^{-1/2})$, which defines this distance, is the Euclidean norm $\| \ \|_F$. The corresponding *infinite-dimensional* affine-invariant Riemannian distance in Section 5.2 will be denoted by d_{aiHS}, where the norm of the corresponding log function is based on the Hilbert-Schmidt norm $\| \ \|_{\mathrm{HS}}$.

Properties of the affine-invariant Riemannian distance.

1. **Affine invariance**. For any invertible $n \times n$ matrix C, the eigenvalues of $(CAC^T)^{-1}(CBC^T) = (C^T)^{-1} A^{-1} B C^T$ are the same as the eigenvalues of $A^{-1} B$, thus we have

$$d_{\mathrm{aiE}}(CAC^T, CBC^T) = d_{\mathrm{aiE}}(A, B), \tag{2.43}$$

which confirms the affine-invariance of the Riemannian distance d_{aiE}.

2. **Scale invariance**. In particular, for $C = \sqrt{s}I$, where $s \in \mathbb{R}, s > 0$, affine invariance becomes scale invariance, that is

$$d_{\mathrm{aiE}}(sA, sB) = d_{\mathrm{aiE}}(A, B). \tag{2.44}$$

3. **Unitary invariance**. For $C^T = C^{-1}$, that is C is a unitary matrix,

$$d_{\mathrm{aiE}}(CAC^T, CBC^T) = d_{\mathrm{aiE}}(A, B), \quad C^T C = I. \tag{2.45}$$

4. **Inversion invariance**.

$$d_{\mathrm{aiE}}(A^{-1}, B^{-1}) = d_{\mathrm{aiE}}(A, B). \tag{2.46}$$

5. **Complete metric space**. Since $\mathrm{Sym}^{++}(n)$ is a geodesically complete Riemannian manifold under the affine-invariant metric, it follows from the Hopf-Rinow Theorem that the metric space $(\mathrm{Sym}^{++}(n), d_{\mathrm{aiE}})$ is complete.

Computational complexity. For two matrices $A, B \in \mathrm{Sym}^{++}(n)$, the computation of $d_{\mathrm{aiE}}(A, B)$ as specified in Eqs. (2.41) and (2.42) requires the computation of the eigenvalues of the matrix $A^{-1}B$ or $A^{-1/2}BA^{-1/2}$. Since matrix inversion requires time complexity $O(n^3)$, matrix multiplication requires time complexity $O(n^3)$, and the eigenvalue computation requires time $O(n^3)$ (see, e.g., [89]) the overall computational complexity of this process is thus $O(n^3)$. Since the computation of $d_{\mathrm{aiE}}(A, B)$ involves computing the eigenvalues of either $A^{-1}B$ or $A^{-1/2}BA^{-1/2}$, in which A and B are *coupled* together, if we have a set of N matrices $\{A_j\}_{j=1}^N$ in $\mathrm{Sym}^{++}(n)$, then the computation of all the pairwise distances $\{d_{\mathrm{aiE}}(A_i, A_j)\}_{i,j=1}^N$ takes time $O(N^2 n^3)$.

2.4.1   CONNECTION WITH THE FISHER-RAO METRIC

The affine-invariant Riemannian metric on $\mathrm{Sym}^{++}(n)$, as described in Section 2.4, is closely connected with the Fisher-Rao Riemannian metric on the statistical manifold of multivariate Gaussian density functions on $\mathbb{R}^n$ with mean zero.

To describe the Fisher-Rao metric, let us first briefly review the concept of *statistical manifold* (see [1] for detail). Let $\mathcal{S}$ be a family of probability density functions P_θ on $\mathcal{X} = \mathbb{R}^n$, parametrized by a parameter $\theta = (\theta^1, \ldots, \theta^k) \in \Theta$, where Θ is an open subset in $\mathbb{R}^k$, for some $k \in \mathbb{N}$, that is

$$\mathcal{S} = \{P_\theta = P(x; \theta) \mid \theta = (\theta^1, \ldots, \theta^k) \in \Theta \subset \mathbb{R}^k\}, \tag{2.47}$$

where the mapping $\theta \to P_\theta$ is assumed to be injective. Such an $\mathcal{S}$ is called a k-dimensional *statistical model* or a *parametric model* on $\mathcal{X}$. Assume further that for each fixed $x \in \mathcal{X}$, the mapping $\theta \to P(x; \theta)$ is C^∞, so that all partial derivatives, such as $\frac{\partial P(x;\theta)}{\partial \theta^i}$, $1 \leq i \leq k$, are well-defined and continuous.

A k-dimensional statistical model $\mathcal{S}$ can be considered as a smooth manifold as follows. With $\mathcal{S} = \{P_\theta \mid \theta \in \Theta\}$, the mapping $\varphi(S) \to \Theta \subset \mathbb{R}^k$, defined by $\varphi(P_\theta) = \theta$, provides a coordinate chart on $\mathcal{S}$. Furthermore, consider the change of coordinates (or re-parametrization) $\psi : \Theta \to \psi(\Theta)$, where $\psi(\Theta)$ is an open subset of $\mathbb{R}^k$. Suppose that ψ is a diffeomorphism, that is it is bijective and both ψ and its inverse ψ^{-1} are C^∞ mappings. Then the re-parametrized family of probability density functions $\{P_{\psi^{-1}(\rho)} \mid \rho \in \psi(\Theta)\}$ is the same as $\mathcal{S}$. Thus, if all diffeomorphic parametrizations are considered to be equivalent to each other, then $\mathcal{S}$ can be considered as a smooth manifold.

Given a k-dimensional statistical manifold $\mathcal{S}$, at each point $\theta \in \Theta$, the *Fisher information matrix* [1] of $\mathcal{S}$ at θ is the $k \times k$ matrix $G(\theta) = [g_{ij}(\theta)]$, $1 \leq i, j \leq k$, with the (i, j)th entry given by

$$g_{ij}(\theta) = \int_{\mathbb{R}^n} \frac{\partial \ln P(x;\theta)}{\partial \theta^i} \frac{\partial \ln P(x;\theta)}{\partial \theta^j} P(x;\theta) dx. \qquad (2.48)$$

It is clear from the definition that the Fisher information matrix $G(\theta)$ is symmetric, positive semi-definite. Assume further that $G(\theta)$ is strictly positive definite $\forall \theta \in \Theta$, then it defines an inner product on the tangent space $T_{P_\theta}(\mathcal{S})$, via the inner product on the basis $\{\frac{\partial}{\partial \theta^j}\}_{j=1}^k$ of $T_{P_\theta}(\mathcal{S})$, by

$$\left\langle \frac{\partial}{\partial \theta^i}, \frac{\partial}{\partial \theta^j} \right\rangle_{P_\theta} = g_{ij}(\theta). \qquad (2.49)$$

This inner product defines a Riemannian metric on $\mathcal{S}$, the so-called *Fisher-Rao metric*, or *Fisher information metric*.

Consider now the family $\mathcal{S}$ of multivariate Gaussian density functions on $\mathbb{R}^n$ with mean zero. Since the corresponding covariance matrices are SPD matrices in $\mathrm{Sym}^{++}(n)$, which are completely determined by the $\frac{n(n+1)}{2}$ upper triangular entries, these Gaussian density functions are parametrized by $\theta \in \mathbb{R}^k$, where $k = \frac{n(n+1)}{2}$. Thus,

$$\mathcal{S} = \left\{ P(x;\theta) = \frac{1}{\sqrt{(2\pi)^n \det(\Sigma(\theta))}} \exp\left(-\frac{1}{2}x^T \Sigma(\theta)^{-1} x\right), \Sigma(\theta) \in \mathrm{Sym}^{++}(n), \theta \in \mathbb{R}^k \right\},$$
$$(2.50)$$

where $k = \frac{n(n+1)}{2}$ and $\theta = [\theta^1, \ldots, \theta^k]$, with the θ^j's corresponding to the upper triangular entries in $\Sigma(\theta)$ according to the following order: $\Sigma(\theta)_{11} = \theta^1$, $\Sigma(\theta)_{12} = \theta^2$, $\ldots$, $\Sigma(\theta)_{22} = \theta^{n+1}$, $\ldots$, $\Sigma(\theta)_{nn} = \theta^{\frac{n(n+1)}{2}}$.

In this case, the Fisher information matrix is given by the following result (see, e.g., [37, 70, 109]).

Theorem 2.9 *For the parametrized family of Gaussian densities on $\mathbb{R}^n$ with mean zero, as given in Eq. (2.50),*

$$g_{ij}(\theta) = \frac{1}{2}\mathrm{tr}[\Sigma^{-1}(\partial_{\theta^i}\Sigma)\Sigma^{-1}(\partial_{\theta^j}\Sigma)], \quad 1 \le i, j \le k, \qquad (2.51)$$

where $\partial_{\theta^i} = \frac{\partial}{\partial \theta^i}, \partial_{\theta^j} = \frac{\partial}{\partial \theta^j}$.

Since the means of the density functions in S are zero, we can identify the statistical manifold $\mathcal{S}$ with the manifold $\mathrm{Sym}^{++}(n)$ and the corresponding tangent space $T_{P_\theta}(\mathcal{S})$ with the tangent space $T_{\Sigma(\theta)}(\mathrm{Sym}^{++}(n)) \cong \mathrm{Sym}(n)$.

For $1 \leq r \leq s \leq n, r, s \in \mathbb{N}$, define the following matrices

$$E_{(r,s)} = \begin{cases} \mathbf{1}_{r,r} & \text{for } r = s, \\ \mathbf{1}_{r,s} + \mathbf{1}_{s,r} & \text{for } r \neq s, \end{cases} \tag{2.52}$$

where $\mathbf{1}_{r,s}$ is the matrix with entry 1 at location (r,s) and 0 everywhere else. Clearly $\{E_{(r,s)}\}_{1 \leq r \leq s \leq n}$ forms a basis for $\text{Sym}(n)$.

Consider the following identification of indices: $1 \to (1,1)$, $2 \to (1,2)$, $3 \to (1,3)$, $\dots, n+1 \to (2,2), \dots, \frac{n(n+1)}{2} \to (n,n)$. By assumption, $\Sigma(\theta) = \sum_{1 \leq r \leq s \leq n} \theta^{(r,s)} E_{(r,s)}$, so that $\frac{\partial \Sigma(\theta)}{\partial \theta^{(r,s)}} = E_{(r,s)}$. Then we can identify the basis $\{\frac{\partial}{\partial \theta^{(r,s)}}\}_{1 \leq r \leq s \leq n}$ of $T_{P_\theta}(\mathcal{S})$ with the basis $\{E_{(r,s)}\}_{1 \leq r \leq s \leq n}$ of $\text{Sym}(n)$. Thus, Eq. (2.51) gives

$$\langle E_{(r_1,s_1)}, E_{(r_2,s_2)} \rangle_\Sigma = \frac{1}{2} \text{tr}[\Sigma^{-1} E_{(r_1,s_1)} \Sigma^{-1} E_{(r_2,s_2)}]. \tag{2.53}$$

Therefore, for any two matrices $A, B \in \text{Sym}(n)$, by expanding in the basis $\{E_{rs}\}_{1 \leq r \leq s \leq n}$, we arrive at the following result (see also [70, 109]).

Theorem 2.10   *The Riemannian metric on* $\text{Sym}^{++}(n)$ *induced by the Fisher information matrix on the statistical manifold of multivariate Gaussian densities on* $\mathbb{R}^n$ *with zero mean is given by*

$$\langle A, B \rangle_\Sigma = \frac{1}{2} \text{tr}[\Sigma^{-1} A \Sigma^{-1} B], \quad A, B \in \text{Sym}(n), \Sigma \in \text{Sym}^{++}(n). \tag{2.54}$$

Thus, the Riemannian metric on $\text{Sym}^{++}(n)$ induced by the Fisher information matrix is precisely half the affine-invariant Riemannian metric as defined in Eq. (2.30) in Section 2.4.

2.5   LOG-EUCLIDEAN METRIC

As discussed in the previous section, the computational complexity of computing all the pairwise distances $\{d_{\text{aiE}}(A_i, A_j)\}_{i,j=1}^N$ for a set of N matrices $\{A_j\}_{j=1}^N$ in $\text{Sym}^{++}(n)$ is $O(N^2 n^3)$. This computational cost becomes very large when N is large. The reduction in computational complexity is one of the motivations for the consideration of the *Log-Euclidean distance* [6], which is defined by

$$d_{\log E}(A, B) = \| \log(A) - \log(B) \|_F. \tag{2.55}$$

If A and B *commute*, that is if $AB = BA$, then the Log-Euclidean distance $d_{\log E}$ and the affine-invariant Riemannian distance d_{aiE} coincide, that is

$$d_{\log E}(A, B) = d_{\text{aiE}}(A, B) = \| \log(A^{-1/2} B A^{-1/2}) \|_F = \| \log(A) - \log(B) \|_F. \tag{2.56}$$

Interpretations. There are (at least) two possible different interpretations for the Log-Euclidean distance $d_{\log E}$, as follows.

1. $d_{\log E}(A, B)$ is an approximation of the affine-invariant Riemannian distance $d_{\text{aiE}}(A, B)$, obtained by first projecting A and B, via the Riemannian log map, to the tangent space $T_I(\text{Sym}^{++}(n))$ at the identity, then computing the Euclidean distance between the projections.

2. $d_{\log E}(A, B)$ is the geodesic distance of a Riemannian metric on $\text{Sym}^{++}(n)$, namely the Log-Euclidean metric, which was formulated in [6].

We discuss these interpretations in detail in Sections 2.5.1 and 2.5.2.

Computational complexity. To compute the distance $d_{\log E}(A, B)$ as defined in Eq. (2.55), we need to compute the principal matrix logarithms $\log(A)$ and $\log(B)$, which involves computing the singular value decomposition (SVD) of A and B, with time complexity $O(n^3)$. However, a key difference between Eq. (2.55) and Eq. (2.41) is that in Eq. (2.55), A and B are *uncoupled*. Thus, when computing all the pairwise distances $\{d_{\log E}(A_i, A_j)\}_{i,j=1}^N$ for a set $\{A_i\}_{i=1}^N$ in $\text{Sym}^{++}(n)$, we can first compute all the functions $\log(A_i)$, $1 \leq i \leq N$, separately, then compute the distance matrix between them. The computational complexity of this process is thus $O(Nn^3)$, which is $O(N)$ times faster than that for the affine-invariant Riemannian distance d_{aiE}. Furthermore, it is straightforward to parallelize the computation of the set $\{\log(A_i)\}_{i=1}^N$, leading to faster actual running time of the overall algorithm.

2.5.1   LOG-EUCLIDEAN DISTANCE AS AN APPROXIMATION OF THE AFFINE-INVARIANT RIEMANNIAN DISTANCE

Let us now consider the first interpretation of the Log-Euclidean distance as defined in Eq. (2.55). We recall that under the affine-invariant Riemannian metric, Eq. (2.40) states that at the identity matrix I, the Riemannian log map is given by $\text{Log}_I(A) = \log(A) \ \forall A \in \text{Sym}^{++}(n)$, and Eq. (2.32) states that the norm on the tangent space $T_I(\text{Sym}^{++}(n))$ at I is the Frobenius norm, that is $||B||_I = ||B||_F \ \forall B \in \text{Sym}(n)$. Thus,

$$||\text{Log}_I(A) - \text{Log}_I(B)||_I = ||\log(A) - \log(B)||_F = d_{\log E}(A, B). \qquad (2.57)$$

Thus, $d_{\log E}(A, B)$ is equal to the distance between the projections of A, B via the Riemannian log map corresponding to the affine-invariant Riemannian metric onto the tangent space $T_I(\text{Sym}^{++}(n))$ at the identity. A geometrical visualization of this interpretation is depicted in Figure 2.4.

Approximation via the Campbell-Baker-Hausdorff (CBH) formula. The following is a more illuminating result illustrating the relationship between the affine-invariant Riemannian distance $d_{\text{aiE}}(A, B)$ and the Log-Euclidean distance $d_{\log E}(A, B)$ when A, B are sufficiently close to the identity matrix I. It is based on the Campbell-Baker-Hausdorff (CBH) formula [42], which states that for any two $n \times n$ matrices A, B sufficiently close to the zero matrix, the

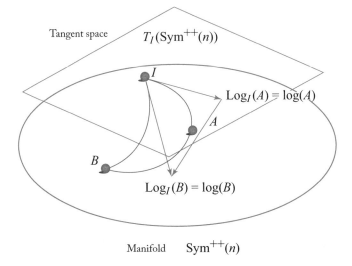

Figure 2.4: The Log-Euclidean distance viewed as an approximation of the affine-invariant Riemannian distance on $\mathrm{Sym}^{++}(n)$. Given two matrices $A, B \in \mathrm{Sym}^{++}(n)$, $\log(A) = \mathrm{Log}_I(A)$ and $\log(B) = \mathrm{Log}_I(B)$ are the projections of A and B, respectively, onto the tangent space $T_I(\mathrm{Sym}^{++}(n))$ at the identity matrix I. The Log-Euclidean distance $d_{\log\mathrm{E}}(A, B) = \|\log(A) - \log(B)\|_F$ is thus the distance between $\log(A)$ and $\log(B)$ in the tangent space $T_I(\mathrm{Sym}^{++}(n))$ and can thus be considered as an approximation of the affine-invariant Riemannian distance $d_{\mathrm{aiE}}(A, B)$ between A and B on the manifold $\mathrm{Sym}^{++}(n)$.

following series expansion converges:

$$\exp(A)\exp(B) = \exp\left(A + B + \frac{1}{2}[A, B] + \frac{1}{12}[A, [A, B]] + \frac{1}{12}[B, [B, A]] + \cdots\right), \quad (2.58)$$

where $[A, B] = AB - BA$ denote the commutator of A and B. Since

$$A^{-1/2}BA^{-1/2} = \exp(-1/2\log(A))\exp(\log(B))\exp(-1/2\log(A)),$$

when $A, B \in \mathrm{Sym}^{++}(n)$ are sufficiently close to the identity matrix, so that $\log(A)$ and $\log(B)$ are close to the zero matrix, by applying the Campbell-Baker-Hausdorff formula twice, we obtain the following convergent series expansion

$$\log(A^{-1/2}BA^{-1/2})$$
$$= -\log(A) + \log(B) - \frac{1}{24}[\log(A), [\log(A), \log(B)]] - \frac{1}{12}[\log(B), [\log(B), \log(A)]] + \cdots$$

From this expansion, we obtain the following result (see also [120] for a detailed derivation and [6] for a comparable result).

Theorem 2.11   *For any pair of matrices $A, B \in \text{Sym}^{++}(n)$ sufficiently close to the identity matrix I,*

$$
\begin{aligned}
|| \log(A^{-1/2} B A^{-1/2}) ||_F^2 &= || \log(A) - \log(B) ||_F^2 \\
&+ \frac{1}{12} \text{tr} \{ [\log(A), [\log(A), \log(B)]](\log(A) - \log(B)) \} \\
&+ \frac{1}{6} \text{tr} \{ [\log(B), [\log(B), \log(A)]](\log(A) - \log(B)) \} + \cdots .
\end{aligned} \tag{2.59}
$$

Thus, by taking only the first term in Eq. (2.59) and truncating the rest, we obtain the Log-Euclidean distance $d_{\text{logE}}(A, B)$ as an approximation of the affine-invariant Riemannian distance $d_{\text{aiE}}(A, B)$ when A, B are sufficiently close to the identity matrix I.

Caveat. While this viewpoint is intuitive and geometrically appealing, further interpretations based upon it need to be made with careful considerations. For example, the fact that A and B are both projected onto the tangent space $T_I(\text{Sym}^{++}(n))$ at the identity matrix I *may* give the impression that the farther A and B are to the identity matrix I, the farther the Log-Euclidean distance $d_{\text{logE}}(A, B)$ is to the affine-invariant Riemannian distance $d_{\text{aiE}}(A, B)$. This is *not necessarily true* in general. We illustrate this phenomenon via the following example.

Let $A, B \in \text{Sym}^{++}(n)$, with the eigenvalues of A and B being $\{(1 + \epsilon_j^A)\}_{j=1}^n$ and $\{(1 + \epsilon_j^B)\}_{j=1}^n$, respectively, where $\epsilon_j^A > 0, \epsilon_j^B > 0, 1 \leq j \leq n$. The distances between A and the identity matrix I and between B and I are then given by

$$
d_{\text{aiE}}(I, A) = d_{\text{logE}}(I, A) = || \log(A) ||_F = \sqrt{ \sum_{j=1}^n \log^2(1 + \epsilon_j^A) },
$$

$$
d_{\text{aiE}}(I, B) = d_{\text{logE}}(I, B) = || \log(B) ||_F = \sqrt{ \sum_{j=1}^n \log^2(1 + \epsilon_j^B) }.
$$

By choosing $\epsilon_j^A, \epsilon_j^B$ arbitrarily small, we can make A and B as close to the identity matrix I as we wish.

We consider now any scalar $s > 0$ along with the scaled matrices sA and sB. We have

$$
d_{\text{aiE}}(I, sA) = d_{\text{logE}}(I, sA) = || \log(sA) ||_F = \sqrt{ \sum_{j=1}^n \log^2[s(1 + \epsilon_j^A)] },
$$

$$
d_{\text{aiE}}(I, sB) = d_{\text{logE}}(I, sB) = || \log(sB) ||_F = \sqrt{ \sum_{j=1}^n \log^2[s(1 + \epsilon_j^B)] }.
$$

By choosing s arbitrarily large, we can make the matrices sA and sB as far away from the identity matrix I as we wish.

On the other hand, by scale invariance, we always have

$$d_{\mathrm{aiE}}(sA, sB) = d_{\mathrm{aiE}}(A, B), \quad d_{\mathrm{logE}}(sA, sB) = d_{\mathrm{logE}}(A, B) \quad \forall s > 0.$$

Thus, in this example, both the Log-Euclidean distance and the affine-invariant Riemannian distance between sA and sB remain the same, no matter how far or how close both sA and sB are from the identity matrix I.

2.5.2   LOG-EUCLIDEAN DISTANCE AS A RIEMANNIAN DISTANCE

Consider now the second interpretation, in which the Log-Euclidean distance is the geodesic distance of a Riemaian metric on $\mathrm{Sym}^{++}(n)$, the so-called Log-Euclidean metric, as formulated by [6]. This metric arises from the following commutative Lie group multiplication on $\mathrm{Sym}^{++}(n)$,

$$\odot : \mathrm{Sym}^{++}(n) \times \mathrm{Sym}^{++}(n) \rightarrow \mathrm{Sym}^{++}(n),$$
$$A \odot B = \exp(\log(A) + \log(B)). \tag{2.60}$$

The Log-Euclidean metric is a *bi-invariant* Riemannian metric on $(\mathrm{Sym}^{++}(n), \odot)$, in the sense that the Riemannian distance on $\mathrm{Sym}^{++}(n)$ under this metric is invariant under the $\odot$ operation, that is

$$d_{\mathrm{logE}}[(A \odot C), (B \odot C)] = d_{\mathrm{logE}}[(C \odot A), (C \odot B)]$$
$$= d_{\mathrm{logE}}(A, B), \quad \forall C \in \mathrm{Sym}^{++}(n), \tag{2.61}$$

as can be readily verified (we refer to, e.g., [28] for a more abstract definition of the concept of bi-invariant metrics).

Riemannian metric. Under the Log-Euclidean metric, the inner product on the tangent space $T_P(\mathrm{Sym}^{++}(n)) \cong \mathrm{Sym}(n)$, $P \in \mathrm{Sym}^{++}(n)$, is given by (see [6], cf. Eq. (2.29))

$$\langle V, W \rangle_P = \langle D \log(P)(V), D \log(P)(W) \rangle_I, \quad V, W \in \mathrm{Sym}(n), \tag{2.62}$$

where $\langle \, , \, \rangle_I$ is any inner product on $T_I(\mathrm{Sym}^{++}(n))$ and $D \log$ denotes the Fréchet derivative of the function $\log : \mathrm{Sym}^{++}(n) \rightarrow \mathrm{Sym}(n)$. For the definition of the Fréchet derivative, see Appendix A.3. The analytical expression for $D \log(P) : \mathrm{Sym}(n) \rightarrow \mathrm{Sym}(n)$ is complicated in general, see Eq. (A.17) in Appendix A.3, with the exception of the case $P = I$, when one has $D \log(I) = \mathrm{id}$. Fortunately, in the present context, knowledge of $D \log$ is not necessary for computing the geodesic curve, under the Log-Euclidean metric, between two points on $\mathrm{Sym}^{++}(n)$ or their Riemannian distance.

The length $|| \, ||_P$ corresponding to the metric in Eq. (2.62) on the tangent space at P is given by (cf. Eq. (2.31))

$$||V||_P = ||D \log(P)(V)||_I, \quad V \in \mathrm{Sym}(n). \tag{2.63}$$

Geodesic curve. The geodesic curve $\gamma : [0, 1] \to \mathrm{Sym}^{++}(n)$ joining two points $A, B \in \mathrm{Sym}^{++}(n)$, with $\gamma(0) = A, \gamma(1) = B$, is given by (cf. Eq. (2.37))

$$\gamma_{AB}(t) = \exp[(1 - t)\log(A) + t\log(B)]. \tag{2.64}$$

Riemannian exponential and logarithm maps. The Riemannian exponential map $\mathrm{Exp}_P :$ $\mathrm{Sym}(n) \to \mathrm{Sym}^{++}(n)$ then has the form (cf. Eq. (2.38))

$$\mathrm{Exp}_P(V) = \exp[\log(P) + D\log(P)(V)]. \tag{2.65}$$

The inverse Riemannian log map $\mathrm{Log}_P : \mathrm{Sym}^{++} \to T_P(\mathrm{Sym}^{++}(n)) \cong \mathrm{Sym}(n)$ is given by (cf. (2.39))

$$\mathrm{Log}_P(A) = D\exp(\log(P))[\log(A) - \log(P)], \quad A \in \mathrm{Sym}^{++}(n). \tag{2.66}$$

In particular, at the identity matrix I,

$$\mathrm{Exp}_I(V) = \exp(V), \quad \mathrm{Log}_I(A) = \log(A), \quad V \in \mathrm{Sym}(n), \quad A \in \mathrm{Sym}^{++}(n). \tag{2.67}$$

Thus, the Riemannian exponential and logarithm maps for the Log-Euclidean metric at the identity I coincide with those for the affine-invariant Riemannian metric (cf. Eq. (2.40)).

Geodesic distance. By Eqs. (2.26), (2.66), and (2.31), the geodesic distance between A and B is given by

$$d_{\mathrm{logE}}(A, B) = \|\mathrm{Log}_A(B)\|_A = \|\log(A) - \log(B)\|_I. \tag{2.68}$$

Equivalently, since the geodesic joining A, B is unique, with length equal to the Riemannian distance between A and B, by Eqs. (2.18) and (2.64),

$$d_{\mathrm{logE}}(A, B) = L(\gamma_{AB}) = \int_0^1 \|\dot{\gamma}_{AB}(t)\|_{\gamma_{AB}(t)}dt = \|\log(A) - \log(B)\|_I.$$

Vector space structure of $\mathrm{Sym}^{++}(n)$. Together with the group operation $\odot$, one can also define the following scalar multiplication on $\mathrm{Sym}^{++}(n)$ [6]

$$\circledast : \mathbb{R} \times \mathrm{Sym}^{++}(n) \to \mathrm{Sym}^{++}(n),$$
$$\lambda \circledast A = \exp(\lambda\log(A)) = A^\lambda, \quad \lambda \in \mathbb{R}. \tag{2.69}$$

Endowed with the commutative group multiplication $\odot$ and the scalar multiplication $\circledast$, the axioms of vector space can be readily verified to show that $(\mathrm{Sym}^{++}(n), \odot, \circledast)$ is a vector space [6].

Inner product space structure on $\mathrm{Sym}^{++}(n)$. On top of the vector space structure $(\mathrm{Sym}^{++}(n), \odot, \circledast)$, we can define the following *Log-Euclidean inner product*:

$$\langle A, B \rangle_{\mathrm{logE}} = \langle \log(A), \log(B) \rangle_F = \mathrm{tr}[\log(A)\log(B)] \tag{2.70}$$

along with the corresponding *Log-Euclidean norm*

$$||A||_{\log E}^2 = \langle \log(A), \log(A) \rangle_F = \text{tr}[\log^2(A)]. \tag{2.71}$$

The axioms of inner product, namely symmetry, positivity, and linearity with respect to the operations $(\odot, \circledast)$ can be verified to show that

$$(\text{Sym}^{++}(n), \odot, \circledast, \langle \, , \, \rangle_{\log E}). \tag{2.72}$$

is an inner product space. This inner product space structure was first discussed in [72]. In terms of the Log-Euclidean inner product and Log-Euclidean norm, the Log-Euclidean distance $d_{\log E}$ in Eq. (2.68) is expressed as

$$d_{\log E}(A, B) = ||\log(A) - \log(B)||_F = ||A \odot B^{-1}||_{\log E}$$
$$= \sqrt{\langle A \odot B^{-1}, A \odot B^{-1} \rangle_{\log E}}. \tag{2.73}$$

Zero curvature. Since the Log-Euclidean distance is induced by the Log-Euclidean inner product in the space $(\text{Sym}^{++}(n), \odot, \circledast, \langle \, , \, \rangle_{\log E})$, it follows that as a Riemannian manifold, $\text{Sym}^{++}(n)$ under the Log-Euclidean metric is flat, that is it has *zero sectional curvature*.

2.5.3   LOG-EUCLIDEAN VS. EUCLIDEAN

Continuing with the previous discussion, it can be verified that

$$\log : (\text{Sym}^{++}(n), \odot, \circledast, \langle \, , \, \rangle_{\log E}) \to (\text{Sym}(n), +, \cdot, \langle \, , \, \rangle_F)$$
$$A \to \log(A) \tag{2.74}$$

is an isometrical isomorphism between inner product spaces, where $(+, \cdot)$ denote the standard matrix addition and scalar multiplication operations, respectively. One can say that the Log-Euclidean metric essentially flattens $\text{Sym}^{++}(n)$ via the map $A \to \log(A)$.

While making $\text{Sym}^{++}(n)$ into an inner product space, it is important to point out that the Log-Euclidean metric is *fundamentally different* from the Euclidean metric. We emphasize that the vector space operations $(\odot, \circledast)$ are *not* the vector space operations in the Euclidean case, namely $(+, \cdot)$, and $(\text{Sym}^{++}(n), \odot, \circledast)$ is *not* a vector subspace of the Euclidean space $(\text{Sym}(n), +, \cdot)$. The crucial differences between the Log-Euclidean and Euclidean distances can be seen more clearly through their invariance properties, as follows.

Properties of the Log-Euclidean distance vs. the Euclidean distance. The Log-Euclidean distance $d_{\log E}$ no longer satisfies the full affine-invariance property as in Eq. (2.43), but it still satisfies many special invariances, including scale invariance, unitary invariance, and invariance under inversion.

1. **Scale invariance**. For any scalar $s > 0$, since $\log(sA) = (\log(s))I + \log(A)$, we immediately have

$$d_{\log E}(sA, sB) = d_{\log E}(A, B). \tag{2.75}$$

In contrast, the Euclidean distance $||A - B||_F$ is clearly *not* scale-invariant.

2. **Unitary invariance**. For any invertible matrix $C \in \mathbb{R}^{n \times n}$ with $C^T = C^{-1}$, that is C is a unitary matrix,

$$d_{\log E}(CAC^T, CBC^T) = d_{\log E}(A, B), \quad C^T C = I. \tag{2.76}$$

Among all the properties listed here, this is the only one that the Euclidean distance shares with the Log-Euclidean distance.

3. **Invariance under inversion**. Since $\log(A^{-1}) = -\log(A)$, we immediately have

$$d_{\log E}(A^{-1}, B^{-1}) = d_{\log E}(A, B). \tag{2.77}$$

In contrast, the Euclidean distance $||A - B||_F$ is clearly *not* inversion-invariant.

4. **Complete metric space**. Since $d_{\log E}$ is the distance induced by an inner product on $\text{Sym}^{++}(n)$, it follows that $(\text{Sym}^{++}(n), d_{\log E})$ is a complete metric space. In contrast, with the Euclidean distance, $(\text{Sym}^{++}(n), || \ ||_F)$ is an *incomplete* metric space.

Thus, in settings that require scale invariance or inversion invariance, for instance, the behavior of the Log-Euclidean distance will be very different from that of the Euclidean distance. We compare their empirical performances in kernel methods in Chapter 3.

2.6 BREGMAN DIVERGENCES

So far we have discussed the affine-invariant Riemannian distance d_{aiE} and the Log-Euclidean distance $d_{\log E}$, both of which are geodesic distances of Riemannian metrics on $\text{Sym}^{++}(n)$. We now turn to the second approach, namely Bregman divergences, in which one defines distance-like functions based on the convex cone structure of $\text{Sym}^{++}(n)$. We focus in particular on the Log-Determinant divergences, which are obtained based on the strictly convex function $\phi(X) = -\log \det(X)$, $X \in \text{Sym}^{++}(n)$. The Log-Determinant divergences are not Riemannian distances on $\text{Sym}^{++}(n)$ and, apart from special cases such as the symmetric Stein divergence, they are generally *not* metric distances, since in general they only satisfy the positivity axiom in the definition of a metric. However, they possess many theoretical properties similar to the affine-invariance Riemannian distance, can be computed efficiently, and have been shown to work well in diverse applications [18, 21, 60, 110, 111].

We first recall the concept of Bregman divergence [13]. Let $\Omega \subset \mathbb{R}^n$ be a convex set and $\phi : \Omega \to \mathbb{R}$ be a differentiable and strictly convex function, then it defines the following *divergence* function on Ω

$$B_\phi(x, y) = \phi(x) - \phi(y) - \langle \nabla \phi(y), x - y \rangle. \tag{2.78}$$

In particular, for $\Omega = \mathbb{R}^n$ and $\phi(x) = ||x||^2$, we obtain the squared Euclidean distance $B_\phi(x, y) = ||x - y||^2$. More generally, ϕ defines following family of divergences [132], parametrized by a parameter $\alpha \in \mathbb{R}$:

$$d_\phi^\alpha(x, y) = \frac{4}{1 - \alpha^2} \left[\frac{1 - \alpha}{2} \phi(x) + \frac{1 + \alpha}{2} \phi(y) - \phi\left(\frac{1 - \alpha}{2} x + \frac{1 + \alpha}{2} y \right) \right], \quad (2.79)$$

with $d_\phi^{\pm 1}$ defined as the limits of d_ϕ^α as $\alpha \to \pm 1$. In fact, we have

$$d_\phi^1(x, y) = \lim_{\alpha \to 1} d_\phi^\alpha(x, y) = B_\phi(x, y), \quad (2.80)$$

$$d_\phi^{-1}(x, y) = \lim_{\alpha \to -1} d_\phi^\alpha(x, y) = B_\phi(y, x). \quad (2.81)$$

In general, it can be readily verified that d_ϕ^α can be expressed in terms of the Bregman divergence B_ϕ $\forall \alpha \in \mathbb{R}$, as follows:

$$d_\phi^\alpha(x, y) = \frac{4}{1 - \alpha^2} \left[\frac{1 - \alpha}{2} B_\phi\left(x, \frac{1 - \alpha}{2} x + \frac{1 + \alpha}{2} y \right) + \frac{1 + \alpha}{2} B_\phi\left(y, \frac{1 - \alpha}{2} x + \frac{1 + \alpha}{2} y \right) \right]. \quad (2.82)$$

In our current context, we consider $\Omega = \mathrm{Sym}^{++}(n)$ together with the strictly convex function $\phi(X) = -\log \det(X)$, $X \in \mathrm{Sym}^{++}(n)$, resulting in the Log-Determinant divergences on $\mathrm{Sym}^{++}(n)$, which we discuss next.

2.6.1 LOG-DETERMINANT DIVERGENCES

We now consider the Alpha Log-Determinant (or Log-Det for short) divergences on $\mathrm{Sym}^{++}(n)$. These are motivated by Ky Fan's inequality [32] on the log-concavity of the matrix determinant function on $\mathrm{Sym}^{++}(n)$ which states that

$$\det[\alpha A + (1 - \alpha)B] \geq \det(A)^\alpha \det(B)^{1 - \alpha},$$
$$\forall A, B \in \mathrm{Sym}^{++}(n), \ 0 \leq \alpha \leq 1. \quad (2.83)$$

For $0 < \alpha < 1$, equality happens if and only if $A = B$.

Thus, the function $\phi(X) = -\log \det(X)$ is strictly convex on $\mathrm{Sym}^{++}(n)$. Hence, based on Eq. (2.79), we obtain the Alpha Log-Determinant divergences, which are a parametrized family of divergences defined by [18]

$$d_{\mathrm{logdet}}^\alpha(A, B) = \frac{4}{1 - \alpha^2} \log \left[\frac{\det(\frac{1 - \alpha}{2} A + \frac{1 + \alpha}{2} B)}{\det(A)^{\frac{1 - \alpha}{2}} \det(B)^{\frac{1 + \alpha}{2}}} \right], \quad -1 < \alpha < 1, \quad (2.84)$$

with the limiting cases $\alpha = \pm 1$, obtained via L'Hopital's rule, given by

$$d_{\mathrm{logdet}}^1(A, B) = \lim_{\alpha \to 1} d_{\mathrm{logdet}}^\alpha(A, B) = \mathrm{tr}(B^{-1}A - I) - \log \det(B^{-1}A), \quad (2.85)$$

$$d_{\mathrm{logdet}}^{-1}(A, B) = \lim_{\alpha \to -1} d_{\mathrm{logdet}}^\alpha(A, B) = \mathrm{tr}(A^{-1}B - I) - \log \det(A^{-1}B). \quad (2.86)$$

By Ky Fan's inequality, the Alpha Log-Det divergences satisfy the *positivity* properties of distance functions, namely

$$d_{\text{logdet}}^{\alpha}(A, B) \geq 0, \tag{2.87}$$

$$d_{\text{logdet}}^{\alpha}(A, B) = 0 \iff A = B. \tag{2.88}$$

Instead of symmetry, $d_{\text{logdet}}^{\alpha}$ satisfies the so-called *dual symmetry* property (see [18]), which states that

$$d_{\text{logdet}}^{\alpha}(A, B) = d_{\text{logdet}}^{-\alpha}(B, A). \tag{2.89}$$

In particular, $d_{\text{logdet}}^{\alpha}$ is symmetric if and only if $\alpha = 0$, that is

$$d_{\text{logdet}}^{0}(A, B) = d_{\text{logdet}}^{0}(B, A). \tag{2.90}$$

The symmetric divergence d_{logdet}^{0}, which is also called the symmetric Stein divergence or Jensen-Bregman LogDet divergence, has been studied extensively, from both mathematical and practical perspectives, see, e.g., [18, 21, 60, 110, 111]. In particular, it is shown in [110, 111] that $\sqrt{d_{\text{logdet}}^{0}(A, B)}$ also satisfies the *triangle inequality*, thus making it a metric on $\text{Sym}^{++}(n)$. Specifically, we have the following result.

Theorem 2.12 [110, 111]. *The function* $d_{\text{stein}} : \text{Sym}^{++}(n) \times \text{Sym}^{++}(n) \to \mathbb{R}^{+}$, *defined by*

$$d_{\text{stein}}(A, B) = \frac{1}{2}\sqrt{d_{\text{logdet}}^{0}(A, B)} = \sqrt{\log \frac{\det(\frac{A+B}{2})}{\sqrt{\det(A)\det(B)}}}, \tag{2.91}$$

is a metric on $\text{Sym}^{++}(n)$.

Invariance properties. The Alpha Log-Det divergences $d_{\text{logdet}}^{\alpha}$ possess many invariance properties as the affine-invariant Riemannian distance d_{aiE}, including the following.

1. **Affine invariance.** For any invertible matrix $C \in \mathbb{R}^{n \times n}$,

$$d_{\text{logdet}}^{\alpha}(CAC^{T}, CBC^{T}) = d_{\text{logdet}}^{\alpha}(A, B). \tag{2.92}$$

2. **Scale invariance.** In particular, for $C = \sqrt{s}I$, with $s > 0$, affine invariance becomes scale invariance, that is

$$d_{\text{logdet}}^{\alpha}(sA, sB) = d_{\text{logdet}}^{\alpha}(A, B). \tag{2.93}$$

3. **Unitary invariance.** For $C^{T} = C^{-1}$, that is C is a unitary matrix,

$$d_{\text{logdet}}^{\alpha}(CAC^{T}, CBC^{T}) = d(A, B), \quad C^{T}C = I. \tag{2.94}$$

4. **Dual invariance under inversion**. Instead of the *invariance under inversion* property of d_{aiE}, in general $d_{\text{logdet}}^{\alpha}$ satisfies the *dual invariance under inversion* property, which states that

$$d_{\text{logdet}}^{\alpha}(A^{-1}, B^{-1}) = d_{\text{logdet}}^{-\alpha}(A, B). \tag{2.95}$$

In particular, $d_{\text{logdet}}^{\alpha}$ satisfies invariance under inversion if and only if $\alpha = 0$, that is

$$d_{\text{logdet}}^{0}(A^{-1}, B^{-1}) = d_{\text{logdet}}^{0}(A, B). \tag{2.96}$$

Computational complexity. For $-1 < \alpha < 1$, the Log-Det divergences can be written as

$$d_{\text{logdet}}^{\alpha}(A, B) = \frac{4}{1 - \alpha^2} \log \det \left(\frac{1 - \alpha}{2} A + \frac{1 + \alpha}{2} B \right)$$
$$- \frac{2}{1 + \alpha} \log \det(A) - \frac{2}{1 - \alpha} \log \det(B). \tag{2.97}$$

Thus, computing $d_{\text{logdet}}^{\alpha}(A, B)$ requires the computation of the log det function of three matrices in $\text{Sym}^{++}(n)$. We first note that the direct computation of $\log \det(A)$, $A \in \text{Sym}^{++}(n)$, is in general only feasible when n is relatively small, typically due to overflow/underflow errors in computing $\det(A)$ when n is large. Fortunately, $\log \det(A)$ can be carried out efficiently via the Cholesky decomposition as follows. We recall that any matrix $A \in \text{Sym}^{++}(n)$ admits a unique Cholesky decomposition, which has the form

$$A = U^T U, \quad U \text{ upper triangular},$$

where all the diagonal entries of U are positive. Thus, it follows that

$$\det(A) = [\det(U)]^2 \Rightarrow \log \det(A) = 2 \log \det(U) = 2 \text{tr} \log(\text{diag}(U)), \tag{2.98}$$

so that only the diagonal entries of U are needed for computing $\log \det(A)$. Since the computational complexity of the Cholesky decomposition is $O(n^3)$ [43], the overall computational complexity for computing $d_{\text{logdet}}^{\alpha}(A, B)$ is $O(n^3)$. Since A and B are coupled together in Eq. (2.97), for a set of N matrices $\{A_j\}_{j=1}^N$ in $\text{Sym}^{++}(n)$, the computational complexity required for computing the matrix of all pairwise divergences $\{d_{\text{logdet}}^{\alpha}(A_i, A_j)\}_{i,j=1}^N$ is $O(N^2 n^3)$.

2.6.2 CONNECTION WITH THE RÉNYI AND KULLBACK-LEIBLER DIVERGENCES

We now show that the Alpha Log-Det divergences $d_{\text{logdet}}^{\alpha}$ are equivalent, up to a multiplicative constant factor, to the Rényi divergences, for $-1 < \alpha < 1$, and the Kullback-Leibler divergences, for $\alpha = \pm 1$, between two multivariate normal density functions on $\mathbb{R}^n$ with zero means.

Let P_1, P_2 be two Borel probability density functions on $\mathbb{R}^n$. For $0 < r < 1$ fixed, the Rényi divergence [99] of order r between P_1 and P_2 is defined to be

$$d_R^r(P_1, P_2) = -\frac{1}{1-r} \log \int_{\mathbb{R}^n} P_1(x)^r P_2(x)^{1-r} dx. \qquad (2.99)$$

As $r \to 1$, the Rényi divergence becomes the Kullback-Leibler divergence [61] between P_1 and P_2, which is given by

$$d_{KL}(P_1, P_2) = \int_{\mathbb{R}^n} P_1(x) \log \frac{P_1(x)}{P_2(x)} dx. \qquad (2.100)$$

For two multivariate normal density functions $P_1 \sim \mathcal{N}(0, C_1)$ and $P_2 \sim \mathcal{N}(0, C_2)$, with zero means and covariance matrices C_1 and C_2, respectively, the Rényi divergence has the following closed form (see, e.g., [91], note that we follow the original definition of Rényi in [99], which differs from the definition in [91] by a multiplication factor of $1/r$)

$$d_R^r(P_1, P_2) = \frac{1}{2(1-r)} \log \left[\frac{\det[(1-r)C_1 + rC_2]}{\det(C_1)^{1-r} \det(C_2)^r} \right] = \frac{r}{2} d_{\text{logdet}}^{(2r-1)}(C_1, C_2), \qquad (2.101)$$

and the Kullback-Leibler divergence has the following closed form

$$d_{KL}(P_1, P_2) = \frac{1}{2}[\text{tr}(C_2^{-1}C_1 - I) - \log \det(C_2^{-1}C_1)] = \frac{1}{2} d_{\text{logdet}}^1(C_1, C_2). \qquad (2.102)$$

By dual invariance under inversion, we have $d_{\text{logdet}}^{-1}(C_1, C_2) = d_{\text{logdet}}^1(C_1^{-1}, C_2^{-1})$, so that

$$d_{KL}(\mathcal{N}(0, C_1^{-1}), \mathcal{N}(0, C_2^{-1})) = \frac{1}{2} d_{\text{logdet}}^{-1}(C_1, C_2). \qquad (2.103)$$

Thus, for all α, $-1 < \alpha \le 1$, $d_{\text{logdet}}^\alpha(C_1, C_2)$ is equivalent to a Rényi divergence (up to a multiplicative constant factor) between two multivariate normal density functions on $\mathbb{R}^n$ with zero means and covariances C_1 and C_2, respectively. For $\alpha = -1$, $d_{\text{logdet}}^{-1}(C_1, C_2)$ is twice the Kullback-Leibler divergence between two multivariate normal density functions on $\mathbb{R}^n$ with zero means and covariances C_1^{-1} and C_2^{-1}, respectively.

2.7 ALPHA-BETA LOG-DET DIVERGENCES

Both the affine-invariant Riemannian distance and the Alpha Log-Det divergences are themselves special cases of a more general family of divergences on $\text{Sym}^{++}(n)$, namely the Alpha-Beta Log-Det divergences [22], which are defined by

$$D^{(\alpha,\beta)}(A, B) = \frac{1}{\alpha\beta} \log \det \left[\frac{\alpha(AB^{-1})^\beta + \beta(AB^{-1})^{-\alpha}}{\alpha + \beta} \right], \quad \alpha > 0, \beta > 0. \qquad (2.104)$$

The affine-invariant Riemannian distance is then obtained via the limit

$$\lim_{\alpha \to 0} D^{(\alpha,\alpha)}(A, B) = \frac{1}{2}|| \log(A^{-1/2}BA^{-1/2})||_F^2 = \frac{1}{2}d_{\text{aiE}}^2(A, B). \tag{2.105}$$

The Alpha Log-Det divergences can be readily verified to be special cases of the Alpha-Beta Log-Det divergences, with

$$d_{\text{logdet}}^\alpha(A, B) = D^{(\frac{1-\alpha}{2}, \frac{1+\alpha}{2})}(A, B). \tag{2.106}$$

Invariances. The Alpha-Beta Log-Det divergences are affine-invariant and in the case $\alpha = \beta$, are also inversion-invariant (see [22]).

Computational complexity. Let $\{\lambda_k\}_{k=1}^n$ be the eigenvalues of AB^{-1}, which are all positive, then

$$D^{(\alpha,\beta)}(A, B) = \frac{1}{\alpha\beta} \sum_{k=1}^n \log \left(\frac{\alpha\lambda_k^\beta + \beta\lambda_k^{-\alpha}}{\alpha + \beta} \right). \tag{2.107}$$

This is the expression that is used to compute $D^{(\alpha,\beta)}(A, B)$ in an actual implementation, except for the case $\beta = 1 - \alpha$, when $D^{(\alpha,1-\alpha)}(A, B) = d_{\text{logdet}}^{1-2\alpha}(A, B)$, which can be computed via the Cholesky decomposition, without the need to compute the eigenvalues of AB^{-1}. In general, for $\beta \neq 1 - \alpha$, since it depends on the eigenvalues $\{\lambda_k\}_{k=1}^n$ of AB^{-1}, the computational complexity of $D^{(\alpha,\beta)}(A, B)$ is essentially the same as that of the affine-invariant Riemannian distance $d_{\text{aiE}}(A, B)$, that is $O(n^3)$. For a set $\{A_i\}_{i=1}^N$ of N matrices in $\text{Sym}^{++}(n)$, the computational complexity required for computing the matrix of all pairwise divergences $\{D^{(\alpha,\beta)}(A_i, A_j)\}_{i,j=1}^N$ is $O(N^2n^3)$.

2.8   POWER EUCLIDEAN METRICS

In [29], the authors proposed the following parametrized family of distances on $\text{Sym}^{++}(n)$

$$d_\alpha(A, B) = \frac{1}{\alpha}||A^\alpha - B^\alpha||_F, \quad \alpha > 0 \tag{2.108}$$

with the case $\alpha = 0$ obtained via the following limit, which is precisely the Log-Euclidean distance.

Lemma 2.13   *For $A, B \in \text{Sym}^{++}(n)$,*

$$\lim_{\alpha \to 0} d_\alpha(A, B) = || \log(A) - \log(B)||_F. \tag{2.109}$$

One advantage of the power Euclidean metrics is that for $\alpha > 0$, they are valid also for the case A, B are positive semi-definite matrices, without the need to carry out any regularization.

However, we note also that for $\alpha > 0$, they do *not* share the same invariance properties of the Log-Euclidean distance. In particular, they are *neither scale-invariant nor inversion-invariant*.

Thus, the power Euclidean metrics do not generalize the Log-Euclidean metrics in the same way that the Alpha-Beta Log-Determinant divergences generalize the affine-invariant Riemannian distance. In terms of computational complexity, for $\alpha \notin \mathbb{N}$, the power-Euclidean metrics also require the SVD of A and B, and thus have the same computational complexity as the Log-Euclidean metric.

2.9 DISTANCES AND DIVERGENCES BETWEEN EMPIRICAL COVARIANCE MATRICES

Let $\mathbf{X} = [x_1, \ldots, x_m] \in \mathbb{R}^{n \times m}$, $\mathbf{Y} = [y_1, \ldots, y_m] \in \mathbb{R}^{n \times m}$ be two data matrices and $C_{\mathbf{X}}, C_{\mathbf{Y}}$ their corresponding $n \times n$ empirical covariance matrices. We can immediately compute their Euclidean inner product and distance according to

$$\langle C_{\mathbf{X}}, C_{\mathbf{Y}} \rangle_F = \mathrm{tr}(C_{\mathbf{X}}^T C_{\mathbf{Y}}) = \mathrm{tr}(C_{\mathbf{X}} C_{\mathbf{Y}}), \tag{2.110}$$
$$d_E(C_{\mathbf{X}}, C_{\mathbf{Y}}) = ||C_{\mathbf{X}} - C_{\mathbf{Y}}||_F. \tag{2.111}$$

The computation of the non-Euclidean distances and divergences, namely the affine-invariant Riemannian distance, Log-Euclidean distance, and Log-Det divergences, generally requires some form of regularization, as we discuss next.

Regularization of empirical covariance matrices. In general, empirical covariance matrices are only guaranteed to be positive semi-definite. Thus, in order to apply the theory and techniques of SPD matrices to compute the non-Euclidean distances and divergences between covariance matrices, it is generally necessary to employ some form of regularization to ensure their positive definiteness. One of the most widely used form of regularization is $(C_{\mathbf{X}} + \gamma I)$, for some regularization parameter $\gamma \in \mathbb{R}, \gamma > 0$, where I is the $n \times n$ identity matrix. This form of regularization is known as *diagonal loading* in the literature (see, e.g., [118], [31] for other forms of regularization). Diagonal loading is straightforward to implement and readily generalizable to the infinite-dimensional setting, as we show later in Chapter 5.

Thus, for two data matrices $\mathbf{X} = [x_1, \ldots, x_m] \in \mathbb{R}^{n \times m}$ and $\mathbf{Y} = [y_1, \ldots, y_m] \in \mathbb{R}^{n \times m}$, instead of computing the non-Euclidean distances/divergences between the covariance matrices $C_{\mathbf{X}}$ and $C_{\mathbf{Y}}$, we compute the non-Euclidean distances/divergences between their corresponding regularized versions $(C_{\mathbf{X}} + \gamma I), (C_{\mathbf{Y}} + \mu I)$, for some regularization parameters $\gamma > 0, \mu > 0$ (note that γ and μ are not required to be the same).

For the affine-invariant Riemannian distance, we thus compute

$$d_{\mathrm{aiE}}[(C_{\mathbf{X}} + \gamma I), (C_{\mathbf{Y}} + \mu I)] = || \log[(C_{\mathbf{X}} + \gamma I)^{-1/2}(C_{\mathbf{Y}} + \mu I)(C_{\mathbf{X}} + \gamma I)^{-1/2}]||_F. \tag{2.112}$$

For the Log-Euclidean distance, we compute

$$d_{\mathrm{logE}}[(C_{\mathbf{X}} + \gamma I), (C_{\mathbf{Y}} + \mu I)] = || \log(C_{\mathbf{X}} + \gamma I) - \log(C_{\mathbf{Y}} + \mu I)||_F. \tag{2.113}$$

For the Log-Euclidean inner product, we compute

$$\langle (C_X + \gamma I), (C_Y + \mu I) \rangle_{\log E} = \langle \log(C_X + \gamma I), \log(C_Y + \mu I) \rangle_F. \tag{2.114}$$

For the Alpha Log-Det divergences, we compute

$$d_{\text{logdet}}^{\alpha}[(C_X + \gamma I), (C_Y + \mu I)] = \frac{4}{1 - \alpha^2} \log \left[\frac{\det(\frac{1-\alpha}{2}(C_X + \gamma I) + \frac{1+\alpha}{2}(C_Y + \mu I))}{\det(C_X + \gamma I)^{\frac{1-\alpha}{2}} \det(C_Y + \mu I)^{\frac{1+\alpha}{2}}} \right],$$
$$- 1 < \alpha < 1, \tag{2.115}$$

$$d_{\text{logdet}}^{1}[(C_X + \gamma I), (C_Y + \mu I)] = \text{tr}[(C_Y + \mu I)^{-1}(C_X + \gamma I) - I]$$
$$- \log \det[(C_Y + \mu I)^{-1}(C_X + \gamma I)], \tag{2.116}$$

$$d_{\text{logdet}}^{-1}[(C_X + \gamma I), (C_Y + \mu I)] = \text{tr}[(C_X + \gamma I)^{-1}(C_Y + \mu I) - I]$$
$$- \log \det[(C_X + \gamma I)^{-1}(C_Y + \mu I)]. \tag{2.117}$$

The mathematical expressions in Eqs. (2.112), (2.113), (2.114), (2.115), (2.116), and (2.117) are those that are computed in actual numerical experiments involving covariance matrices.

2.10   RUNNING TIME COMPARISON

In the previous sections, we have presented the computational complexities of the distances and divergences considered in this chapter. In this section, we present the actual running time for the computation of the Euclidean distance, Log-Euclidean distance, affine-invariant Riemannian distance, and symmetric Stein divergence.

In order to do so, we carried out the following experiments. We generated N data matrices $\{X_j\}_{j=1}^{N}$, for $N = 500, 1000$, and 5000. Each data matrix X_j, $1 \leq j \leq N$, has size $n \times m$ where $n = 25$ (corresponding to the number of features) and $m = 1024$ (corresponding to the number of observations). The entries in each data matrix X_j are randomly generated according to the Gaussian probability distribution $\mathcal{N}(0, 1)$. The regularization parameter is set to be a fixed $\gamma = 10^{-8}$. We then computed the $N \times N$ matrix of all pairwise distances/divergences between all the (regularized) covariance matrices C_{X_j} associated with the data matrices X_j, $1 \leq j \leq N$. The actual running times (in seconds) are reported in Table 2.3. We stress that the running time is both *program-dependent* and *system-dependent*. The current experiments were run using MATLAB R2017a on a Dell Precision T5600, with two processors Intel Xeon E5-2620 and 32 GB RAM.

As can be seen from Table 2.3, the Euclidean distance is the fastest to compute, as expected, followed by the Log-Euclidean distance. Even though they have similar computational complexities in the $O()$ notation, the Stein divergence is considerably faster to compute than the affine-invariant Riemannian distance, which is the most computationally expensive. This is because the Stein divergence involves the Cholesky decompositions, which are faster to compute than the combination of matrix inversion and SVD required in the computation of the affine-invariant Riemannian distance.

Table 2.3: Comparison of running time for the different distances and divergences, in seconds, using MATLAB R2017a, on a Dell Precision T5600, with two processors Intel Xeon E5-2620 and 32 GB RAM. We stress that the running time reported is *implementation-dependent*. Here each covariance matrix is of size 25×25.

Number of Matrices	Euclidean	Log-Euclidean	Stein	Affine-Invariant
500	0.149	0.162	1.076	6.334
1,000	0.2036	0.2625	3.010	22.279
5,000	1.121	1.270	64.732	601.586

Another important aspect to notice from Table 2.3 is the scaling of the running time with respect to the number of data matrices N. According to the theoretical analysis of computational complexities, in both $d_{\mathrm{aiE}}[(C_{\mathbf{X}_i} + \gamma I), (C_{\mathbf{X}_j} + \gamma I)]$ and $d_{\mathrm{stein}}[(C_{\mathbf{X}_i} + \gamma I), (C_{\mathbf{X}_j} + \gamma I)]$, the covariance matrices $C_{\mathbf{X}_i}$ and $C_{\mathbf{X}_j}$ are uncoupled, and thus we need to carry out an SVD (for d_{aiE}), or a Cholesky decomposition (for d_{stein}) for *each pair* of covariance matrices. This requires a loop of size $O(N^2)$. Thus the running time for the case $N = 5000$ should be about 25 times the running time for the case $N = 1000$. This is indeed the case, as can be seen from Table 2.3. On the other hand, as we noted before, in $d_{\mathrm{logE}}[(C_{\mathbf{X}_i} + \gamma I), (C_{\mathbf{X}_j} + \gamma I)]$, the covariance matrices $C_{\mathbf{X}_i}$ and $C_{\mathbf{X}_j}$ are uncoupled, thus only a loop of size N is required for computing the SVD and log function of each covariance matrix. Then, the Euclidean distances between the principal logarithms of the covariance matrices can be computed very efficiently via vectorized code in MATLAB, leading to much faster running time, as can be observed in Table 2.3. The same observation is true for $d_E(C_{\mathbf{X}_i}, C_{\mathbf{X}_j})$. Thus it is much more efficient to scale the Euclidean and Log-Euclidean distances to large datasets than the affine-invariant Riemannian distance and Stein divergence.

2.11 SUMMARY

In this chapter, we presented the following metrics and divergences on $\mathrm{Sym}^{++}(n)$.

- The Euclidean metric.

- The affine-invariant Riemannian metric and its close connection to the Fisher-Rao metric on the manifold of multivariate Gaussian probability density functions with mean zero, along with the corresponding affine-invariant Riemannian distance.

- The Log-Euclidean metric as a bi-invariant Riemannian metric, along with the corresponding Log-Euclidean inner product structure on $\mathrm{Sym}^{++}(n)$. We also discussed the alternative interpretation of the Log-Euclidean distance as an approximation of the affine-invariant Riemannian distance.

- The Alpha Log-Determinant divergences (which include the symmetric Stein divergence as a special case) and their connections to the Kullback-Leibler and Rényi divergences between multivariate Gaussian probability density functions with mean zero.

- The highly general Alpha-Beta Log-Det divergences, which include both the affine-invariant Riemannian distance and Alpha Log-Determinant divergences as special cases, and the power Euclidean distances, which include the Log-Euclidean distance as a special case.

- We also discussed the different invariance properties, such as affine invariance and scale invariance, along with the corresponding interpretations and motivations.

- We presented a comparison of the actual running time, in MATLAB, of the different distances and divergences, showing that the Euclidean and Log-Euclidean distances are the most efficient computationally, followed by the symmetric Stein divergence, and finally the affine-invariant Riemannian distance.

CHAPTER 3

Kernel Methods on Covariance Matrices

Having represented images by covariance matrices, which from this point on we assume to be SPD matrices, and presented various different notions of distances and divergences between them, we now discuss some of the most important problems encountered in practical applications, namely classification and regression on SPD matrices. In machine learning, a prominent paradigm for solving classification and regression problems is that of kernel methods [102, 104]. Since most traditional kernel methods employ positive definite kernels based on the Euclidean metric, in order to exploit the non-Euclidean distances and divergences *intrinsic* to SPD matrices, as described in Chapter 2, it is necessary to define new positive definite kernels based on these distances and divergences. In this chapter, we describe these kernels and the corresponding kernel methods.

3.1 POSITIVE DEFINITE KERNELS AND REPRODUCING KERNEL HILBERT SPACES

We first present a brief overview of the concepts of positive definite kernels and the associated reproducing kernel Hilbert spaces (RKHS), which play a fundamental role in many areas of machine learning, statistics, and applications. For more comprehensive treatment, we refer to e.g., [4, 103, 104].

Positive definite kernels. Let $\mathcal{X}$ be an arbitrary non-empty set. A function $K : \mathcal{X} \times \mathcal{X} \to \mathbb{R}$ is said to be a real-valued positive definite kernel if it is symmetric, that is $K(x, y) = K(y, x)$ $\forall x, y \in \mathcal{X}$, and satisfies

$$\sum_{i,j=1}^{N} a_i a_j K(x_i, x_j) \geq 0 \qquad (3.1)$$

for any set of points $\mathbf{X} = \{x_i\}_{i=1}^{N}$ in $\mathcal{X}$ and any set of real numbers $\{a_i\}_{i=1}^{N}$. In other words, the $N \times N$ matrix $K[\mathbf{X}]$ defined by $(K[\mathbf{X}])_{ij} = K(x_i, x_j)$ is symmetric, positive semi-definite. The matrix $K[\mathbf{X}]$ is called the *Gram matrix* induced by the kernel K on the set of points $\mathbf{X}$.

The following are examples of some commonly used positive definite kernels in machine learning.

1. Gaussian kernel $K(x, y) = \exp\left(-\frac{1}{\sigma^2}||x - y||^2\right)$, $\sigma \neq 0$, for $x, y \in \mathbb{R}^n$, $n \in \mathbb{N}$.

2. Generalized Gaussian kernels $K(x, y) = \exp\left(-\frac{1}{\sigma^2}||x - y||^p\right)$, $\sigma \neq 0$, $0 < p \leq 2$, for $x, y \in \mathbb{R}^n$, $n \in \mathbb{N}$.

3. Polynomial kernels $K(x, y) = (\langle x, y \rangle + c)^d$, $c \geq 0$, $d \in \mathbb{N}$, for $x, y \in \mathbb{R}^n$.

Reproducing kernel Hilbert spaces (RKHS). Each positive definite kernel $K : \mathcal{X} \times \mathcal{X} \to \mathbb{R}$ corresponds to a unique Hilbert space of real-valued functions on $\mathcal{X}$ as follows. For each $x \in \mathcal{X}$, there corresponds a function $K_x : \mathcal{X} \to \mathbb{R}$ defined by $K_x(y) = K(x, y)$ $\forall y \in \mathcal{X}$. Consider the set $\mathcal{H}_0$ of all finite linear combinations of functions of the form K_x, $x \in \mathcal{X}$, that is

$$\mathcal{H}_0 = \left\{ \sum_{j=1}^{N} a_j K_{x_j} \; : \; a_j \in \mathbb{R}, x_j \in \mathcal{X}, N \in \mathbb{N} \right\}. \tag{3.2}$$

On $\mathcal{H}_0$, we define the following inner product

$$\left\langle \sum_{i=1}^{N} a_i K_{x_i}, \sum_{j=1}^{M} b_j K_{y_j} \right\rangle_{\mathcal{H}_K} = \sum_{i=1}^{N}\sum_{j=1}^{M} a_i b_j K(x_i, y_j). \tag{3.3}$$

From the assumption that K is a positive definite kernel, it can be verified that $\langle \, , \, \rangle_{\mathcal{H}_K}$ is well-defined as an inner product, that is it satisfies all the axioms of inner product, namely symmetry, positivity, and linearity. Thus, $(\mathcal{H}_0, \langle \, , \, \rangle_{\mathcal{H}_K})$ is an inner product space, with the corresponding norm $|| \, ||_{\mathcal{H}_K}$. Let $\mathcal{H}_K$ be the Hilbert completion of $\mathcal{H}_0$, obtained by adding the limits of all the Cauchy sequences in $\mathcal{H}_0$ under the norm $|| \, ||_{\mathcal{H}_K}$, then $\mathcal{H}_K$ is a Hilbert space of functions on $\mathcal{X}$, called the *reproducing kernel Hilbert space* (RKHS) induced by the kernel K.

The *reproducing property*, which gives rise to the name RKHS, states that for all $f \in \mathcal{H}_K$ and all $x \in \mathcal{X}$,

$$f(x) = \langle f, K_x \rangle_{\mathcal{H}_K}. \tag{3.4}$$

The correspondence between the kernel K and the Hilbert space $\mathcal{H}_K$ is one-to-one.

3.2   POSITIVE DEFINITE KERNELS ON SPD MATRICES

In the following, we present positive definite kernels defined using the Euclidean metric, Log-Euclidean metric, and symmetric Stein divergence on $\mathrm{Sym}^{++}(n)$. A summary of the kernels commonly employed in practice is given in Table 3.1.

Table 3.1: Common positive definite kernels defined using different distances, inner products, and divergences on $\text{Sym}^{++}(n)$

Kernels by Euclidean inner product and distance

$$K(A, B) = (\langle A, B \rangle_F + c)^d, c \geq 0, d \in \mathbb{N}$$
$$K(A, B) = \exp(-\tfrac{1}{\sigma^2}\|A - B\|_F^p), \sigma \neq 0, 0 < p \leq 2$$

Kernels by Log-Euclidean inner product and distance

$$K(A, B) = (\langle \log(A), \log(B) \rangle_F + c)^d, c \geq 0, d \in \mathbb{N}$$
$$K(A, B) = \exp(-\tfrac{1}{\sigma^2}\|\log(A) - \log(B)\|_F^p), \sigma \neq 0, 0 < p \leq 2$$

Kernels by Symmetric Stein divergence

$$K(A, B) = \exp[-\sigma d_{\text{stein}}^2(A, B)],$$
$$\text{where}$$
$$\sigma \in \{\tfrac{1}{2}, 1, \ldots, \tfrac{n-1}{2}\} \cup \{\sigma \in \mathbb{R}, \sigma > \tfrac{n-1}{2}\},$$
$$d_{\text{stein}}^2(A, B) = \log \det(\tfrac{A+B}{2}) - \tfrac{1}{2}\log \det(AB)$$

3.2.1 POSITIVE DEFINITE KERNELS WITH THE EUCLIDEAN METRIC

Since the set $\text{Sym}^{++}(n)$ of $n \times n$ SPD matrices is an open subset of the Euclidean space $\mathbb{R}^{n \times n}$, it automatically inherits the Euclidean metric on $\mathbb{R}^{n \times n}$, as discussed in Section 2.1. Thus, $\text{Sym}^{++}(n)$ also inherits all positive definite kernels that can be defined on Euclidean space, using the Euclidean distance $\|A - B\|_F$ and Euclidean inner product $\langle A, B \rangle_F$, where $A, B \in \mathbb{R}^{n \times n}$.

Some common positive definite kernels (or kernels for short) $K : \mathbb{R}^{n \times n} \times \mathbb{R}^{n \times n} \to \mathbb{R}$ are the following.

1. Polynomial kernels

$$K(A, B) = (\langle A, B \rangle_F + c)^d = [\text{tr}(A^T B) + c]^d, \quad d \in \mathbb{N}, c \geq 0. \tag{3.5}$$

2. Gaussian and Gaussian-like kernels

$$K(A, B) = \exp\left(-\frac{1}{\sigma^2}\|A - B\|_F^p\right), \quad \sigma \neq 0, 0 < p \leq 2. \tag{3.6}$$

These kernels are straightforward to implement and efficient to compute. However, as discussed in Chapter 2, they do not reflect the *intrinsic* geometry of the set $\mathrm{Sym}^{++}(n)$ and therefore tend to be sup-optimal in practical applications.

3.2.2   POSITIVE DEFINITE KERNELS WITH THE LOG-EUCLIDEAN METRIC

As we discussed in Section 2.5 in Chapter 2,

$$(\mathrm{Sym}^{++}(n), \odot, \circledast, \langle\,,\,\rangle_{\mathrm{logE}})$$

is an inner product space, with the Log-Euclidean inner product $\langle A, B\rangle_{\mathrm{logE}} = \langle \log(A), \log(B)\rangle_F$ and the corresponding Log-Euclidean norm $||A||_{\mathrm{logE}} = \sqrt{\langle A, A\rangle_{\mathrm{logE}}}$. The Log-Euclidean distance is then $d_{\mathrm{logE}}(A, B) = ||A \odot B^{-1}||_{\mathrm{logE}} = ||\log(A) - \log(B)||_F$, where $A, B \in \mathrm{Sym}^{++}(n)$.

Consequently, we can define positive definite kernels on $\mathrm{Sym}^{++}(n)$ using the inner product $\langle\,,\,\rangle_{\mathrm{logE}}$ and the norm $||\,||_{\mathrm{logE}}$. The following are the Log-Euclidean counterparts of the Euclidean kernels in Section 3.2.1.

Theorem 3.1   *The following kernels* $K : \mathrm{Sym}^{++}(n) \times \mathrm{Sym}^{++}(n) \to \mathbb{R}$ *are positive definite*

$$K(A, B) = (\langle A, B\rangle_{\mathrm{logE}} + c)^d = (\langle\log(A), \log(B)\rangle_F + c)^d, \quad c \geq 0, d \in \mathbb{N}. \tag{3.7}$$

$$K(A, B) = \exp\left(-\frac{1}{\sigma^2}||A \odot B^{-1}||_{\mathrm{logE}}^p\right)$$

$$= \exp\left(-\frac{1}{\sigma^2}||\log(A) - \log(B)||_F^p\right), \quad \sigma \neq 0, 0 < p \leq 2. \tag{3.8}$$

Remark 3.2   A proof of Theorem 3.1 can be found in [81]. The generalized Gaussian kernel K in Eq. (3.8) in particular generalizes the results in [55, 56, 72], which show that K is positive definite for $p = 2$.

The key difference between kernels defined using the Log-Euclidean inner product $\langle\,,\,\rangle_{\mathrm{logE}}$ and Log-Euclidean norm $||\,||_{\mathrm{logE}}$, in contrast to the kernels defined using the Euclidean inner product $\langle\,,\,\rangle_F$ and Euclidean norm $||\,||_F$ in Section 3.2.1, is that they are *intrinsic* to $\mathrm{Sym}^{++}(n)$. With these kernels, we can apply kernel methods, such as SVM, *directly* on $\mathrm{Sym}^{++}(n)$. For a binary classification problem with input in $\mathrm{Sym}^{++}(n)$, for example, this means that the decision boundary is a curve lying on $\mathrm{Sym}^{++}(n)$, instead of a surface in the much larger ambient space $\mathbb{R}^{n \times n}$.

3.2.3 POSITIVE DEFINITE KERNELS WITH THE SYMMETRIC STEIN DIVERGENCE

Among all the Alpha Log-Det divergences d_{logdet}^α on $\text{Sym}^{++}(n)$, as defined in Section 2.6.1, only d_{logdet}^0 is symmetric and furthermore, $\sqrt{d_{\text{logdet}}^0}$ is a metric on $\text{Sym}^{++}(n)$, that is it also satisfies the triangle inequality, as shown in [110, 111]. It is then natural to ask whether one can construct the Gaussian kernel using d_{logdet}^0. Following [110, 111], we define

$$d_{\text{stein}}^2(A, B) = \frac{1}{4} d_{\text{logdet}}^0(A, B) = \log \det \left(\frac{A + B}{2} \right) - \frac{1}{2} \log \det(AB). \qquad (3.9)$$

Since this divergence does not arise from an inner product, it is far from trivial to determine whether the Gaussian kernel $\exp[-\sigma d_{\text{stein}}^2(A, B)]$ is positive definite. It turns out that $\exp[-\sigma d_{\text{stein}}^2(A, B)]$ is positive definite for specific choices of σ, as shown in the following result by Sra [110, 111].

Theorem 3.3 [110, 111]. *The kernel $K : \text{Sym}^{++}(n) \times \text{Sym}^{++}(n) \to \mathbb{R}$, defined by*

$$K(A, B) = \exp[-\sigma d_{\text{stein}}^2(A, B)], \qquad (3.10)$$

is positive definite if and only if σ satisfies

$$\sigma \in \left\{ \frac{1}{2}, 1, \ldots, \frac{n-1}{2} \right\} \cup \left\{ \sigma \in \mathbb{R}, \sigma > \frac{n-1}{2} \right\}. \qquad (3.11)$$

Thus, general kernel methods are applicable on $\text{Sym}^{++}(n)$ using the kernel $K(A, B) = \exp[-\sigma d_{\text{stein}}^2(A, B)]$, with σ in the range specified in Theorem 3.3. However, when performing parameter tuning on σ, care needs to be taken to ensure that σ remains in the specified range to guarantee the positive definiteness of the kernel.

3.2.4 POSITIVE DEFINITE KERNELS WITH THE AFFINE-INVARIANT RIEMANNIAN METRIC

It is natural to ask whether one can construct a Gaussian kernel on $\text{Sym}^{++}(n)$ using the affine-invariant Riemannian distance $d_{\text{aiE}}(A, B) = \|\log(A^{-1/2} B A^{-1/2})\|_F$, $A, B \in \text{Sym}^{++}(n)$, that is a kernel of the form

$$K(A, B) = \exp[-\sigma d_{\text{aiE}}^2(A, B)], \quad \sigma > 0. \qquad (3.12)$$

It turns out that K is positive definite for *every* value of $\sigma > 0$ if and only if the Riemannian manifold is flat, i.e., has zero sectional curvature, as shown in [38]. This is not the case with the affine-invariant Riemannian metric, under which $\text{Sym}^{++}(n)$ is a Riemannian manifold with nonpositive sectional curvature. Thus, $K(A, B) = \exp[-\sigma d_{\text{aiE}}^2(A, B)]$ cannot be positive definite for *every* $\sigma > 0$.

It would be of interest, both theoretically and practically, to determine whether the kernel $K(A, B) = \exp[-\sigma d_{\text{aiE}}^2(A, B)]$ is positive definite for *some* value of $\sigma > 0$, as is the case with the symmetric Stein divergence (Theorem 3.3). However, at the time of writing, we are not aware of any theoretical result of this kind.

3.3 KERNEL METHODS ON COVARIANCE MATRICES

Having constructed positive definite kernels on $\text{Sym}^{++}(n)$, we can now apply directly on $\text{Sym}^{++}(n)$ any known kernel method, such as classification, regression, and kernel K-means. The schematic diagram for SVM classification with kernels defined using the Log-Euclidean distance is illustrated graphically in Figure 3.1 and procedurally in Algorithm 3.1. The Log-Euclidean distance (Log-E stage) in Figure 3.1 can be replaced by the Euclidean distance and inner product, the Log-Euclidean inner product, and the symmetric Stein divergence, with appropriate values of the parameter σ. Likewise, the final stage in Figure 3.1, namely SVM classification, can be replaced by any other kernel method. In the Log-Euclidean case, this approach was proposed in [55, 56, 72, 120], with the linear kernel already being employed in [127].

We demonstrate the empirical performance of this framework on the task of image classification in the next section.

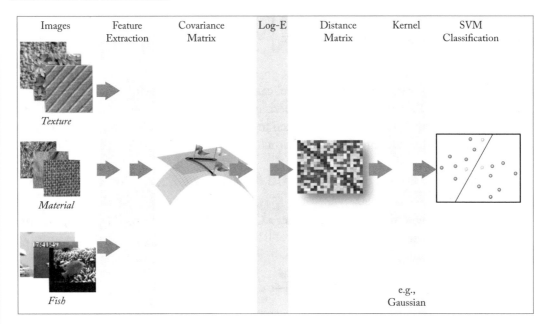

Figure 3.1: Kernel methods for image classification with the Log-Euclidean metric.

Algorithm 3.1 Kernel machine on covariance matrices with the Log-Euclidean distance/Log-Euclidean inner product, as depicted in Figure 3.1. Other alternative machines can be obtained by using the Euclidean distance/Euclidean inner product/symmetric Stein divergence instead.

Input: Set of N data matrices $\mathbf{X}_i$, $1 \leq i \leq N$, each of size $n \times m$

(For image classification, each image gives rise to one such data matrix $\mathbf{X}_i$, with each column being a feature vector extracted from the image. For simplicity, all regularization parameters γ_i's can be set to be the same.)

Output: Kernel matrix (used as input to a kernel method, e.g., SVM classification)

Parameters:

Positive definite kernel K

Regularization parameters $\gamma_i > 0$, $1 \leq i \leq N$

Procedure:

1. For data matrix $\mathbf{X}_i$, $1 \leq i \leq N$, compute the corresponding covariance matrix $C_{\mathbf{X}_i}$ according to Eq. (1.3).

2. For each pair of regularized covariance matrices $(C_{\mathbf{X}_i} + \gamma_i I)$ and $(C_{\mathbf{X}_j} + \gamma_j I)$, compute the corresponding Log-Euclidean distance, according to Eq. (2.113), or the corresponding Log-Euclidean inner product, according to Eq. (2.114), using regularization parameters γ_i, γ_j, respectively.

3. Using kernel K, compute an $N \times N$ kernel matrix using the above Log-Euclidean distances, e.g., according to Eq. (3.8), or above Log-Euclidean inner products, e.g., according to Eq. (3.7).

3.4 EXPERIMENTS ON IMAGE CLASSIFICATION

In this section, we present a set of empirical results obtained on the task of image classification using the kernel framework with the Log-Euclidean metric, as depicted in Figure 3.1. These experiments were carried out and reported in [76, 83, 84]. They will be compared with results obtained later on using SVM classification with infinite-dimensional covariance operators in Section 6.4.

3.4.1 DATASETS

The following are the two image classification tasks performed in the experiments, along with the corresponding datasets.

Material classification. For this task, the KTH-TIPS2b dataset [14] was employed. This dataset contains images of 11 materials captured under 4 different illuminations, in 3 poses, and at 9 scales. The total number of images for each sample in a category is 108, with 4 samples

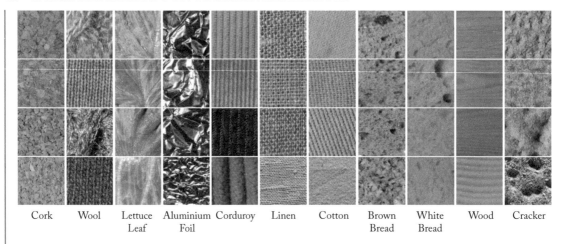

| Cork | Wool | Lettuce Leaf | Aluminium Foil | Corduroy | Linen | Cotton | Brown Bread | White Bread | Wood | Cracker |

Figure 3.2: Samples from the four splits of the KTH-TIPS2b dataset [14].

Figure 3.3: Samples from the ETH-80 dataset [69].

per material. Figure 3.2 shows some sample images from this dataset. The same experimental protocol as in [44] was employed. At the pixel at location (x, y), the following 23-dimensional low-level feature vector was extracted,

$$\mathbf{f}(x, y) = \left[R(x, y), G(x, y), B(x, y), |G^{0,0}(x, y)|, \dots |G^{3,4}(x, y)| \right], \tag{3.13}$$

where $R(x, y), G(x, y), B(x, y)$ are the three color channels red, green, and blue, respectively, and $|G^{o,s}(x, y)|$ are the 20 Gabor filters at 4 orientations and 5 scales. For each sample, 3 images were used for training, with the rest used for testing. The mean and the standard deviation values for all the 4 splits of the dataset are reported.

Object recognition. For this task, the **ETH80 dataset** [69] was employed. This dataset contains images of eight object categories: apples, cows, cups, dogs, horses, pears, tomatoes, and cars. Each category includes ten object subcategories (e.g., various dogs) in 41 orientations, resulting in 410 images per category. Figure 3.3 shows some sample images from this dataset.

For the classification task 21 images were randomly chosen for training, with the rest used for testing. This process was repeated 10 times. For this dataset, following [55], at each pixel the following 5-dimensional feature vector was extracted

$$\mathbf{f}(x, y) = [x, y, I(x, y), |I_x|, |I_y|], \tag{3.14}$$

where I denotes the intensity function and I_x and I_y denote the partial derivative of I along the x and y directions, respectively.

3.4.2 RESULTS

In Table 3.2, we report results obtained on the material classification task, using the KTH-TIPS2b dataset, and the object recognition task, using the ETH-80 dataset. Here the classification was carried out using LIBSVM [17] with the Gaussian kernels, using the Euclidean and Log-Euclidean distances (Figure 3.1). All parameters were chosen by cross-validation. For comparison, we also list results obtained using the symmetric Stein divergence, under the Nearest Neighbor approach. As can be seen from Table 3.2, on these two datasets, the Log-Euclidean distance and symmetric Stein divergence, which are intrinsic to $\mathrm{Sym}^{++}(n)$, both considerably outperform the extrinsic Euclidean distance.

Table 3.2: Experimental results obtained by SVM classification with the Gaussian kernels, defined using the Euclidean (E) and Log-Euclidean (*Log-E*) distances, on the KTH-TIPS2b and ETH-80 datasets. By comparison, the experiments *Stein*, using the symmetric Stein divergence, were carried out using the Nearest Neighbor approach. The results in this table should be compared with those in Table 6.3.

Method	KTH-TIPS2b	ETH-80
E	55.3%	64.4%
	(±7.6%)	(±0.9%)
Stein [21]	73.1%	67.5%
	(±8.0%)	(±0.4%)
Log-E	74.1%	71.1%
	(±7.4%)	(±1.0%)

3.5   RELATED APPROACHES

In this chapter, we focused on positive definite kernels and in particular the SVM on covariance matrices. In [55, 56], the authors also studied other commonly used kernel methods, including kernel K-means, multiple kernel learning (MKL), and kernel PCA on $\mathrm{Sym}^{++}(n)$. We remark that there is also a line of ongoing research that seeks to generalize other machine learning methods from the Euclidean setting to the manifold setting of SPD matrices, such as boosting [123], sparse coding and dictionary learning [19, 20, 46, 72, 108, 129], metric learning [52, 74], and dimensionality reduction [45].

PART II

Covariance Operators and Applications

CHAPTER 4

Data Representation by Covariance Operators

In Chapter 1, we reviewed the data representation framework using finite-dimensional covariance matrices, which encode *linear correlations* between input features. In this chapter, by employing the feature map viewpoint of kernel methods in machine learning, we generalize covariance matrices to infinite-dimensional covariance operators in RKHS. Since they encode *nonlinear correlations* between input features, they can be employed as a powerful form of data representation, which we explore in subsequent chapters.

From a geometrical viewpoint, kernel feature maps transform covariance matrices, which lie on a finite-dimensional Riemannian manifold, into covariance operators, whose regularized versions lie on an infinite-dimensional Riemannian manifold; see Figure 4.1. We study this infinite-dimensional manifold structure in detail in Chapter 5.

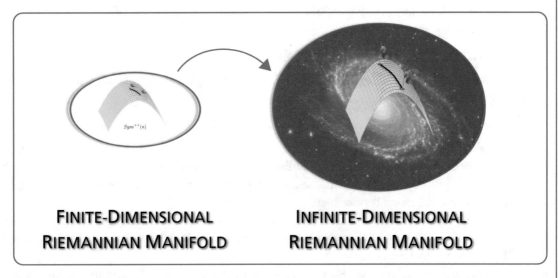

FINITE-DIMENSIONAL RIEMANNIAN MANIFOLD

INFINITE-DIMENSIONAL RIEMANNIAN MANIFOLD

Figure 4.1: Feature maps, which are induced by positive definite kernels, transform covariance matrices, which lie on the finite-dimensional Riemannian manifold $\text{Sym}^{++}(n)$, into covariance operators, whose regularized versions lie on an infinite-dimensional Riemannian manifold.

The material presented in this chapter follows that from [75, 76, 81], see also [16, 44, 135].

4.1   POSITIVE DEFINITE KERNELS AND FEATURE MAPS

A geometrically appealing view of positive definite kernels that is widely exploited in machine learning and pattern recognition is that of *feature spaces* and *feature maps*. Specifically, if $K : \mathcal{X} \times \mathcal{X} \to \mathbb{R}$ is a positive definite kernel, then there exists a Hilbert space $\mathcal{H}$, called a *feature space*, and a map $\Phi : \mathcal{X} \to \mathcal{H}$, called a *feature map*, such that

$$K(x, y) = \langle \Phi(x), \Phi(y) \rangle_{\mathcal{H}} \quad \forall x, y \in \mathcal{H}. \tag{4.1}$$

The following is a well-known example of feature maps. Consider the quadratic polynomial kernel $K : \mathbb{R}^2 \times \mathbb{R}^2 \to \mathbb{R}$ defined by $K(x, y) = \langle x, y \rangle^2 = (x_1 y_1 + x_2 y_2)^2$. It can be readily verified, via a simple algebraic calculation, that the following is a 3-dimensional feature map for K, with the feature space being $\mathbb{R}^3$,

$$\Phi : \mathbb{R}^2 \to \mathbb{R}^3, \quad \Phi(x) = (x_1^2, \sqrt{2} x_1 x_2, x_2^2) \in \mathbb{R}^3.$$

We see that $\Phi(x)$ is a quadratic, i.e., *nonlinear* function of the coordinates (x_1, x_2) of x.

If K is a nonlinear kernel on $\mathbb{R}^n \times \mathbb{R}^n$, then $\Phi(x)$ is necessarily a nonlinear function of x and gives rise to the *kernel trick*, or *kernelization* in general, in machine learning. Any *linear* algorithm, which is expressed in terms of the inner product $\langle x, y \rangle$ of input examples in Euclidean space, can be transformed into a *nonlinear* algorithm, simply by replacing $\langle x, y \rangle$ with $\langle \Phi(x), \Phi(y) \rangle_{\mathcal{H}} = K(x, y)$ for some nonlinear kernel K.

In general, for any positive definite kernel K, from the definition of the RKHS $\mathcal{H}_K$ and the reproducing property, we have

$$K(x, y) = K_x(y) = \langle K_x, K_y \rangle_{\mathcal{H}_K} \quad \forall (x, y) \in \mathcal{X} \times \mathcal{X}. \tag{4.2}$$

It follows that the RKHS $\mathcal{H}_K$ induced by K is a feature space associated with K, with corresponding feature map $\Phi : \mathcal{X} \to \mathcal{H}_K$, defined by

$$\Phi(x) = K_x \quad \forall x \in \mathcal{X}. \tag{4.3}$$

This is called the *canonical feature map* associated with K, see e.g., [82]. The paper [82] contains many examples of feature maps, including analytical expressions in many cases, along with further detailed discussion. In general, feature maps are *not unique*, but they are all essentially equivalent to the canonical feature map.

For the Gaussian kernel on $\mathcal{X} \times \mathcal{X}$, if $\mathcal{X} \subset \mathbb{R}^n$ is a set with non-empty interior, then $\dim(\mathcal{H}_K) = \infty$ (see [77]), so that the feature map Φ is infinite-dimensional. Hence $\Phi(x)$ is a highly nonlinear function of x.

In general, whenever $\dim(\mathcal{H}_K) = \infty$, so that the feature map Φ is infinite-dimensional (or high-dimensional, as in the case of polynomial kernels of high degrees), then $\Phi(x)$ is a highly nonlinear function of x. We can then apply this property to define to covariance operators in RKHS, which encode *nonlinear correlations* between input features.

4.2   COVARIANCE OPERATORS IN RKHS

Let us now generalize the mean and covariance matrix in Section 1.2 via the infinite-dimensional feature map Φ.

Let $\mathcal{X}$ be an arbitrary non-empty set. Let $(\mathcal{H}_K, \langle,\rangle_{\mathcal{H}_K})$ be the RKHS of functions on $\mathcal{X}$ induced by K and $\Phi : \mathcal{X} \to \mathcal{H}_K$ be the corresponding canonical feature map given by

$$\Phi(x) = K_x,$$
$$\Phi(x)(y) = K(x, y), \quad \forall(x, y) \in \mathcal{X} \times \mathcal{X}. \tag{4.4}$$

The reproducing property states that

$$f(x) = \langle f, \Phi(x)\rangle_{\mathcal{H}_K}, \quad \forall f \in \mathcal{H}_K, x \in \mathcal{X}, \tag{4.5}$$
$$\langle\Phi(x), \Phi(y)\rangle_{\mathcal{H}_K} = K(x, y), \quad \forall(x, y) \in \mathcal{X} \times \mathcal{X}. \tag{4.6}$$

RKHS mean and covariance operator. Assume that ρ is a Borel probability distribution on $\mathcal{X}$, with

$$\int_{\mathcal{X}} \|\Phi(x)\|^2_{\mathcal{H}_K} d\rho(x) = \int_{\mathcal{X}} K(x, x) d\rho(x) < \infty. \tag{4.7}$$

Under this assumption, the feature map $\Phi : \mathcal{X} \to \mathcal{H}_K$ induces the mean vector

$$\mu_\Phi = \int_{\mathcal{X}} \Phi(x) d\rho(x) \in \mathcal{H}_K, \tag{4.8}$$

which satisfies

$$\langle\mu_\Phi, f\rangle_{\mathcal{H}_K} = \int_{\mathcal{X}} \langle f, \Phi(x)\rangle_{\mathcal{H}_K} = \int_{\mathcal{X}} f(x) d\rho(x) = \mathbb{E}_\rho[f] \quad \forall f \in \mathcal{H}_K. \tag{4.9}$$

Similarly, Φ induces the covariance operator $C_\Phi : \mathcal{H}_K \to \mathcal{H}_K$, defined by

$$C_\Phi = \int_{\mathcal{X}} (\Phi(x) - \mu_\Phi) \otimes (\Phi(x) - \mu_\Phi) d\rho(x) = \int_{\mathcal{X}} \Phi(x) \otimes \Phi(x) d\rho(x) - \mu_\Phi \otimes \mu_\Phi. \tag{4.10}$$

Here for two vectors $u, v \in \mathcal{H}_K$, the notation $u \otimes v$ denotes the rank-one operator $u \otimes v : \mathcal{H}_K \to \mathcal{H}_K$ defined by $(u \otimes v)w = \langle v, w\rangle_{\mathcal{H}_K} u \; \forall w \in \mathcal{H}_K$. It is the generalization of the rank-one matrix uv^T in the case $u, v \in \mathbb{R}^n$. For any pair of functions $f, g \in \mathcal{H}_K$, we then have

$$\langle f, C_\Phi g\rangle_{\mathcal{H}_K} = \mathbb{E}_\rho[fg] - \mathbb{E}_\rho(f)\mathbb{E}_\rho(g), \tag{4.11}$$
$$\langle f, C_\Phi f\rangle_{\mathcal{H}_K} = \mathbb{E}_\rho(f^2) - [\mathbb{E}_\rho(f)]^2. \tag{4.12}$$

When K is the linear kernel on $\mathbb{R}^n$, that is $K(x, y) = \langle x, y\rangle$, then $\Phi(x) = x$, $\mathcal{H}_K = \mathbb{R}^n$, and we readily recover the mean and covariance matrix in Section 1.2.

The following is a key property of covariance operators, which, in the RKHS setting, follows from Mercer's Theorem for continuous positive definite kernel [25].

Theorem 4.1 *Let $\mathcal{X}$ be a complete, separable metric space and $K : \mathcal{X} \times \mathcal{X} \to \mathbb{R}$ be a continuous, positive definite kernel. Let ρ be a Borel probability measure on $\mathcal{X}$. Assume that Eq. (4.7) is satisfied. Then the covariance operator $C_\Phi : \mathcal{H}_K \to \mathcal{H}_K$, as defined in Eq. (4.10), is a positive trace class operator. In other words, C_Φ possesses a countable set of eigenvalues $\{\lambda_k\}_{k=1}^\infty$, $\lambda_k \geq 0 \ \forall k \in \mathbb{N}$, and*

$$\sum_{k=1}^{\infty} \lambda_k < \infty. \tag{4.13}$$

Proof. See Appendix A.5. $\square$

Separable RKHS. The hypotheses of Theorem 4.1 that $\mathcal{X}$ is a complete separable metric space and K is continuous also imply that the RKHS $\mathcal{H}_K$ is separable, that is it possesses a countable orthonormal basis (see [113], Lemma 4.33). We take this as an underlying assumption throughout the rest of the book.

Empirical mean and covariance operator. Let $\mathbf{X} = [x_1, \ldots, x_m]$ be a data matrix randomly sampled from $\mathcal{X}$ according to the probability distribution ρ, where $m \in \mathbb{N}$ is the number of observations. The feature map Φ gives rise to the following bounded linear operator $\Phi(\mathbf{X}) : \mathbb{R}^m \to \mathcal{H}_K$, defined by

$$\Phi(\mathbf{X})w = \sum_{i=1}^{m} w_i \Phi(x_i) = \sum_{i=1}^{m} w_i K(x_i, .), \quad w = (w_i)_{i=1}^{m} \in \mathbb{R}^m. \tag{4.14}$$

Its adjoint operator $\Phi(\mathbf{X})^* : \mathcal{H}_K \to \mathbb{R}^m$ is given by

$$\Phi(\mathbf{X})^* f = (\langle f, \Phi(x_i) \rangle)_{i=1}^{m} = (f(x_i))_{i=1}^{m}, \quad f \in \mathcal{H}_K. \tag{4.15}$$

Given the data matrix $\mathbf{X}$, the empirical mean vector corresponding to μ_Φ is given by

$$\mu_{\Phi(\mathbf{X})} = \frac{1}{m} \sum_{i=1}^{m} \Phi(x_i) = \frac{1}{m} \Phi(\mathbf{X}) \mathbf{1}_m, \quad \text{where } \mathbf{1}_m = (1, \ldots, 1)^T \in \mathbb{R}^m. \tag{4.16}$$

Similarly, the empirical covariance operator corresponding to C_Φ is given by

$$C_{\Phi(\mathbf{X})} = \frac{1}{m} \sum_{i=1}^{m} \Phi(x_i) \otimes \Phi(x_i) - \mu_{\Phi(\mathbf{X})} \otimes \mu_{\Phi(\mathbf{X})}. \tag{4.17}$$

In terms of $\Phi(\mathbf{X})$, the empirical covariance operator is given by

$$C_{\Phi(\mathbf{X})} = \frac{1}{m} \Phi(\mathbf{X}) J_m \Phi(\mathbf{X})^* : \mathcal{H}_K \to \mathcal{H}_K. \tag{4.18}$$

This can be readily seen as the generalization of the empirical covariance matrix C_X in Section 1.1 via the feature map Φ. In particular, if $X = \mathbb{R}^n$ and $K(x, y) = \langle x, y \rangle_{\mathbb{R}^n}$, then $C_{\Phi(X)} = C_X$.

Finite-rank operator. While $C_{\Phi(X)}$ is an infinite-dimensional operator, it has finite rank, which is at most $m - 1$, since $\mathrm{rank}(J_m) = m - 1$.

Infinite matrix viewpoint. Informally, both $\Phi(X)$ and $C_{\Phi(X)}$ can be viewed as a (potentially infinite) matrices as follows.

Given the data matrix $\mathbf{X} = [x_1, \ldots, x_m]$, one can view $\Phi(\mathbf{X})$ as the feature matrix

$$\Phi(\mathbf{X}) = [\Phi(x_1), \ldots, \Phi(x_m)] \tag{4.19}$$

of size $\dim(\mathcal{H}_K) \times m$ in the space $\mathcal{H}_K$, with each column being a vector in $\mathcal{H}_K$. With this view, the operation $\Phi(\mathbf{X})w$ in Eq. (4.14) can be viewed simply as a (matrix $\times$ vector) operation.

With the matrix viewpoint, the covariance operator $C_{\Phi(X)}$ can then be viewed as the (potentially infinite) covariance matrix associated with the feature matrix $\Phi(\mathbf{X})$ in the feature space $\mathcal{H}_K$.

Connection between feature maps and Gram matrices. Consider the $m \times m$ Gram matrix $K[\mathbf{X}]$ defined by $(K[\mathbf{X}])_{ij} = K(x_i, x_j)$, $1 \leq i, j \leq m$, and the operator $\Phi(\mathbf{X})^*\Phi(\mathbf{X}) : \mathbb{R}^m \to \mathbb{R}^m$. We have

$$[\Phi(\mathbf{X})^*\Phi(\mathbf{X})]w = \left(\sum_{j=1}^{m} w_j \langle \Phi(x_i), \Phi(x_j) \rangle_{\mathcal{H}_K} \right)_{i=1}^{m}$$

$$= \left(\sum_{j=1}^{m} K(x_i, x_j)w_j \right)_{i=1}^{m} = K[\mathbf{X}]w, \quad \forall w \in \mathbb{R}^m. \tag{4.20}$$

Thus, it follows that

$$\Phi(\mathbf{X})^*\Phi(\mathbf{X}) = K[\mathbf{X}]. \tag{4.21}$$

Similarly, if $\mathbf{Y} = [y_1, \ldots, y_m]$ is another data matrix, then

$$\Phi(\mathbf{X})^*\Phi(\mathbf{Y}) = K[\mathbf{X}, \mathbf{Y}], \tag{4.22}$$

where $(K[\mathbf{X}, \mathbf{Y}])_{ij} = K(x_i, y_j)$, $1 \leq i, j \leq m$.

These relations are employed in the subsequent computations of all distances and inner products between RKHS covariance operators in Chapter 5.

4.3   DATA REPRESENTATION BY RKHS COVARIANCE OPERATORS

Having defined RKHS covariance operators, let us describe how they can be used as a framework for data representation. This framework is a generalization of the covariance matrix representation described in Section 1.1.

For concreteness, let us focus on image representation. As in Section 1.1, for each image, let $\mathbf{X} = [x_1, \ldots, x_m]$ be the data matrix of size $n \times m$, with each column being the vector of features $x_i \in \mathbb{R}^n$ sampled at pixel i, $1 \leq i \leq m$. Now let $K : \mathbb{R}^n \times \mathbb{R}^n \to \mathbb{R}$ be a continuous positive definite kernel, such as the Gaussian kernel. Then K induces a feature map $\Phi : \mathbb{R}^n \to \mathcal{H}_K$, where $\mathcal{H}_K$ is the RKHS induced by K, which is a separable Hilbert space. As discussed in the previous section, the map Φ induces feature matrix in $\mathcal{H}_K$

$$\Phi(\mathbf{X}) = [\Phi(x_1), \ldots \Phi(x_m)], \tag{4.23}$$

which can be viewed informally as a (potentially infinite) matrix of size $\dim(\mathcal{H}_K) \times m$, along with the RKHS covariance operator

$$C_{\Phi(\mathbf{X})} = \frac{1}{m}\Phi(\mathbf{X})J_m\Phi(\mathbf{X})^* : \mathcal{H}_K \to \mathcal{H}_K, \tag{4.24}$$

which can be viewed informally as a (potentially infinite) matrix of size $\dim(\mathcal{H}_K) \times \dim(\mathcal{H}_K)$.

The original image is now represented by the covariance operator $C_{\Phi(\mathbf{X})}$. If K is nonlinear, then $\Phi(x)$ is a nonlinear function of $x \in \mathbb{R}^n$ and thus $C_{\Phi(\mathbf{X})}$ encodes *nonlinear correlations* between all the different extracted features. This representation is particularly rich when $\dim(\mathcal{H}_K) = \infty$, when the corresponding feature $\Phi(x)$ is a highly nonlinear function of the original input x.

Covariance matrix representation as a special case. For the linear kernel $K(x, y) = \langle x, y \rangle$ on $\mathbb{R}^n \times \mathbb{R}^n$, we have $\Phi(x) = x$ and $C_{\Phi(\mathbf{X})} = C_{\mathbf{X}}$, so that we recover the covariance matrix representation in Chapter 1.

Implicit and explicit representations. While the covariance matrix representation $C_{\mathbf{X}}$ is explicit, in general the *exact* RKHS covariance operator representation is *implicit*, that is neither the infinite-dimensional feature matrix $\Phi(\mathbf{X})$ nor the infinite-dimensional covariance operator $C_{\Phi(\mathbf{X})}$ is explicitly computed. Instead, all the necessary computations involving $\Phi(\mathbf{X})$ and $C_{\Phi(\mathbf{X})}$ are performed via the corresponding Gram matrices. This is the case for the all distances and inner products between RKHS covariance operators in Chapter 5. However, to reduce computational complexity of the exact methods, we also carry out *explicit finite-dimensional approximations* of the feature matrix $\Phi(\mathbf{X})$ and covariance operator $C_{\Phi(\mathbf{X})}$. This is the case of the approximate kernel methods on covariance operators in Chapter 6.

We next turn to the question of computing distances/similarity measures between covariance operators in Chapter 5.

CHAPTER 5

Geometry of Covariance Operators

Having described the image representation framework by RKHS covariance operators, we now describe the distances and divergences between covariance operators. These distances and divergences can then be directly employed in a practical application, e.g., image classification. We emphasize, however, that the concepts we present below are general and applicable in any application involving the comparison of covariance operators.

Generalizing the finite-dimensional geometrical structures along with the corresponding distances and inner products between covariance matrices in Chapter 2, in this chapter we consider the following geometrical structures and the corresponding distances/divergences and inner products between infinite-dimensional covariance operators.

1. The Hilbert-Schmidt distance and Hilbert-Schmidt inner product, which are the infinite-dimensional generalizations, respectively, of the Euclidean distance and Euclidean inner product. In particular, for RKHS covariance operators $C_{\Phi(X)}$, which are Hilbert-Schmidt operators, both the Hilbert-Schmidt distance and Hilbert-Schmidt inner product admit closed form expressions via the corresponding Gram matrices.

2. The *infinite-dimensional Hilbert manifold* of *positive definite Hilbert–Schmidt operators*, which is the infinite-dimensional generalization of the finite-dimensional smooth manifold $\text{Sym}^{++}(n)$ of SPD matrices. Each point on this manifold has the form $A + \gamma I > 0$, $\gamma > 0$, where A is a Hilbert-Schmidt operator. In particular, *regularized* RKHS covariance operators $(C_{\Phi(X)} + \gamma I)$, $\gamma > 0$, are positive definite Hilbert-Schmidt operators.

3. The affine-invariant Riemannian distance between positive definite Hilbert-Schmidt operators, which is the infinite-dimensional generalization of the affine-invariant Riemannian distance between SPD matrices. In particular, for *regularized* RKHS covariance operators $(C_{\Phi(X)} + \gamma I)$, $\gamma > 0$, the affine-invariant Riemannian distance admits a closed form expressions via the corresponding Gram matrices.

4. The Log-Hilbert-Schmidt distance and Log-Hilbert-Schmidt inner product between positive definite Hilbert-Schmidt operators, which are the infinite-dimensional generalizations, respectively, of the Log-Euclidean distance and Log-Euclidean inner product between SPD matrices. In particular, for *regularized* RKHS covariance operators

$(C_{\Phi(X)} + \gamma I)$, $\gamma > 0$, both the Log-Hilbert-Schmidt distance and Log-Hilbert-Schmidt inner product admit closed form expressions via the corresponding Gram matrices.

5. The *infinite-dimensional convex cone* of *positive definite trace class operators*, which also generalizes the finite-dimensional convex cone $\mathrm{Sym}^{++}(n)$ of SPD matrices. However, in contrast to the finite-dimensional case, in the infinite-dimensional case, this convex cone is a *strict subset* of the manifold of positive definite Hibert-Schmidt operators. Each point in this cone has the form $A + \gamma I > 0$, $\gamma > 0$, where A is a trace class operator. In particular, *regularized* RKHS covariance operators $(C_{\Phi(X)} + \gamma I)$, $\gamma > 0$, are positive definite trace class operators.

6. The Alpha Log-Determinant divergences between positive definite trace class operators, which are the infinite-dimensional generalizations of the Alpha Log-Determinant divergences between SPD matrices. In particular, for *regularized* RKHS covariance operators $(C_{\Phi(X)} + \gamma I)$, $\gamma > 0$, which are positive definite trace class operators, the Alpha Log-Determinant divergences admit closed form expressions via the corresponding Gram matrices.

Among the three distances treated in this chapter, the Hilbert-Schmidt distance is obtained by treating covariance operators as Hilbert-Schmidt operators, without taking into account their positivity. The other two distances, namely affine-invariant Riemannian and Log-Hilbert-Schmidt distances, arise by viewing the set of positive definite Hilbert-Schmidt operators as an *infinite-dimensional Riemannian manifold*. They were developed in [64, 76, 78], see also [81], and are the generalizations of, respectively, the affine-invariant Riemannian distance and Log-Euclidean distance between SPD matrices to the infinite-dimensional setting. On the other hand, the Alpha Log-Determinant divergences arise by viewing the set of positive definite trace class operators, a strict subset of the above manifold, as an *infinite-dimensional convex cone*. They were formulated in [75] and are the generalizations of the Alpha Log-Determinant divergences between SPD matrices in Section 2.6.1.

An important point that we wish to point out is that, in general, with the exception of the Euclidean and Hilbert-Schmidt distances and inner products between RKHS covariance operators, the distance/divergence/inner product formulas for the finite and infinite-dimensional cases are *different* and the infinite-dimensional formulas are generally *not* the limits of the finite-dimensional ones as the dimension approaches infinity. For RKHS covariance operators, all the distances/divergences/inner products presented here admit closed forms in terms of Gram matrices. Thus they are straightforward to implement and apply in practice. Summaries of the concepts discussed in this chapter are presented in Tables 5.1 and 5.2.

Remark 5.1   Bregman divergences.   In [44, 135], the authors considered several Bregman divergences between infinite-dimensional RKHS covariance matrices and their applications

Table 5.1: Several distances and inner products on the Hilbert manifold $\Sigma(\mathcal{H})$ of positive definite Hilbert-Schmidt operators on an infinite-dimensional separable Hilbert space $\mathcal{H}$

Hilbert-Schmidt operators
$$\mathrm{HS}(\mathcal{H}) = \{A \: : \: ||A||_{\mathrm{HS}}^2 = \textstyle\sum_{k=1}^{\infty} ||Ae_k||^2 < \infty\}$$
for any orthonormal basis $\{e_k\}_{k=1}^{\infty}$ in $\mathcal{H}$
Hilbert-Schmidt distance and inner product
$$d_{\mathrm{HS}}(A, B) = ||A - B||_{\mathrm{HS}}$$
$$\langle A, B \rangle_{\mathrm{HS}} = \mathrm{tr}(A^*B) = \textstyle\sum_{k=1}^{\infty} \langle Ae_k, Be_k \rangle$$
$$A, B \in \mathrm{HS}(\mathcal{H})$$

Affine-invariant Riemannian distance
$$d_{\mathrm{aiHS}}[(A + \gamma I), (B + \mu I)] = || \log[(A + \gamma I)^{-1/2}(B + \mu I)(A + \gamma I)^{-1/2})||_{\mathrm{eHS}}$$
$$(A + \gamma I), (B + \mu I) \in \Sigma(\mathcal{H})$$

Log-Hilbert-Schmidt distance and inner product
$$d_{\mathrm{logHS}}(A, B) = || \log(A + \gamma I) - \log(B + \mu I)||_{\mathrm{eHS}}$$
$$\langle (A + \gamma I), (B + \mu I) \rangle_{\mathrm{logHS}} = \langle \log(A + \gamma I), \log(B + \mu I) \rangle_{\mathrm{eHS}}$$
$$(A + \gamma I), (B + \mu I) \in \Sigma(\mathcal{H})$$

Hilbert manifold $\Sigma(\mathcal{H})$ of positive definite Hilbert-Schmidt operators
$$\Sigma(\mathcal{H}) = \{A + \gamma I > 0 \: : \: A = A^*, A \in \mathrm{HS}(\mathcal{H}), \gamma \in \mathbb{R}\}$$
Tangent space at any point $P \in \Sigma(\mathcal{H})$
$$T_P(\Sigma(\mathcal{H})) \cong \mathcal{H}_{\mathbb{R}} = \{A + \gamma I \: : \: A = A^*, A \in \mathrm{HS}(\mathcal{H}), \gamma \in \mathbb{R}\}$$
Extended Hilbert-Schmidt inner product
$$\langle (A + \gamma I), (B + \mu I) \rangle_{\mathrm{eHS}} = \langle A, B \rangle_{\mathrm{HS}} + \gamma \mu$$
$$(A + \gamma I), (B + \mu I) \in \mathcal{H}_{\mathbb{R}}$$

---

in computer vision. These divergences were obtained by essentially *kernelizing* the finite-dimensional versions, without considering the geometry of infinite-dimensional covariance operators, and are, strictly speaking, valid for *finite-dimensional* RKHS.

In Section 5.3 below, we presents results developed in [75], which contains a rigorous mathematical formulation for the infinite-dimensional Alpha Log-Determinant divergences between *positive definite trace class operators*, with closed form expressions in terms of Gram matrices for the case of RKHS covariance operators. This formulation generalizes the finite-dimensional Alpha Log-Determinant divergences between SPD matrices in Section 2.6.1 and includes in particular the infinite-dimensional Stein divergence as a special case. We have recently general-

Table 5.2: Alpha Log-Determinant divergences on the cone of positive definite trace class operators on an infinite-dimensional separable Hilbert space $\mathcal{H}$. Note that for simplicity, we have only listed the formulas for the special case $\gamma = \mu$. For the general case, see Section 5.3.

Trace class operators

$$\text{Tr}(\mathcal{H}) = \{A \ : \ ||A||_{\text{tr}} = \sum_{k=1}^{\infty} \langle e_k, (A^*A)^{1/2} e_k \rangle < \infty\}$$
$$\text{for any orthonormal basis } \{e_k\}_{k=1}^{\infty} \text{ in } \mathcal{H}$$
$$\text{tr}(A) = \sum_{k=1}^{\infty} \lambda_k, \qquad \{\lambda_k\}_{k=1}^{\infty} = \text{eigenvalues of } A$$

Extended trace class operators

$$\text{Tr}_X(\mathcal{H}) = \{A + \gamma I \ : \ A \in \text{Tr}(\mathcal{H}), \gamma \in \mathbb{R}\}$$

Extended trace

$$\text{tr}_X(A + \gamma I) = \gamma + \text{tr}(A) = \gamma + \sum_{k=1}^{\infty} \lambda_k$$

Fredholm determinant

$$\det(A + I) = \prod_{k=1}^{\infty} (\lambda_k + 1), \qquad A \in \text{Tr}(\mathcal{H})$$

Extended Fredholm determinant

$$\det_X(A + \gamma I) = \gamma \det[(A/\gamma) + I], \qquad (A + \gamma I) \in \text{Tr}_X(\mathcal{H}), \gamma \neq 0$$

Convex cone of positive definite trace class operators

$$\text{PTr}(\mathcal{H}) = \{A + \gamma I > 0 \ : \ A^* = A, A \in \text{Tr}(\mathcal{H}), \gamma \in \mathbb{R}\}$$

Alpha Log-Determinant divergences

between $(A + \gamma I), (B + \mu I) \in \text{PTr}(\mathcal{H})$ when $\gamma = \mu$

$$d^{\alpha}_{\text{logdet}}[(A + \gamma I), (B + \gamma I)] = \frac{4}{1-\alpha^2} \log \left[\frac{\det_X\left(\frac{1-\alpha}{2}(A+\gamma I) + \frac{1+\alpha}{2}(B+\gamma I)\right)}{\det_X(A+\gamma I)^{\frac{1-\alpha}{2}} \det_X(B+\gamma I)^{\frac{1+\alpha}{2}}} \right]$$
$$-1 < \alpha < 1$$

$$d^{1}_{\text{logdet}}[(A + \gamma I), (B + \gamma I)] = \text{tr}_X[(B + \gamma I)^{-1}(A + \gamma I) - I]$$
$$- \log \det_X[(B + \gamma I)^{-1}(A + \gamma I)]$$

$$d^{-1}_{\text{logdet}}[(A + \gamma I), (B + \gamma I)] = \text{tr}_X(A + \gamma I)^{-1}(B + \gamma I) - I]$$
$$- \log \det_X[(A + \gamma I)^{-1}(B + \gamma I)]$$

ized the formulation in [75] further to the infinite-dimensional Alpha-Beta Log-Determinant divergences [79, 80] between *positive definite Hilbert-Schmidt operators*. These divergences generalize the finite-dimensional Alpha-Beta divergences in Section 2.7 and include the infinite-dimensional affine-invariant Riemannian distance in Section 5.2 below as a special case. The interested reader is referred to [75], [79], and [80] for the full mathematical detail.

5.1   HILBERT-SCHMIDT DISTANCE

Since covariance operators are trace class operators and hence Hilbert-Schmidt operators, a natural distance between them is the Hilbert-Schmidt distance, which is the infinite-dimensional generalization of the Euclidean distance given by the Frobenius norm $|| \, ||_F$. We first consider the generalization of the Frobenius norm in Eq. (1.22) to the infinite-dimensional setting. Throughout the following, let $\mathcal{H}$ denote a separable Hilbert space, that is it possesses a countable orthonormal basis, with $\dim(\mathcal{H}) = \infty$, unless explicitly stated otherwise.

Let us first recall the two closely related concepts of trace class and Hilbert-Schmidt operators on $\mathcal{H}$ (see e.g., [98] for a comprehensive treatment). A bounded linear operator $A : \mathcal{H} \to \mathcal{H}$ is said to be *trace class* if for any orthonormal basis $\{e_k\}_{k=1}^{\infty}$ in $\mathcal{H}$,

$$||A||_{\mathrm{tr}} = \sum_{k=1}^{\infty} \langle e_k, |A|e_k \rangle = \sum_{k=1}^{\infty} \langle e_k, (A^*A)^{1/2} e_k \rangle < \infty, \tag{5.1}$$

where $|A| = (A^*A)^{1/2}$ denotes the unique square root of the positive operator A^*A. The quantity $||A||_{\mathrm{tr}}$ is called the *trace norm* of A and is independent of the choice of the orthonormal basis $\{e_k\}_{k=1}^{\infty}$.

Let $\mathrm{Tr}(\mathcal{H})$ denote the set of all trace class operators on $\mathcal{H}$. For $A \in \mathrm{Tr}(\mathcal{H})$, its *trace* is defined to be

$$\mathrm{tr}(A) = \sum_{k=1}^{\infty} \langle e_k, Ae_k \rangle, \tag{5.2}$$

which can be shown to be independent of the choice of the orthonormal basis $\{e_k\}_{k=1}^{\infty}$. A trace class operator A is in particular a compact operator, so that it possesses a countable set of eigenvalues $\{\lambda_k\}_{k=1}^{\infty}$. A fundamental result linking the trace and eigenvalues of A is Lidskii's Trace Theorem (see e.g., [107]), which states that

$$\mathrm{tr}(A) = \sum_{k=1}^{\infty} \lambda_k, \tag{5.3}$$

which is a natural generalization of the corresponding finite-dimensional result on traces of square matrices. One important point to note here is that if $\dim(\mathcal{H}) = \infty$, then the identity operator I is not trace class, since obviously

$$||I||_{\mathrm{tr}} = \mathrm{tr}(I) = \infty.$$

This fact plays a crucial role in the formulations of infinite-dimensional generalization of the Alpha Log-Determinant divergences below.

A bounded linear operator $A : \mathcal{H} \to \mathcal{H}$ is said to be a Hilbert-Schmidt operator if

$$||A||_{\mathrm{HS}}^2 = \mathrm{tr}(A^*A) = \sum_{k=1}^{\infty} ||Ae_k||^2 < \infty, \tag{5.4}$$

for any countable orthonormal basis $\{e_k\}_{k \in \mathbb{N}}$ in $\mathcal{H}$. The quantity $||A||_{\mathrm{HS}}$ is called the Hilbert-Schmidt norm of A, which is the infinite-dimensional version of the Frobenius norm in Eq. (1.22). Another important point to note here is that if $\dim(\mathcal{H}) = \infty$, then the identity operator I is not Hilbert-Schmidt, since

$$||I||_{\mathrm{HS}} = \infty.$$

This fact plays a crucial role in the formulations of infinite-dimensional generalization of the affine-invariant and Log-Euclidean distances below.

Let $\mathrm{HS}(\mathcal{H})$ denote the set of all Hilbert-Schmidt operators on $\mathcal{H}$. The Hilbert-Schmidt norm is the Hilbert space norm corresponding to the Hilbert-Schmidt inner product on $\mathrm{HS}(\mathcal{H})$, which is defined by

$$\langle A, B \rangle_{\mathrm{HS}} = \mathrm{tr}(A^*B) = \sum_{k=1}^{\infty} \langle Ae_k, Be_k \rangle, \quad A, B \in \mathrm{HS}(\mathcal{H}). \tag{5.5}$$

Under this inner product and norm structure, $\mathrm{HS}(\mathcal{H})$ itself forms a Hilbert space. For a self-adjoint operator $A \in \mathrm{HS}(\mathcal{H})$, A is compact and hence possesses a countable spectrum $\{\lambda_k\}_{k=1}^{\infty}$, with $\lim_{k \to \infty} \lambda_k = 0$, and

$$||A||_{\mathrm{HS}}^2 = \sum_{k=1}^{\infty} \lambda_k^2 < \infty. \tag{5.6}$$

Furthermore, assuming also that A is self-adjoint, then

$$||A||_{\mathrm{HS}}^2 = \sum_{k=1}^{\infty} \lambda_k^2 \leq \left(\sum_{k=1}^{\infty} |\lambda_k| \right)^2 = ||A||_{\mathrm{tr}}^2.$$

Thus, if $A \in \mathrm{Tr}(\mathcal{H})$, so that $||A||_{\mathrm{tr}} < \infty$, then also $||A||_{\mathrm{HS}} < \infty$, so that $A \in \mathrm{HS}(\mathcal{H})$. The converse is not true, however, as can be seen by taking the sequence $\{\lambda_k = \frac{1}{k}\}_{k=1}^{\infty}$, which satisfies $\sum_{k=1}^{\infty} \frac{1}{k^2} = \frac{\pi^2}{6} < \infty$ but $\sum_{k=1}^{\infty} \frac{1}{k} = \infty$. Hence, the corresponding operator A satisfies $A \in \mathrm{HS}(\mathcal{H})$, but $A \notin \mathrm{Tr}(\mathcal{H})$.

In general, when $\dim(\mathcal{H}) = \infty$, it can be shown that we have the *strict inclusion*

$$\mathrm{Tr}(\mathcal{H}) \subsetneq \mathrm{HS}(\mathcal{H}). \tag{5.7}$$

RKHS covariance operators as positive Hilbert-Schmidt operators. In particular, for the RKHS covariance operator C_Φ in Eq. (4.10), which is a positive trace class operator by Theorem 4.1, its eigenvalues satisfy

$$\sum_{k=1}^{\infty} \lambda_k^2 \le \left(\sum_{k=1}^{\infty} \lambda_k \right)^2 < \infty, \tag{5.8}$$

thus C_Φ is automatically a positive Hilbert-Schmidt operator. The corresponding empirical RKHS covariance operator $C_{\Phi(\mathbf{X})}$, being finite-rank, is also automatically a positive Hilbert-Schmidt operator.

For two RKHS covariance operators $C_{\Phi(\mathbf{X})}$ and $C_{\Phi(\mathbf{Y})}$, their Hilbert-Schmidt distance and inner product are expressed explicitly in terms of the corresponding Gram matrices, as follows. Let $\mathcal{X}$ be an arbitrary non-empty input space and $K : \mathcal{X} \times \mathcal{X} \to \mathbb{R}$ be a positive definite kernel, along with a corresponding feature map $\Phi : \mathcal{X} \to \mathcal{H}$. Let $\mathbf{X} = [x_1, \ldots, x_m]$, $\mathbf{Y} = [y_1, \ldots, y_m]$ be two data matrices sampled from $\mathcal{X}$, with $x_i, y_i \in \mathcal{X}$, $1 \le i \le m$.

Let $K[\mathbf{X}]$, $K[\mathbf{Y}]$, $K[\mathbf{X}, \mathbf{Y}]$ denote the $m \times m$ Gram matrices defined by

$$(K[\mathbf{X}])_{ij} = K(x_i, x_j), \quad (K[\mathbf{Y}])_{ij} = K(y_i, y_j), \tag{5.9}$$
$$(K[\mathbf{X}, \mathbf{Y}])_{ij} = K(x_i, y_j), \quad 1 \le i, j \le m. \tag{5.10}$$

By definition of feature maps, we have $K(x, y) = \langle \Phi(x), \Phi(y) \rangle_{\mathcal{H}} \; \forall (x, y) \in \mathcal{X} \times \mathcal{X}$, so that the Gram matrices and the feature maps are closely related as follows. Let

$$\Phi(\mathbf{X}) = [\Phi(x_1), \ldots, \Phi(x_m)], \quad \Phi(\mathbf{Y}) = [\Phi(y_1), \ldots, \Phi(y_m)], \tag{5.11}$$

which, as discussed in Chapter 4, can be viewed alternately as bounded linear operators $\Phi(\mathbf{X}), \Phi(\mathbf{Y}) : \mathbb{R}^m \to \mathcal{H}$, or as feature matrices of size $\dim(\mathcal{H}) \times m$. Then

$$K[\mathbf{X}] = \Phi(\mathbf{X})^* \Phi(\mathbf{X}), \quad K[\mathbf{Y}] = \Phi(\mathbf{Y})^* \Phi(\mathbf{Y}), \quad K[\mathbf{X}, \mathbf{Y}] = \Phi(\mathbf{X})^* \Phi(\mathbf{Y}). \tag{5.12}$$

Lemma 5.2 *The Hilbert-Schmidt distance between two RKHS covariance operators $C_{\Phi(\mathbf{X})}$ and $C_{\Phi(\mathbf{Y})}$ is given by*

$$||C_{\Phi(\mathbf{X})} - C_{\Phi(\mathbf{Y})}||_{\mathrm{HS}}^2 = \frac{1}{m^2} \langle J_m K[\mathbf{X}], K[\mathbf{X}] J_m \rangle_F - \frac{2}{m^2} \langle J_m K[\mathbf{X}, \mathbf{Y}], K[\mathbf{X}, \mathbf{Y}] J_m \rangle_F$$
$$+ \frac{1}{m^2} \langle J_m K[\mathbf{Y}], K[\mathbf{Y}] J_m \rangle_F. \tag{5.13}$$

The Hilbert–Schmidt inner product between $C_{\Phi(\mathbf{X})}$ and $C_{\Phi(\mathbf{Y})}$ is given by

$$\langle C_{\Phi(\mathbf{X})}, C_{\Phi(\mathbf{Y})}\rangle_{\mathrm{HS}} = \frac{1}{m^2}\langle J_m K[\mathbf{X}, \mathbf{Y}], K[\mathbf{X}, \mathbf{Y}]J_m\rangle_F. \tag{5.14}$$

Remark 5.3   We note that Eqs. (5.13) and (5.14) have the same form, regardless of whether $\dim(\mathcal{H}_K) = \infty$ (e.g., in the case of the Gaussian kernel) or $\dim(\mathcal{H}_K) < \infty$ (e.g., in the case of the polynomial kernels). This does *not* hold true for the affine-invariant Riemannian distance and the Log-Hilbert-Schmidt distance and Log-Hilbert-Schmidt inner product, which we consider next. For the linear kernel $K(x, y) = \langle x, y\rangle_{\mathbb{R}^n}$, we have $\Phi(\mathbf{X}) = \mathbf{X}$, $\Phi(\mathbf{Y}) = \mathbf{Y}$ and thus Eq. (5.13) gives us the Euclidean distance $||C_{\mathbf{X}} - C_{\mathbf{Y}}||_F$ and Eq. (5.14) gives us the Euclidean inner product $\langle C_{\mathbf{X}}, C_{\mathbf{Y}}\rangle_F$.

Computational complexity. The computation of Eqs. (5.13) and (5.14) requires the calculation of $m \times m$ Gram matrices and the pointwise multiplication of these matrices. Thus, the computational complexity required for computing the Hilbert-Schmidt distance/inner product between a pair of covariance operators $C_{\Phi(\mathbf{X})}$ and $C_{\Phi(\mathbf{Y})}$ is $O(m^2)$. If we have a set of N data matrices $\{X_j\}_{j=1}^N$, then for computing all the pairwise Hilbert-Schmidt distances/inner products between the corresponding covariance operators $\{C_{\Phi(\mathbf{X}_j)}\}_{j=1}^N$, the computational complexity required is $O(N^2 m^2)$.

The Hilbert-Schmidt distance (and Hilbert-Schmidt inner product) is the most computationally efficient distance considered in this chapter. However, just like the Euclidean distance, the Hilbert-Schmidt distance does *not* reflect the *positivity* of covariance operators. In order to do so, as with $\mathrm{Sym}^{++}(n)$, we need to consider the intrinsic geometrical structures of positive definite operators. This is the content of the remaining part of this chapter.

5.2   RIEMANNIAN DISTANCES BETWEEN COVARIANCE OPERATORS

We now present the generalizations of the affine-invariant Riemannian metric and the Log-Euclidean metric in Sections 2.4 and 2.5.2, respectively, to the infinite-dimensional settings, specifically to self-adjoint, positive definite Hilbert-Schmidt operators on a separable Hilbert space $\mathcal{H}$. These generalizations were carried out recently in [63, 64, 78], for the affine-invariant Riemannian metric, and in [76] for the Log-Euclidean metric, see also [81] for further detail.

We first present two key concepts that are required for a proper generalization of the affine-invariant Riemannian and Log-Euclidean metrics (in [76, 81] we presented different, but equivalent, motivations of these concepts, see further below).

1. *Positive definite operators and regularization.* In the finite-dimensional case, the regularization $(C_{\mathbf{X}} + \gamma I)$ is often necessary *empirically* since in general $C_{\mathbf{X}}$ is not guaranteed to be

positive definite. In contrast, when $\dim(\mathcal{H}) = \infty$, for a covariance operator A, the regularization form $(A + \gamma I)$ is necessary both *theoretically* and *empirically*, even if A is strictly positive. This is because in this case, A possesses infinitely many positive eigenvalues, with accumulation point 0. Thus A^{-1} is *always unbounded* and one must always consider the regularized form $(A + \gamma I)$, for some regularization parameter $\gamma > 0$, so that $(A + \gamma I)^{-1}$ is bounded.

2. *Extended Hilbert-Schmidt inner product and extended Hilbert-Schmidt norm.* While the natural generalization of the Frobenius inner product $\langle \, , \rangle_F$ is the Hilbert-Schmidt inner product in Section 5.1, it is *not sufficient* for the purpose of generalizing the affine-invariant Riemannian and Log-Euclidean metrics. This is because when $\dim(\mathcal{H}) = \infty$, the identity operator I is not Hilbert-Schmidt, so that when using the regularization $(A + \gamma I)$ above, neither $(A + \gamma I)$ nor its inverse $(A + \gamma I)^{-1}$ is Hilbert-Schmidt, with infinite Hilbert-Schmidt norm. The same is true for the operator $\log(A + \gamma I)$. This issue is resolved by the introduction of the extended Hilbert-Schmidt inner product and corresponding extended Hilbert-Schmidt norm.

Positive definite operators and regularization. Let us first motivate the concept of positive definite operators in the infinite-dimensional setting. We recall the definition of the affine-invariant Riemannian metric on the manifold $\mathrm{Sym}^{++}(n)$ in Section 2.4. The inner product on the tangent space $T_P(\mathrm{Sym}^{++}(n)) \cong \mathrm{Sym}(n)$ that defines the Riemannian metric is given by

$$\langle A, B \rangle_P = \mathrm{tr}(P^{-1}AP^{-1}B) = \langle AP^{-1}, P^{-1}B \rangle_F, \quad A, B \in \mathrm{Sym}(n). \tag{5.15}$$

Let us consider the generalization of this inner product to the infinite-dimensional setting.

First consider the inverse operation P^{-1}. Let $P \in \mathrm{Sym}^{++}(n)$. Let $\{\lambda_k\}_{k=1}^n$ be the eigenvalues of P, arranged in decreasing order, $\lambda_k > 0$, $1 \le k \le n$, with corresponding orthonormal eigenvectors $\{\mathbf{u}_k\}_{k=1}^n$. Then P admits the following spectral decomposition

$$P = \sum_{k=1}^n \lambda_k \mathbf{u}_k \mathbf{u}_k^T, \tag{5.16}$$

and the inverse of P is well-defined and is given by

$$P^{-1} = \sum_{k=1}^n \frac{1}{\lambda_k} \mathbf{u}_k \mathbf{u}_k^T.$$

Consider now an infinite-dimensional separable Hilbert space $\mathcal{H}$. Let $\mathcal{L}(\mathcal{H})$ denote the set of all bounded linear operators on $\mathcal{H}$. Let $\mathrm{Sym}(\mathcal{H}) \subset \mathcal{L}(\mathcal{H})$ denote the set of all bounded, self-adjoint operators on $\mathcal{H}$. Let $\mathrm{Sym}^{++}(\mathcal{H}) \subset \mathcal{L}(\mathcal{H})$ denote the set of all bounded, self-adjoint, strictly positive operators on $\mathcal{H}$, so that

$$A \in \mathrm{Sym}^{++}(\mathcal{H}) \iff A = A^*, \ \langle x, Ax \rangle > 0 \ \forall x \in \mathcal{H}, x \ne 0.$$

Let P be a strictly positive Hilbert-Schmidt operator on $\mathcal{H}$, that is $P \in \text{Sym}^{++}(\mathcal{H}) \cap \text{HS}(\mathcal{H})$. Then P possesses a countable set of eigenvalues $\{\lambda_k\}_{k=1}^{\infty}$, arranged in decreasing order, where $\lambda_k > 0 \ \forall k \in \mathbb{N}$ and $\lim_{k \to \infty} \lambda_k = 0$, with corresponding orthonormal eigenvectors $\{\mathbf{u}_k\}_{k=1}^{\infty}$. Thus P admits the following spectral decomposition, which generalizes Eq. (5.16),

$$P = \sum_{k=1}^{\infty} \lambda_k \mathbf{u}_k \otimes \mathbf{u}_k.$$

Here the operator $\mathbf{u}_k \otimes \mathbf{u}_k : \mathcal{H} \to \mathcal{H}$ generalizes the matrix $\mathbf{u}_k \mathbf{u}_k^T$ and is given by $(\mathbf{u}_k \otimes \mathbf{u}_k)x = \langle \mathbf{u}_k, x \rangle \mathbf{u}_k \ \forall x \in \mathcal{H}$. However, since $\lim_{k \to \infty} \lambda_k = 0$, the inverse of P, namely

$$P^{-1} = \sum_{k=1}^{\infty} \frac{1}{\lambda_k} \mathbf{u}_k \otimes \mathbf{u}_k \tag{5.17}$$

is *unbounded*, since $\lim_{k \to \infty} \frac{1}{\lambda_k} = \infty$.

Remark 5.4 Here we note that since the vectors $\{\mathbf{u}_k\}_{k=1}^{\infty}$ form an orthonormal basis in $\mathcal{H}$, each operator $\mathbf{u}_k \otimes \mathbf{u}_k$ corresponds to the orthogonal projection onto the direction $\mathbf{u}_k$. Let $\{a_k\}_{k=1}^{\infty}$ be a sequence of real numbers, then for the operator $A : \mathcal{H} \to \mathcal{H}$ defined by

$$A = \sum_{k=1}^{\infty} a_k (\mathbf{u}_k \otimes \mathbf{u}_k),$$

the eigenvalues of A are precisely $\{a_k\}_{k=1}^{\infty}$, with corresponding orthonormal eigenvectors $\{\mathbf{u}_k\}_{k=1}^{\infty}$. Thus, by definition, the operator norm of A is

$$\|A\| = \sup_{x \in \mathcal{H}, x \neq 0} \frac{\|Ax\|}{\|x\|} = \sup_{k \in \mathbb{N}} |a_k|.$$

Therefore, A is a bounded operator if and only if $\sup_{k \in \mathbb{N}} |a_k| < \infty$. In Eq. (5.17), $\sup_{k \in \mathbb{N}}(\frac{1}{\lambda_k}) = \infty$ and hence P^{-1} is unbounded.

Thus, a direct generalization of the inner product in Eq. (2.30) is *not* possible. The issue arising from the unboundedness of P^{-1} can be resolved via regularization as follows. Instead of $P \in \text{HS}(\mathcal{H})$, we consider operators of the form $P + \gamma I$, where $\gamma \in \mathbb{R}$, $\gamma > 0$. Then from Remark 5.4, the inverse of the regularized operator $P + \gamma I$, namely

$$(P + \gamma I)^{-1} = \sum_{k=1}^{\infty} \frac{1}{\lambda_k + \gamma} \mathbf{u}_k \otimes \mathbf{u}_k, \tag{5.18}$$

is a bounded operator, with operator norm $\|(P + \gamma I)^{-1}\| = \sup_{k \in \mathbb{N}}(\frac{1}{\lambda_k + \gamma}) = \frac{1}{\gamma} < \infty$.

The operator $P + \gamma I$ is a member of the set of self-adjoint *positive definite operator* on $\mathcal{H}$, see, e.g., [93], which is defined by

$$\mathbb{P}(\mathcal{H}) = \{B \in \mathcal{L}(\mathcal{H}) : B = B^*, \exists M_B > 0 \text{ such that } \langle x, Bx \rangle \geq M_B ||x||^2 \; \forall x \in \mathcal{H}\}. \quad (5.19)$$

If $B \in \mathbb{P}(\mathcal{H})$, which we denote by the notation $B > 0$, then the eigenvalues of B, if they exist, are all bounded below by the constant $M_B > 0$. It can be shown that

$$B \text{ positive definite} \iff B \text{ strictly positive and invertible}. \quad (5.20)$$

While in the finite-dimensional case, i.e., $B \in \text{Sym}^{++}(n)$, positive definiteness and strict positivity are the same, since strict positivity also implies invertibility, in the infinite-dimensional setting, invertibility is separate from strict positivity and thus positive definiteness is a stronger requirement than strict positivity.

Operators of the form $A + \gamma I > 0$, where $A \in \text{HS}(\mathcal{H})$, are called *positive definite unitized (or extended) Hilbert-Schmidt operators*, or *positive definite Hilbert-Schmidt operators* for short.

Remark 5.5 In [76, 78, 81], the positive definite operators $A + \gamma I > 0$, were A is Hilbert-Schmidt, is motivated by a different, but equivalent viewpoint, as follows. Recall the finite-dimensional affine-invariant Riemannian distance in Eq. (2.41) and the Log-Euclidean distance in Eq. (2.55),

$$d_{\text{aiE}}(A, B) = || \log(A^{-1/2} B A^{-1/2}) ||_F, \quad d_{\text{logE}}(A, B) = || \log(A) - \log(B) ||_F. \quad (5.21)$$

For $A \in \text{Sym}^{++}(n)$, its principal logarithm function, which appears in the formulas for both distances above, is always well-defined by

$$\log(A) = \sum_{k=1}^{n} \log(\lambda_k) \mathbf{u}_k \mathbf{u}_k^T. \quad (5.22)$$

However, in the infinite-dimensional setting, for $A \in \text{Sym}^{++}(\mathcal{H}) \cap \text{HS}(\mathcal{H})$, its principal logarithm

$$\log(A) = \sum_{k=1}^{\infty} \log(\lambda_k) \mathbf{u}_k \otimes \mathbf{u}_k \quad (5.23)$$

is unbounded, since $\lim_{k \to \infty} \log(\lambda_k) = -\infty$. The resolution of this issue also leads to the consideration of the positive definite Hilbert-Schmidt operators $A + \gamma I > 0$, so that

$$\log(A + \gamma I) = \sum_{k=1}^{\infty} \log(\lambda_k + \gamma) \mathbf{u}_k \otimes \mathbf{u}_k \quad (5.24)$$

is a bounded operator on $\mathcal{H}$. In fact, by Remark 5.4, the operator norm of $\log(A + \gamma I)$ is

$$\| \log(A + \gamma I) \| = \sup_{k \in \mathbb{N}} |\log(\lambda_k + \gamma)| = \max\{|\log(\lambda_1 + \gamma)|, |\log(\gamma)|\} < \infty.$$

Extended Hilbert-Schmidt inner product and norm. From the previous discussion, we see that for the infinite-dimensional generalization of $\mathrm{Sym}^{++}(n)$, instead of the set $\mathrm{Sym}^{++}(\mathcal{H})$, we need to consider the set

$$\Sigma(\mathcal{H}) = \{A + \gamma I > 0 \ : \ A = A^*, A \in \mathrm{HS}(\mathcal{H}), \gamma \in \mathbb{R}\}. \tag{5.25}$$

We recall that in the finite-dimensional case, $\forall P \in \mathrm{Sym}^{++}(n)$, the tangent space at P is $T_P(\mathrm{Sym}^{++}(n)) \cong \mathrm{Sym}(n)$ and $A \in \mathrm{Sym}^{++}(n) \iff \log(A) \in \mathrm{Sym}(n)$. In the Hilbert space setting, we have the following result.

Proposition 5.6 *Assume that $A + \gamma I > 0$ where $\gamma > 0$ and A is a self-adjoint, compact operator. Then*

$$A + \gamma I \in \Sigma(\mathcal{H}) \iff \log(A + \gamma I) \in \mathcal{H}_{\mathbb{R}}, \tag{5.26}$$

where

$$\begin{aligned} \mathcal{H}_{\mathbb{R}} &= \{A + \gamma I \ : \ A^* = A, \ A \in \mathrm{HS}(\mathcal{H}), \ \gamma \in \mathbb{R}\} \\ &\subset \mathrm{HS}_X(\mathcal{H}) = \{A + \gamma I \ : \ A \in \mathrm{HS}(\mathcal{H}), \ \gamma \in \mathbb{R}\} \end{aligned} \tag{5.27}$$

Proposition 5.6 suggests that, for the generalization of $\mathrm{Sym}(n)$ to the Hilbert space setting, instead of the space $\mathrm{Sym}(\mathcal{H})$, we need to consider the set $\mathcal{H}_{\mathbb{R}}$ as defined in Eq. (5.27). Let us now attempt to generalize the inner product in Eq. (5.15), with the Frobenius inner product replaced by its natural generalization, namely the Hilbert-Schmidt inner product,

$$\langle (A + \gamma I), (B + \mu I) \rangle_{(P + \lambda I)} = \langle (A + \gamma I)(P + \lambda I)^{-1}, (P + \lambda I)^{-1}(B + \mu I) \rangle_{\mathrm{HS}}, \tag{5.28}$$

where $(A + \gamma I), (B + \mu I) \in \mathcal{H}_{\mathbb{R}}$ and $(P + \lambda I) \in \Sigma(\mathcal{H})$. However, the right-hand side of Eq. (5.28) is generally infinite. To see this, note that

$$(A + \gamma I)(P + \lambda I)^{-1} = A(P + \lambda I)^{-1} - \frac{\gamma}{\lambda}P(P + \lambda I)^{-1} + \frac{\gamma}{\lambda}I = C_1 + \gamma_1 I \in \mathrm{HS}_X(\mathcal{H}),$$

$$(B + \mu I)(P + \lambda I)^{-1} = B(P + \lambda I)^{-1} - \frac{\mu}{\lambda}P(P + \lambda I)^{-1} + \frac{\mu}{\lambda}I = C_2 + \gamma_2 I \in \mathrm{HS}_X(\mathcal{H}),$$

where $C_1 = A(P + \lambda I)^{-1} - \frac{\gamma}{\lambda}P(P + \lambda I)^{-1} \in \mathrm{HS}(\mathcal{H})$, $C_2 = B(P + \lambda I)^{-1} - \frac{\mu}{\lambda}P(P + \lambda I)^{-1} \in \mathrm{HS}(\mathcal{H})$. Thus, the right-hand side of Eq. (5.28) has the form

$$\langle (C_1 + \gamma_1 I), (C_2 + \gamma_2 I) \rangle_{\mathrm{HS}}, \quad \text{where} \ (C_1 + \gamma_1 I), (C_2 + \gamma_2 I) \in \mathrm{HS}_X(\mathcal{H}).$$

This inner product is infinite for $\gamma_1 \neq 0, \gamma_2 \neq 0$, since as noted above, $||I||_{\mathrm{HS}} = \infty$, that is the identity operator is not Hilbert-Schmidt.

Thus, the appropriate infinite-dimensional generalization of the Frobenius inner product in Eq. (5.15) is *not* the Hilbert-Schmidt inner product. The resolution of this issue is the *extended Hilbert-Schmidt inner product*, as considered in [63, 64], which is defined by

$$\langle (C_1 + \gamma_1 I), (C_2 + \gamma_2 I) \rangle_{\mathrm{eHS}} = \langle C_1, C_2 \rangle_{\mathrm{HS}} + \gamma_1 \gamma_2. \tag{5.29}$$

The extended Hilbert-Schmidt inner product is clearly finite for all pairs $(C_1 + \gamma_1 I), (C_2 + \gamma_2 I) \in \mathrm{HS}_X(\mathcal{H})$.

The corresponding *extended Hilbert-Schmidt norm* is then given by

$$||A + \gamma I||^2_{\mathrm{eHS}} = ||A||^2_{\mathrm{HS}} + \gamma^2. \tag{5.30}$$

We see that under the extended Hilbert-Schmidt inner product, the scalar operators γI are orthogonal to the Hilbert-Schmidt operators and the identity operator has norm 1, that is $||I||_{\mathrm{eHS}} = 1$, in contrast to the infinite Hilbert-Schmidt norm $||I||_{\mathrm{HS}} = \infty$.

Remark 5.7   In [76, 78, 81], we motivate the extended Hilbert-Schmidt inner product and the corresponding extended Hilbert-Schmidt norm from a different viewpoint. Let us attempt to generalize the Frobenius norm in the finite-dimensional affine-invariant Riemannian distance and Log-Euclidean distance in Eq. (5.21), with the matrices $A, B \in \mathrm{Sym}^{++}(n)$ now replaced by positive definite Hilbert-Schmidt operators $A + \gamma I > 0, B + \mu I > 0$. We first have the following result.

Proposition 5.8 [81]   *Assume that $A + I > 0, \gamma > 0$, where A is a self-adjoint, compact operator on $\mathcal{H}$. Then $\log(A + I) \in \mathrm{HS}(\mathcal{H})$ if and only if $A \in \mathrm{HS}(\mathcal{H})$.*

For $\gamma > 0, \gamma \neq 1$, we have the decomposition

$$\log(A + \gamma I) = \log\left(\frac{A}{\gamma} + I\right) + (\log \gamma)I, \tag{5.31}$$

where on the right-hand side, $\log(\frac{A}{\gamma} + I) \in \mathrm{HS}(\mathcal{H})$ by Proposition 5.8 and $\log(\gamma)I \notin \mathrm{HS}(\mathcal{H})$. Thus it follows that for $\gamma \neq 1$, $\log(A + \gamma I) \notin \mathrm{HS}(\mathcal{H})$, i.e.,

$$||\log(A + \gamma I)||_{\mathrm{HS}} = \infty, \quad \gamma \neq 1.$$

Thus, the appropriate infinite-dimensional generalization of the Frobenius norm in Eq. (5.21) is *not* the Hilbert-Schmidt norm. The resolution of this issue is also the extended Hilbert-Schmidt inner product and corresponding extended Hilbert-Schmidt norm, which gives

$$|| \log(A + \gamma I)||^2_{\mathrm{eHS}} = \left\| \log \left(\frac{A}{\gamma} + I \right) \right\|^2_{\mathrm{HS}} + (\log \gamma)^2 < \infty, \tag{5.32}$$

for all $A + \gamma I \in \Sigma(\mathcal{H})$.

Thus the proper generalization of either the finite-dimensional Riemannian metric in Eq. (5.15) or the corresponding finite-dimensional Riemannian distances in Eq. (5.21) both lead to the positive definite unitized Hilbert-Schmidt operators $A + \gamma I > 0$ and the extended Hilbert-Schmidt inner product and norm.

The Hilbert manifold of positive definite unitized Hilbert-Schmidt operators. In the finite-dimensional setting, a smooth n-dimensional manifold is locally homeomorphic to the Euclidean space $\mathbb{R}^n$. A natural generalization of this concept to the infinite-dimensional setting is a *Hilbert manifold* (see, e.g., [62]), which is locally homeomorphic to an infinite-dimensional Hilbert space $\mathcal{H}$.

Under the extended Hilbert-Schmidt inner product and corresponding extended Hilbert-Schmidt norm, the vector space

$$\mathcal{H}_{\mathbb{R}} = \{A + \gamma I \ : \ A^* = A, \ A \in \mathrm{HS}(\mathcal{H}), \ \gamma \in \mathbb{R}\}$$

becomes a Hilbert space. The set

$$\Sigma(\mathcal{H}) = \mathbb{P}(\mathcal{H}) \cap \mathcal{H}_{\mathbb{R}} = \{A + \gamma I > 0 \ : \ A^* = A, \ A \in \mathrm{HS}(\mathcal{H}), \ \gamma \in \mathbb{R}\},$$

which is an open subset in the Hilbert space $\mathcal{H}_{\mathbb{R}}$, is then an *infinite-dimensional Hilbert manifold*, first introduced by [63, 64]. For each point $P \in \Sigma(\mathcal{H})$, the tangent space at P is

$$T_P(\Sigma(\mathcal{H})) \cong \mathcal{H}_{\mathbb{R}}.$$

We next describe the generalization of the affine-invariant Riemannian metric in Section 2.4 on this Hilbert manifold.

5.2.1   THE AFFINE-INVARIANT RIEMANNIAN METRIC

The finite-dimensional affine-invariant Riemannian metric on $\mathrm{Sym}^{++}(n)$ was generalized to the Hilbert manifold $\Sigma(\mathcal{H})$ by [63, 64]. The Riemannian metric is defined by the following inner product on the tangent space $T_{(P+\lambda I)}(\Sigma(\mathcal{H})) \cong \mathcal{H}_{\mathbb{R}}$,

$$\langle (A + \gamma I), (B + \mu I) \rangle_{(P+\lambda I)} = \langle (A + \gamma I)(P + \lambda I)^{-1}, (P + \lambda I)^{-1}(B + \mu I) \rangle_{\mathrm{eHS}}, \tag{5.33}$$

for any $(P + \lambda I) \in \Sigma(\mathcal{H})$, and $(A + \gamma I), (B + \mu I) \in \mathcal{H}_{\mathbb{R}}$.

Under the Riemannian metric defined in Eq. (5.33), $\Sigma(\mathcal{H})$ becomes an *infinite-dimensional Riemannian manifold* (see Figure 5.1). Specifically, we have the following key result from [64].

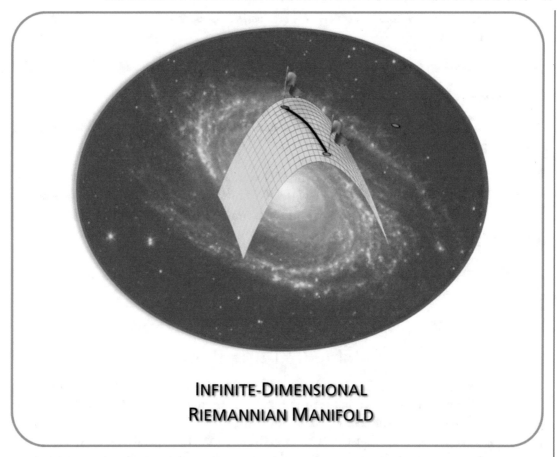

Figure 5.1: The set of positive definite Hilbert-Schmidt operators viewed as an infinite-dimensional Riemannian manifold.

Theorem 5.9 [64]. *Under the Riemannian metric define in Eq. (5.33), $\Sigma(\mathcal{H})$ becomes an infinite-dimensional Cartan-Hadamard manifold, that is it is simply connected, geodesically complete, and has nonpositive sectional curvature. For any $(P + \lambda I) \in \Sigma(\mathcal{H})$, the exponential map at $(P + \lambda I)$ is given by*

$$\mathrm{Exp}_{(P+\lambda I)}(V + \mu I) = (P + \lambda I)^{1/2} \exp[(P + \lambda I)^{-1/2}(V + \mu I)(P + \lambda I)^{-1/2}](P + \lambda I)^{1/2}, \tag{5.34}$$

for any $V + \mu I \in \mathcal{H}_{\mathbb{R}} \cong T_{(P+\lambda I)}(\Sigma(\mathcal{H}))$.

The Riemannian distance between any two positive definite operators $(A + \gamma I), (B + \mu I) \in \Sigma(\mathcal{H})$ is given by

$$d_{\text{aiHS}}[(A + \gamma I), (B + \mu I)] = \| \log[(A + \gamma I)^{-1/2}(B + \mu I)(A + \gamma I)^{-1/2}] \|_{\text{eHS}}. \quad (5.35)$$

Furthermore, the metric space $(\Sigma(\mathcal{H}), d_{\text{aiHS}})$ is complete.

The following result shows that the distance $d_{\text{aiHS}}[(A + \gamma I), (B + \mu I)]$ is always finite for any pair of operators $(A + \gamma I), (B + \mu I) \in \Sigma(\mathcal{H})$.

Proposition 5.10   [81] *Assume that $\dim(\mathcal{H}) = \infty$. For any two operators $(A + \gamma I), (B + \mu I) \in \Sigma(\mathcal{H})$, write $(A + \gamma I)^{-1/2}(B + \mu I)(A + \gamma I)^{-1/2} = Z + \nu I > 0$, where $\nu = \frac{\mu}{\gamma}$ and $Z = (A + \gamma I)^{-1/2}B(A + \gamma I)^{-1/2} - \frac{\mu}{\gamma}A(A + \gamma I)^{-1}$, with $Z \in \text{Sym}(\mathcal{H}) \cap \text{HS}(\mathcal{H})$. Then the affine-invariant Riemannian distance $d_{\text{aiHS}}[(A + \gamma I), (B + \mu I)]$ admits the following decomposition*

$$d_{\text{aiHS}}^2[(A + \gamma I), (B + \mu I)] = \| \log(Z + \nu I) \|_{\text{eHS}} = \left\| \log\left(\frac{Z}{\nu} + I\right) \right\|_{\text{HS}}^2 + (\log \nu)^2. \quad (5.36)$$

In Proposition 5.10, if $A = B = 0$, then $Z = 0$ and Eq. (5.36) gives

$$d_{\text{aiHS}}[\gamma I, \mu I] = |\log \nu| = |\log(\gamma/\mu)|. \quad (5.37)$$

Thus, the second term on the right-hand side of Eq. (5.36) is precisely the squared affine-invariant Riemannian distance between the scalar operators γI and μI (this distance would be infinite if measured in the Hilbert-Schmidt norm).

The RKHS setting. Consider now two RKHS covariance operators $C_{\Phi(X)}, C_{\Phi(Y)}$, which are positive Hilbert-Schmidt operators on the RKHS $\mathcal{H}_K$. Their regularized versions, namely $(C_{\Phi(X)} + \gamma I)$ and $(C_{\Phi(Y)} + \mu I)$, are positive definite Hilbert-Schmidt operators on $\mathcal{H}_K$. We can thus compute the affine-invariant Riemannian distance between them, that is

$$d_{\text{aiHS}}[(C_{\Phi(X)} + \gamma I_{\mathcal{H}_K}), (C_{\Phi(Y)} + \mu I_{\mathcal{H}_K})]. \quad (5.38)$$

This distance admits a closed form in terms of the corresponding Gram matrices, which was given by [78], as follows.

Theorem 5.11   [78]. *Assume that $\dim(\mathcal{H}_K) = \infty$. Let $\gamma > 0, \mu > 0$. Then*

$$d_{\text{aiHS}}^2[(C_{\Phi(X)} + \gamma I_{\mathcal{H}_K}), (C_{\Phi(Y)} + \mu I_{\mathcal{H}_K})] = \text{tr}\left\{ \log\left[\begin{pmatrix} C_{11} & C_{12} & C_{13} \\ C_{21} & C_{22} & C_{23} \\ C_{11} & C_{12} & C_{13} \end{pmatrix} + I_{3m} \right] \right\}^2$$

$$+ \left(\log \frac{\gamma}{\mu} \right)^2, \quad (5.39)$$

where the $m \times m$ matrices C_{ij}, $i = 1, 2$, $j = 1, 2, 3$, are given by

$$C_{11} = \frac{1}{\mu m} J_m K[\mathbf{Y}] J_m,$$

$$C_{12} = -\frac{1}{\sqrt{\gamma \mu} m} J_m K[\mathbf{Y}, \mathbf{X}] J_m \left(I_m + \frac{1}{\gamma m} J_m K[\mathbf{X}] J_m \right)^{-1},$$

$$C_{13} = -\frac{1}{\gamma \mu m^2} J_m K[\mathbf{Y}, \mathbf{X}] J_m \left(I_m + \frac{1}{\gamma m} J_m K[\mathbf{X}] J_m \right)^{-1} J_m K[\mathbf{X}, \mathbf{Y}] J_m,$$

$$C_{21} = \frac{1}{\sqrt{\gamma \mu} m} J_m K[\mathbf{X}, \mathbf{Y}] J_m,$$

$$C_{22} = -\frac{1}{\gamma m} J_m K[\mathbf{X}] J_m \left(I_m + \frac{1}{\gamma m} J_m K[\mathbf{X}] J_m \right)^{-1},$$

$$C_{23} = -\frac{1}{\gamma m} J_m K[\mathbf{X}] J_m \left(I_m + \frac{1}{\gamma m} J_m K[\mathbf{X}] J_m \right)^{-1} \frac{1}{\sqrt{\gamma \mu} m} J_m K[\mathbf{X}, \mathbf{Y}] J_m.$$

The previous theorem applies to, for example, the case of the Gaussian kernel on $\mathbb{R}^n$, where $\dim(\mathcal{H}_K) = \infty$. For comparison, the following is the finite-dimensional version for the case $\dim(\mathcal{H}_K) < \infty$, such as the case of the polynomial kernels on $\mathbb{R}^n$.

Theorem 5.12 [78]. *Assume that* $\dim(\mathcal{H}_K) < \infty$. *Let* $\gamma > 0, \mu > 0$. *Then*

$$d_{\text{aiHS}}^2[(C_{\Phi(\mathbf{X})} + \gamma I_{\mathcal{H}_K}), (C_{\Phi(\mathbf{Y})} + \mu I_{\mathcal{H}_K})] = \text{tr} \left\{ \log \left[\begin{pmatrix} C_{11} & C_{12} & C_{13} \\ C_{21} & C_{22} & C_{23} \\ C_{11} & C_{12} & C_{13} \end{pmatrix} + I_{3m} \right] \right\}^2$$

$$- 2 \left(\log \frac{\gamma}{\mu} \right) \text{tr} \left\{ \log \left[\begin{pmatrix} C_{11} & C_{12} & C_{13} \\ C_{21} & C_{22} & C_{23} \\ C_{11} & C_{12} & C_{13} \end{pmatrix} + I_{3m} \right] \right\} + \left(\log \frac{\gamma}{\mu} \right)^2 \dim(\mathcal{H}_K), \quad (5.40)$$

where the $m \times m$ matrices C_{ij}'s, $i = 1, 2$, $j = 1, 2, 3$, are as in Theorem 5.11.

Remark 5.13 We see that the formula for the affine-invariant distance for the case $\dim(\mathcal{H}_K) = \infty$ is generally different from that for the case $\dim(\mathcal{H}_K) < \infty$, except when $\gamma = \mu$, in which case they are identical. One can see that for $m \in \mathbb{N}$ fixed, $\gamma \neq \mu$, the right-hand side of Eq. (5.40) approaches infinity as $\dim(\mathcal{H}_K) \to \infty$. Thus, for $\gamma \neq \mu$, one *cannot* approximate the infinite-dimensional distance in Eq. (5.39) by the finite-dimensional distance in Eq. (5.40).

Computational complexity. In both Theorems 5.11 and 5.12, for the computation of the affine-invariant Riemannian distance between two regularized RKHS covariance operators $(C_{\Phi(\mathbf{X})} + \gamma I_{\mathcal{H}_K})$ and $(C_{\Phi(\mathbf{Y})} + \mu I_{\mathcal{H}_K})$, we need to carry out multiplications and inversions of

$m \times m$ matrices, and the eigenvalue computation for a $3m \times 3m$ matrix. Thus, the total computational complexity required is $O(m^3)$. If we have a set of N data matrices $\{\mathbf{X}_j\}_{j=1}^N$, in order to compute all the pairwise distances between the corresponding regularized covariance operators, the total computational complexity is $O(N^2 m^3)$.

5.2.2 LOG-HILBERT-SCHMIDT METRIC

We now describe the generalization of the Log-Euclidean distance [6] on $\mathrm{Sym}^{++}(n)$, as described in Section 2.5.2, to the Log-Hilbert-Schmidt distance on $\Sigma(\mathcal{H})$. This generalization was first carried out in [76], see also [81].

The operations $(\odot, \circledast)$ on $\mathrm{Sym}^{++}(n)$ defined in [6], as described in Section 2.5.2, can be readily generalized to $\Sigma(\mathcal{H})$ as follows [76]. First, the commutative Lie group multiplication operation $\odot$ on $\Sigma(\mathcal{H})$ is defined by

$$\odot : \Sigma(\mathcal{H}) \times \Sigma(\mathcal{H}) \to \Sigma(\mathcal{H})$$
$$(A + \gamma I) \odot (B + \mu I) = \exp(\log(A + \gamma I) + \log(B + \mu I)). \tag{5.41}$$

The Log-Hilbert-Schmidt distance between $(A + \gamma I), (B + \mu I) \in \Sigma(\mathcal{H})$ is then defined to be [76]

$$d_{\mathrm{logHS}} : \Sigma(\mathcal{H}) \times \Sigma(\mathcal{H}) \to \mathbb{R}^+,$$
$$d_{\mathrm{logHS}}[(A + \gamma I), (B + \mu I)] = ||\log[(A + \gamma I) \odot (B + \mu I)^{-1}]||_{\mathrm{eHS}} \tag{5.42}$$
$$= ||\log(A + \gamma I) - \log(B + \mu I)||_{\mathrm{eHS}}.$$

The following result shows that $d_{\mathrm{logHS}}[(A + \gamma I), (B + \mu I)]$ is always well-defined and finite for any pair of operators $(A + \gamma I), (B + \mu I) \in \Sigma(\mathcal{H})$.

Proposition 5.14 [76, 81] *For any pair of operators $(A + \gamma I), (B + \mu I) \in \Sigma(\mathcal{H})$, the distance $d_{\mathrm{logHS}}[(A + \gamma I), (B + \mu I)] = ||\log(A + \gamma I) - \log(B + \mu I)||_{\mathrm{eHS}}$ is always finite. Furthermore, when $\dim(\mathcal{H}) = \infty$,*

$$||\log(A + \gamma I) - \log(B + \mu I)||_{\mathrm{eHS}}^2 = \left\| \log\left(\frac{A}{\gamma} + I\right) - \log\left(\frac{B}{\mu} + I\right) \right\|_{\mathrm{HS}}^2 + \left(\log\frac{\gamma}{\mu}\right)^2. \tag{5.43}$$

In particular, for $A = B = 0$, Eq. (5.43) gives

$$d_{\mathrm{logHS}}[\gamma I, \mu I] = ||\log(\gamma I) - \log(\mu I)||_{\mathrm{eHS}} = |\log(\gamma/\mu)|. \tag{5.44}$$

Thus, the second term on the right-hand side of Eq. (5.43) is precisely the squared Log-Hilbert-Schmidt distance between the scalar operators γI and μI (this distance would be infinite if measured in the Hilbert-Schmidt norm $||\ ||_{\mathrm{HS}}$). We also note that $d_{\mathrm{aiHS}}[\gamma I, \mu I] = d_{\mathrm{logHS}}[\gamma I, \mu I]$, since the operators γI and μI trivially commute.

Vector space structure of $\Sigma(\mathcal{H})$. Together with the group operation $\odot$, one also defines the following scalar multiplication on $\Sigma(\mathcal{H})$

$$\circledast : \mathbb{R} \times \Sigma(\mathcal{H}) \to \Sigma(\mathcal{H}),$$
$$\lambda \circledast (A + \gamma I) = \exp(\lambda \log(A + \gamma I)) = (A + \gamma I)^{\lambda}, \quad \lambda \in \mathbb{R}. \tag{5.45}$$

Endowed with the commutative group multiplication $\odot$ and the scalar multiplication $\circledast$, the axioms of vector space can be readily verified to show that $(\Sigma(\mathcal{H}), \odot, \circledast)$ is a vector space (see [76] for the detailed proofs).

Hilbert space structure on $\Sigma(\mathcal{H})$. On top of the vector space structure $(\Sigma(\mathcal{H}), \odot, \circledast)$, we can define the following *Log-Hilbert-Schmidt inner product* on $\Sigma(\mathcal{H})$ by

$$\langle (A + \gamma I), (B + \mu I) \rangle_{\text{logHS}} = \langle \log(A + \gamma I), \log(B + \mu I) \rangle_{\text{eHS}}, \tag{5.46}$$

along with the corresponding *Log-Hilbert-Schmidt norm*

$$||A + \gamma I||^2_{\text{logHS}} = \langle \log(A + \gamma I), \log(A + \gamma I) \rangle_{\text{eHS}}. \tag{5.47}$$

The axioms of inner product, namely symmetry, positivity, and linearity with respect to the operations $(\odot, \circledast)$ can be verified (see [76]) to show that

$$(\Sigma(\mathcal{H}), \odot, \circledast, \langle \, , \, \rangle_{\text{logHS}}) \tag{5.48}$$

is a complete inner product space, that is a Hilbert space. This Hilbert space structure was first discussed in [76] and generalizes the finite-dimensional inner product space

$$(\text{Sym}^{++}(n), \odot, \circledast, \langle \, , \, \rangle_{\text{logE}})$$

in Section 2.5.2.

As a generalization from Section 2.5.2, it can be shown that the map

$$\log : (\Sigma(\mathcal{H}), \odot, \circledast, \langle \, , \, \rangle_{\text{logHS}}) \to (\mathcal{H}_{\mathbb{R}}, +, \cdot, \langle \, , \, \rangle_{\text{eHS}}) \tag{5.49}$$

is an isometrical isomorphism of Hilbert spaces, where the operations $(+, \cdot)$ are the standard addition and scalar multiplication operations, respectively.

In terms of the Log-Hilbert-Schmidt inner product and Log-Hilbert-Schmidt norm, the Log-Hilbert-Schmidt distance d_{logHS} in Eq. (5.42) is expressed as

$$
\begin{aligned}
d_{\text{logHS}}(A + \gamma I), (B + \mu I)] &= || \log(A + \gamma I) - \log(B + \mu I)||_{\text{eHS}} \\
&= ||(A + \gamma I) \odot (B + \mu I)^{-1}||_{\text{logHS}} \\
&= \sqrt{\langle (A + \gamma I) \odot (B + \mu I)^{-1}, (A + \gamma I) \odot (B + \mu I)^{-1} \rangle_{\text{logHS}}}.
\end{aligned}
\tag{5.50}
$$

The RKHS setting. As in the case of the affine-invariant Riemannian distance, in the case of regularized RKHS covariance operators, both the Log-Hilbert-Schmidt distance

$$d_{\text{logHS}}[C_{\Phi(X)} + \gamma I, C_{\Phi(Y)} + \mu I] = || \log(C_{\Phi(X)} + \gamma I) - \log(C_{\Phi(Y)} + \mu I)||_{\text{eHS}} \tag{5.51}$$

and the Log-Hilbert-Schmidt inner product

$$\langle(C_{\Phi(\mathbf{X})} + \gamma I), (C_{\Phi(\mathbf{Y})} + \mu I)\rangle_{\text{logHS}} \tag{5.52}$$

admit closed forms, expressed explicitly via the Gram matrices corresponding to $\mathbf{X}$ and $\mathbf{Y}$ [76]. To state this explicit form, we first define the following operators

$$A = \frac{1}{\sqrt{\gamma m}}\Phi(\mathbf{X})J_m : \mathbb{R}^m \to \mathcal{H}_K, \quad B = \frac{1}{\sqrt{\mu m}}\Phi(\mathbf{Y})J_m : \mathbb{R}^m \to \mathcal{H}_K, \tag{5.53}$$

so that

$$A^*A = \frac{1}{\gamma m}J_m K[\mathbf{X}]J_m, \quad B^*B = \frac{1}{\mu m}J_m K[\mathbf{Y}]J_m, \quad A^*B = \frac{1}{\sqrt{\gamma\mu m}}J_m K[\mathbf{X}, \mathbf{Y}]J_m. \tag{5.54}$$

Let N_A and N_B be the numbers of nonzero eigenvalues of A^*A and B^*B, respectively. Let Σ_A and Σ_B be the diagonal matrices of size $N_A \times N_A$ and $N_B \times N_B$, and U_A and U_B be the matrices of size $m \times N_A$ and $m \times N_B$, respectively, which are obtained from the spectral decompositions

$$A^*A = \frac{1}{\gamma m}J_m K[\mathbf{X}]J_m = U_A\Sigma_A U_A^T, \quad B^*B = \frac{1}{\mu m}J_m K[\mathbf{Y}]J_m = U_B\Sigma_B U_B^T. \tag{5.55}$$

Let $\circ$ denote the Hadamard (element-wise) matrix product and define

$$C_{AB} = \mathbf{1}_{N_A}^T \log(I_{N_A} + \Sigma_A)\Sigma_A^{-1}(U_A^T A^* B U_B \circ U_A^T A^* B U_B)\Sigma_B^{-1}\log(I_{N_B} + \Sigma_B)\mathbf{1}_{N_B}. \tag{5.56}$$

In terms of the quantities just defined, the Log-Hilbert-Schmidt distance and Log-Hilbert-Schmidt inner product between $(C_{\Phi(\mathbf{X})} + \gamma I)$ and $(C_{\Phi(\mathbf{Y})} + \mu I)$ are expressed as follows.

Theorem 5.15 [76]. *Assume that* $\dim(\mathcal{H}_K) = \infty$. *Let* $\gamma > 0$, $\mu > 0$. *Then the Log-Hilbert-Schmidt distance between* $(C_{\Phi(\mathbf{X})} + \gamma I_{\mathcal{H}_K})$ *and* $(C_{\Phi(\mathbf{Y})} + \mu I_{\mathcal{H}_K})$ *is given by*

$$d_{\text{logHS}}^2[(C_{\Phi(\mathbf{X})} + \gamma I_{\mathcal{H}_K}), (C_{\Phi(\mathbf{Y})} + \mu I_{\mathcal{H}_K})] = \text{tr}[\log(I_{N_A} + \Sigma_A)]^2 + \text{tr}[\log(I_{N_B} + \Sigma_B)]^2$$
$$- 2C_{AB} + (\log\gamma - \log\mu)^2. \tag{5.57}$$

The Log-Hilbert-Schmidt inner product between the two operators $(C_{\Phi(\mathbf{X})} + \gamma I_{\mathcal{H}_K})$ *and* $(C_{\Phi(\mathbf{Y})} + \mu I_{\mathcal{H}_K})$ *is given by*

$$\langle(C_{\Phi(\mathbf{X})} + \gamma I_{\mathcal{H}_K}), (C_{\Phi(\mathbf{Y})} + \mu I_{\mathcal{H}_K})\rangle_{\text{logHS}} = C_{AB} + (\log\gamma)(\log\mu). \tag{5.58}$$

The Log-Hilbert-Schmidt norm of the operator $(C_{\Phi(\mathbf{X})} + \gamma I_{\mathcal{H}_K})$ *is given by*

$$\|(C_{\Phi(\mathbf{X})} + \gamma I_{\mathcal{H}_K})\|_{\text{logHS}}^2 = \text{tr}[\log(I_{N_A} + \Sigma_A)]^2 + (\log\gamma)^2. \tag{5.59}$$

The two expressions (5.58) and (5.59) are identical if $\mathbf{X} = \mathbf{Y}$ *and* $\gamma = \mu$.

Remark 5.16 In Theorem 5.15, the first two expressions are from [76], whereas the last expression is a straightforward corollary of the second expression and Eq. (5.55).

We now present the formulas corresponding to those in Theorem 5.15 in the case $\dim(\mathcal{H}_K) < \infty$, e.g., in the case of the polynomial kernels. As in the case of the affine-invariant Riemannian distance, the formulas for the Log-Hilbert-Schmidt distance, Log-Hilbert-Schmidt inner product, and Log-Hilbert-Schmidt norm are different in the case $\dim(\mathcal{H}_K) < \infty$ compared to the case $\dim(\mathcal{H}_K) < \infty$, with the finite-dimensional quantities generally approaching infinity as $\dim(\mathcal{H}_K) \to \infty$.

Theorem 5.17 [76]. *Assume that* $\dim(\mathcal{H}_K) < \infty$. *Let* $\gamma > 0$, $\mu > 0$. *Then the Log-Hilbert-Schmidt distance between* $(C_{\Phi(\mathbf{X})} + \gamma I_{\mathcal{H}_K})$ *and* $(C_{\Phi(\mathbf{Y})} + \mu I_{\mathcal{H}_K})$ *is given by*

$$
\begin{aligned}
d_{\text{logHS}}^2[(C_{\Phi(\mathbf{X})} + \gamma I_{\mathcal{H}_K}), (C_{\Phi(\mathbf{Y})} + \mu I_{\mathcal{H}_K})] = {} & \text{tr}[\log(I_{N_A} + \Sigma_A)]^2 + \text{tr}[\log(I_{N_B} + \Sigma_B)]^2 - 2C_{AB} \\
& + 2\left(\log\frac{\gamma}{\mu}\right)(\text{tr}[\log(I_{N_A} + \Sigma_A)] - \text{tr}[\log(I_{N_B} + \Sigma_B)]) \\
& + (\log\gamma - \log\mu)^2 \dim(\mathcal{H}_K).
\end{aligned}
\tag{5.60}
$$

The Log-Hilbert-Schmidt inner product between $(C_{\Phi(\mathbf{X})} + \gamma I_{\mathcal{H}_K})$ *and* $(C_{\Phi(\mathbf{Y})} + \mu I_{\mathcal{H}_K})$ *is given by*

$$
\begin{aligned}
\langle(C_{\Phi(\mathbf{X})} + \gamma I_{\mathcal{H}_K}), (C_{\Phi(\mathbf{Y})} + \mu I_{\mathcal{H}_K})\rangle_{\text{logHS}} = {} & C_{AB} + (\log\mu)\text{tr}[\log(I_{N_A} + \Sigma_A)] \\
& + (\log\gamma)\text{tr}[\log(I_{N_B} + \Sigma_B)] + (\log\gamma \log\mu)\dim(\mathcal{H}_K).
\end{aligned}
\tag{5.61}
$$

The Log-Hilbert-Schmidt norm of $(C_{\Phi(\mathbf{X})} + \gamma I_{\mathcal{H}_K})$ *is given by*

$$
\begin{aligned}
||(C_{\Phi(\mathbf{X})} + \gamma I_{\mathcal{H}_K})||_{\text{logHS}}^2 = {} & \text{tr}[\log(I_{N_A} + \Sigma_A)]^2 + 2(\log\gamma)\text{tr}[\log(I_{N_A} + \Sigma_A)] \\
& + (\log\gamma)^2 \dim(\mathcal{H}_K).
\end{aligned}
\tag{5.62}
$$

The two expressions (5.61) and (5.62) are identical if $\mathbf{X} = \mathbf{Y}$ *and* $\gamma = \mu$.

Remark 5.18 In Theorem 5.17, the first two expressions are from [76], whereas the last expression is a straightforward corollary of the second expression and Eq. (5.55). In the case of the linear kernel $K(x, y) = \langle x, y\rangle$, $x, y \in \mathbb{R}^n$, Theorem 5.17 gives the Log-Euclidean distance $||\log(C_{\mathbf{X}} + \gamma I) - \log(C_{\mathbf{Y}} + \mu I)||$, Log-Euclidean inner product $\langle\log(C_{\mathbf{X}} + \gamma I), \log(C_{\mathbf{Y}} + \mu I)\rangle_F$, and Log-Euclidean norm $||\log(C_{\mathbf{X}} + \gamma I)||_F$.

Computational complexity. Let n be the number of features and m be the number of observations for each input sample. For computing the Log-Euclidean distance or Log-Euclidean inner product between two $n \times n$ covariance matrices, the computational complexity required is $O(n^2 m + n^3)$, since the computational complexity required for computing the covariance matrices themselves is $O(n^2 m)$ and the computational complexity for computing the SVD of an $n \times n$

matrix is $O(n^3)$. On the other hand, for computing the Log-Hilbert-Schmidt distance or Log-Hilbert-Schmidt inner product between two covariance operators in an infinite-dimensional RKHS, where we need to carry out SVD and multiplications with Gram matrices of size $m \times m$, the computational complexity required is $O(m^3)$. This is of the same order as the computational complexity for computing the Stein and Jeffreys divergences in RKHS in [44]. If we have a set of N data matrices $\{\mathbf{X}_j\}_{j=1}^N$, then the computational complexity required for computing all pairwise distances between the corresponding regularized covariance operators is $O(N^2 m^3)$.

5.3 INFINITE-DIMENSIONAL ALPHA LOG-DETERMINANT DIVERGENCES

In this section, we generalize the Alpha Log-Determinant divergences $d_{\mathrm{logdet}}^\alpha$ on $\mathrm{Sym}^{++}(n)$, as described in Section 2.6.1, to the infinite-dimensional setting. The formulation presented here was developed in [75].

From Eq. (2.84), which defines $d_{\mathrm{logdet}}^\alpha(A, B)$ for $A, B \in \mathrm{Sym}^{++}(n)$, we see that the infinite-dimensional generalization of $d_{\mathrm{logdet}}^\alpha$ involves the generalizations of the determinant det and log-determinant $\log \det$ functions. Let $A \in \mathrm{Sym}^{++}(n)$ and let $\{\lambda_k\}_{k=1}^n$ be its eigenvalues, then

$$\det(A) = \prod_{k=1}^n \lambda_k = \exp\left(\sum_{k=1}^n \log \lambda_k\right) = \exp[\mathrm{tr}(\log(A))], \tag{5.63}$$

$$\log \det(A) = \mathrm{tr}(\log(A)). \tag{5.64}$$

Consider the generalization of these functions to a positive compact operator A on a separable, infinite-dimensional Hilbert space $\mathcal{H}$. This setting includes in particular RKHS covariance operators. From Eqs. (5.63) and (5.64), we see that the following two conditions are necessary:

1. $\log(A)$ is well-defined and is a bounded operator on $\mathcal{H}$.

2. The trace $\mathrm{tr}(\log(A))$ is finite.

For the first condition, as in the case of the affine-invariant Riemannian and Log-Hilbert-Schmidt distances, instead of simply considering a positive operator A, we need to consider regularized operators of the form $(A + \gamma I) > 0$, $\gamma \in \mathbb{R}, \gamma > 0$, so that $\log(A + \gamma I)$ is bounded.

Let $\{\lambda_k\}_{k=1}^\infty$ be the eigenvalues of A, with $\lambda_k \geq 0$, $\lim_{k\to\infty} \lambda_k = 0$. The second condition then becomes

$$\mathrm{tr}[\log(A + \gamma I)] = \sum_{k=1}^\infty \log(\lambda_k + \gamma) \ \text{ is finite.} \tag{5.65}$$

Since $\lambda_k \geq 0$, $\lim_{k\to\infty} \lambda_k = 0$, for $\gamma = 1$, we have by the limit $\lim_{x\to 0} \frac{\log(1+x)}{x} = 1$ that the series $\mathrm{tr}[\log(A + I)] = \sum_{k=1}^\infty \log(\lambda_k + 1)$ converges if and only if the series $\sum_{k=1}^\infty \lambda_k$ converges, that is if and only if $A \in \text{Tr}(\mathcal{H})$. However, for $\gamma \neq 1$, we have

$$\lim_{k \to \infty} \log(\lambda_k + \gamma) = \log(\gamma) \neq 0$$

and thus the series in Eq. (5.65) always diverges. This can also be seen from the following decomposition:

$$\text{tr}[\log(A + \gamma I)] = \text{tr}\left[\log\left(\frac{A}{\gamma} + I\right) + (\log \gamma)I\right] = \text{tr}\left[\log\left(\frac{A}{\gamma} + I\right)\right] + (\log \gamma)\text{tr}(I). \quad (5.66)$$

On the right-hand side of Eq. (5.66), the first term $\text{tr}[\log(\frac{A}{\gamma} + I)]$ is finite for $A \in \text{Tr}(\mathcal{H})$, but the second term is always infinite when $\dim(\mathcal{H}) = \infty$, because the identity operator is not trace class, with $\text{tr}(I) = \infty$. Thus, we have an issue similar to that caused by the fact that the identity operator is not Hilbert-Schmidt, with $||I||_{\text{HS}} = \infty$, when we attempted to generalize the affine-invariant Riemannian and Log-Euclidean metrics to the infinite-dimensional settings in Section 5.2.

Fredholm determinant. The case $\gamma = 1$ above is closely connected to the definition of the infinite-dimensional Fredholm determinant (see e.g., [106]). Specifically, if $A \in \text{Tr}(\mathcal{H})$, then the *Fredholm determinant* of the operator $(A + I)$ is defined by

$$\det(A + I) = \prod_{k=1}^{\infty}(\lambda_k + 1). \quad (5.67)$$

This allows us to define the Alpha Log-Determinant divergences of the form $d_{\text{logdet}}^{\alpha}[(A + I), (B + I)]$, where $A + I > 0, B + I > 0, A, B \in \text{Tr}(\mathcal{H})$. However, a similar argument as above shows that the Fredholm determinant is not defined for operators of the form $(A + \gamma I)$ where $\gamma \neq 1$.

Extended trace class operators. To resolve the issue with the case $\gamma \neq 1$, similar to the extended Hilbert-Schmidt operators and extended Hilbert-Schmidt inner product in Section 5.2, we introduce the *extended trace class operators* and *extended trace*, as follows. Given the set of trace class operators $\text{Tr}(\mathcal{H})$, the set of extended (or unitized) trace class operators is defined to be

$$\text{Tr}_X(\mathcal{H}) = \{A + \gamma I : A \in \text{Tr}(\mathcal{H}), \gamma \in \mathbb{R}\}. \quad (5.68)$$

This set becomes a Banach space under the following *extended trace norm*

$$||A + \gamma I||_{\text{tr}_X} = ||A||_{\text{tr}} + |\gamma|.$$

For $(A + \gamma I) \in \text{Tr}_X(\mathcal{H})$, its *extended trace* is defined to be

$$\text{tr}_X(A + \gamma I) = \text{tr}(A) + \gamma. \quad (5.69)$$

In particular, by this definition

$$\text{tr}_X(I) = 1, \quad \text{in contrast to} \quad \text{tr}(I) = \infty.$$

Positive definite trace class operators. Similar to the positive definite Hilbert-Schmidt operators in Section 5.2, we define the set of *positive definite unitized (or extended) trace class operators*, or *positive definite trace class operators* for short, to be

$$\text{PTr}(\mathcal{H}) = \{A + \gamma I > 0 \; : \; A^* = A, A \in \text{Tr}(\mathcal{H}), \gamma \in \mathbb{R}\}. \tag{5.70}$$

This is an *open convex cone* in the infinite-dimensional Banach space $\text{Tr}_X(\mathcal{H})$. There is a one-to-one correspondence between the set $\text{PTr}(\mathcal{H})$ of positive definite trace class operators and the set $\text{Sym}(\mathcal{H}) \cap \text{Tr}_X(\mathcal{H})$ of self-adjoint extended trace class operators. Specifically, we have the following result, which is analogous to Proposition 5.6 in the Hilbert-Schmidt case.

Proposition 5.19 [75]

$$(A + \gamma I) \in \text{PTr}(\mathcal{H}) \iff \log(A + \gamma I) \in \text{Sym}(\mathcal{H}) \cap \text{Tr}_X(\mathcal{H}). \tag{5.71}$$

In particular, for $\gamma = 1$,

$$(A + I) > 0 \iff \log(A + I) \in \text{Sym}(\mathcal{H}) \cap \text{Tr}(\mathcal{H}). \tag{5.72}$$

Extended Fredholm determinant for positive definite trace class operators. By Proposition 5.19, if $(A + \gamma I) \in \text{PTr}(\mathcal{H})$, then $\log(A + \gamma I) \in \text{Tr}_X(\mathcal{H})$ and hence $\text{tr}_X(A + \gamma I)$ is finite. This enables us to define the following *extended Fredholm determinant* of $(A + \gamma I)$, which generalizes the corresponding finite-dimensional formula in Eq. (5.63), namely

$$\text{det}_X(A + \gamma I) = \exp(\text{tr}_X[\log(A + \gamma I)]). \tag{5.73}$$

The extended Fredholm determinant det_X is related to the Fredholm determinant det via the following factorization formula

$$\text{det}_X(A + \gamma I) = \gamma \det[(A/\gamma) + I]. \tag{5.74}$$

Extended Fredholm determinant for extended trace class operators. The expression of det_X as given in Eq. (5.73) requires explicitly that $(A + \gamma I) \in \text{PTr}(\mathcal{H})$. By using the factorization property in Eq. (5.74), we can define det_X for all operators $(A + \gamma I) \in \text{Tr}_X(\mathcal{H})$ with $\gamma \neq 0$, as follows.

Definition 5.20 (Extended Fredholm determinant).   Let $\mathcal{H}$ be a separable Hilbert space with $\dim(\mathcal{H}) = \infty$. For an operator $(A + \gamma I) \in \text{Tr}_X(\mathcal{H})$, $\gamma \neq 0$, its extended Fredholm determinant is defined to be.

$$\text{det}_X(A + \gamma I) = \gamma \det[(A/\gamma) + I], \tag{5.75}$$

where det on the right-hand side denotes the Fredholm determinant.

If $\dim(\mathcal{H}) < \infty$, then we define $\det_X(A + \gamma I) = \det(A + \gamma I)$, the standard matrix determinant.

Remark 5.21   We emphasize that for $\gamma \neq 1$, the definition of $\det_X$ as given in Eq. (5.75) is *strictly* for the case $\dim(\mathcal{H}) = \infty$. When $\dim(\mathcal{H}) < \infty$, we have

$$\det_X(A + \gamma I) = \det(A + \gamma I) = \gamma^{\dim(\mathcal{H})} \det[(A/\gamma) + I].$$

This expression coincides with that in Eq. (5.75) if and only if $\gamma = 1$.

Generalization of the Log-determinant Concavity. We recall in the finite-dimensional setting in Section 2.6.1 that the Alpha Log-Determinant divergence d^α_{logdet} is based on Ky Fan's inequality on the log-concavity of the determinant function on the set $\text{Sym}^{++}(n)$. The following is the generalization of of Ky Fan's inequality to the extended Fredholm determinant $\det_X$ on $\text{PTr}(\mathcal{H})$.

Theorem 5.22   [75].   *For* $(A + \gamma I), (B + \mu I) \in \text{PTr}(\mathcal{H})$, *for* $0 \leq \alpha \leq 1$,

$$\det_X[\alpha(A + \gamma I) + (1 - \alpha)(B + \mu I)] \geq (\gamma/\mu)^{\alpha - \delta} \det_X(A + \gamma I)^\delta \det_X(B + \mu I)^{1-\delta} \quad (5.76)$$

where $\delta = \frac{\alpha\gamma}{(\alpha\gamma + (1-\alpha)\mu)}$. *For* $0 < \alpha < 1$, *equality occurs if and only if* $A = B$ *and* $\gamma = \mu$. *For* $\gamma = \mu$,

$$\det_X[\alpha(A + \gamma I) + (1 - \alpha)(B + \gamma I)] \geq \det_X(A + \gamma I)^\alpha \det_X(B + \gamma I)^{1-\alpha}. \quad (5.77)$$

In particular, in Eq. (5.77), if we set $A, B \in \text{Sym}^{++}(n)$ and $\gamma = 0$, then we recover Ky Fan's inequality, as stated in Eq. (2.83).

Infinite-dimensional Alpha Log-determinant divergences. Motivated by Theorem 5.22 and the finite-dimensional setting in Section 2.6.1, the following is our definition of the Alpha Log-determinant divergences in the infinite-dimensional setting.

Definition 5.23   (Alpha Log-Determinant divergences between positive definite trace class operators [75]).   Assume that $\dim(\mathcal{H}) = \infty$. For $-1 < \alpha < 1$, the Alpha Log-Determinant divergence $d^\alpha_{\text{logdet}}[(A + \gamma I), (B + \mu I)]$ between $(A + \gamma I), (B + \mu I) \in \text{PTr}(\mathcal{H})$ is defined to be

$$d^\alpha_{\text{logdet}}[(A + \gamma I), (B + \mu I)]$$
$$= \frac{4}{1 - \alpha^2} \log \left[\frac{\det_X \left(\frac{1-\alpha}{2}(A + \gamma I) + \frac{1+\alpha}{2}(B + \mu I) \right)}{\det_X(A + \gamma I)^\beta \det_X(B + \mu I)^{1-\beta}} \left(\frac{\gamma}{\mu} \right)^{\beta - \frac{1-\alpha}{2}} \right], \quad (5.78)$$

where $\beta = \frac{(1-\alpha)\gamma}{(1-\alpha)\gamma+(1+\alpha)\mu}$ and $1-\beta = \frac{(1+\alpha)\mu}{(1-\alpha)\gamma+(1+\alpha)\mu}$.

For $\alpha = \pm 1$, we define $d_{\text{logdet}}^{\pm 1}$ based on limits of $d_{\text{logdet}}^{\alpha}$ as $\alpha \to \pm 1$, respectively.

Definition 5.24   (Limiting cases).

$$
\begin{aligned}
d_{\text{logdet}}^{1}[(A + \gamma I), (B + \mu I)] &= \lim_{\alpha \to 1^-} d_{\text{logdet}}^{\alpha}[(A + \gamma I), (B + \mu I)] \\
&= \left(\frac{\gamma}{\mu} - 1\right) \log \frac{\gamma}{\mu} + \text{tr}_X[(B + \mu I)^{-1}(A + \gamma I) - I] \\
&\quad - \frac{\gamma}{\mu} \log \det_X[(B + \mu I)^{-1}(A + \gamma I)].
\end{aligned}
\tag{5.79}
$$

$$
\begin{aligned}
d_{\text{logdet}}^{-1}[(A + \gamma I), (B + \mu I)] &= \lim_{\alpha \to -1^+} d_{\text{logdet}}^{\alpha}[(A + \gamma I), (B + \mu I)] \\
&= \left(\frac{\mu}{\gamma} - 1\right) \log \frac{\mu}{\gamma} + \text{tr}_X\left[(A + \gamma I)^{-1}(B + \mu I) - I\right] \\
&\quad - \frac{\mu}{\gamma} \log \det_X[(A + \gamma I)^{-1}(B + \mu I)].
\end{aligned}
\tag{5.80}
$$

The following key result confirms that $d_{\text{logdet}}^{\alpha}[(A + \gamma I), (B + \mu I)]$ is indeed a divergence function on $\text{PTr}(\mathcal{H})$.

Theorem 5.25   (Positivity [75]).   *Let $-1 \leq \alpha \leq 1$ be fixed. For any pair $(A + \gamma I), (B + \mu I) \in \text{PTr}(\mathcal{H})$,*

$$d_{\text{logdet}}^{\alpha}[(A + \gamma I), (B + \mu I)] \geq 0, \tag{5.81}$$
$$d_{\text{logdet}}^{\alpha}[(A + \gamma I), (B + \mu I)] = 0 \iff A = B, \gamma = \mu. \tag{5.82}$$

Special cases. For $\gamma = \mu$, the formulas for $d_{\text{logdet}}^{\alpha}[(A + \gamma I), (B + \mu I)]$ are much simpler than in the general case and are direct generalizations of the finite-dimensional formulas in Section 2.6.1. With $\gamma = \mu$, we have $\beta = \frac{1-\alpha}{2}$, $1 - \beta = \frac{1+\alpha}{2}$, and Eq. (5.78) becomes

$$
\begin{aligned}
&d_{\text{logdet}}^{\alpha}[(A + \gamma I), (B + \gamma I)] \\
&= \frac{4}{1-\alpha^2} \log \left[\frac{\det_X \left(\frac{1-\alpha}{2}(A + \gamma I) + \frac{1+\alpha}{2}(B + \gamma I)\right)}{\det_X(A + \gamma I)^{\frac{1-\alpha}{2}} \det_X(B + \gamma I)^{\frac{1+\alpha}{2}}} \right], \quad -1 < \alpha < 1,
\end{aligned}
\tag{5.83}
$$

which is the direct generalization of Eq. (2.84). In particular, for $A, B \in \text{Sym}^{++}(n)$, by setting $\gamma = 0$ in Eq. (5.83), we recover Eq. (2.84).

Similarly, with $\gamma = \mu$, Eqs. (5.79) and (5.80) become, respectively

$$
\begin{aligned}
&d_{\text{logdet}}^{1}[(A + \gamma I), (B + \gamma I)] \\
&= \text{tr}_X[(B + \gamma I)^{-1}(A + \gamma I) - I] - \log \det_X[(B + \gamma I)^{-1}(A + \gamma I)],
\end{aligned}
\tag{5.84}
$$

$$d_{\text{logdet}}^{-1}[(A + \gamma I), (B + \gamma I)]$$
$$= \text{tr}_X(A + \gamma I)^{-1}(B + \gamma I) - I] - \log \det_X[(A + \gamma I)^{-1}(B + \gamma I)], \tag{5.85}$$

which directly generalize Eqs. (2.85) and (2.86), respectively. For $A, B \in \text{Sym}^{++}(n)$, by setting $\gamma = 0$, we recover Eqs. (2.85) and (2.86), respectively.

The RKHS setting. As in the case of the affine-invariant Riemannian and Log-Hilbert-Schmidt distances in Section 5.2, in the case of RKHS covariance operators, the Alpha Log-Det divergences

$$d_{\text{logdet}}^{\alpha}[(C_{\Phi(X)} + \gamma I_{\mathcal{H}_K}), (C_{\Phi(Y)} + \mu I_{\mathcal{H}_K})] \tag{5.86}$$

admit closed forms, expressed via the Gram matrices corresponding to **X** and **Y**, as follows.

Theorem 5.26 [75]. *Assume that* $\dim(\mathcal{H}_K) = \infty$. *Let* $\gamma > 0$, $\mu > 0$. *For* $-1 < \alpha < 1$, *the divergence* $d_{\text{logdet}}^{\alpha}[(C_{\Phi(X)} + \gamma I), (C_{\Phi(Y)} + \mu I)]$ *is given by*

$$d_{\text{logdet}}^{\alpha}[(C_{\Phi(X)} + \gamma I), (C_{\Phi(Y)} + \mu I)] \tag{5.87}$$
$$= \frac{4}{1 - \alpha^2} \text{logdet} \left[\frac{1}{ms(\gamma, \mu, \alpha)} \begin{pmatrix} (1 - \alpha) J_m K[X] J_m & \sqrt{1 - \alpha^2} J_m K[X, Y] J_m \\ \sqrt{1 - \alpha^2} J_m K[Y, X] J_m & (1 + \alpha) J_m K[Y] J_m \end{pmatrix} + I_{2m} \right]$$
$$- \frac{4\beta}{1 - \alpha^2} \text{logdet} \left(\frac{J_m K[X] J_m}{m\gamma} + I_m \right) - \frac{4(1 - \beta)}{1 - \alpha^2} \text{logdet} \left(\frac{J_m K[Y] J_m}{m\mu} + I_m \right) + c(\alpha, \gamma, \mu).$$

Here the quantities $s(\gamma, \mu, \alpha)$ *and* $c(\alpha, \gamma, \mu)$ *are given by*

$$s(\gamma, \mu, \alpha) = (1 - \alpha)\gamma + (1 + \alpha)\mu, \tag{5.88}$$
$$c(\alpha, \gamma, \mu) = \frac{4 \log(s(\gamma, \mu, \alpha)/2)}{1 - \alpha^2} - \frac{2 \log \gamma}{1 + \alpha} - \frac{2 \log \mu}{1 - \alpha}. \tag{5.89}$$

The corresponding formula when $\dim(\mathcal{H}_K) < \infty$ is given by the following result.

Theorem 5.27 [75]. *Assume that* $\dim(\mathcal{H}_K) < \infty$. *Let* $\gamma > 0$, $\mu > 0$. *Then for* $-1 < \alpha < 1$,

$$d_{\text{logdet}}^{\alpha}[(C_{\Phi(X)} + \gamma I), (C_{\Phi(Y)} + \mu I)]$$
$$= \frac{4}{1 - \alpha^2} \text{logdet} \left[\frac{1}{ms(\gamma, \mu, \alpha)} \begin{pmatrix} (1 - \alpha) J_m K[X] J_m & \sqrt{1 - \alpha^2} J_m K[X, Y] J_m \\ \sqrt{1 - \alpha^2} J_m K[Y, X] J_m & (1 + \alpha) J_m K[Y] J_m \end{pmatrix} + I_{2m} \right]$$
$$- \frac{2}{1 + \alpha} \log \det \left(\frac{1}{m\gamma} J_m K[X] J_m + I_m \right) - \frac{2}{1 - \alpha} \log \det \left(\frac{1}{m\mu} J_m K[Y] J_m + I_m \right)$$
$$+ c(\alpha, \gamma, \mu) \dim(\mathcal{H}_K). \tag{5.90}$$

Remark 5.28   It can be shown that $c(\alpha, \gamma, \mu) \geq 0$, with equality if and only if $\gamma = \mu$. The kernel matrices $K[\mathbf{X}]$, $K[\mathbf{Y}]$, $K[\mathbf{X}, \mathbf{Y}]$, $K[\mathbf{Y}, \mathbf{X}]$ have finite sizes $m \times m$. Thus, for $m \in \mathbb{N}$ fixed and $\gamma \neq \mu$, so that $c(\alpha, \gamma, \mu) > 0$, the right-hand side of Eq. (5.90) approaches infinity as $\dim(\mathcal{H}_K) \to \infty$. Thus, except in the case $\gamma = \mu$, the infinite-dimensional case *cannot* be obtained from the finite-dimensional case as the dimension approaches infinity.

Consider now the limiting cases $\alpha = \pm 1$. The following gives the formula for $d_{\text{logdet}}^{-1}[(C_{\Phi(\mathbf{X})} + \gamma I_{\mathcal{H}_K}), (C_{\Phi(\mathbf{Y})} + \mu I_{\mathcal{H}_K})]$ when $\dim(\mathcal{H}_K) = \infty$. For $\alpha = 1$, we use the dual symmetry formula (see [75])

$$d_{\text{logdet}}^{1}[(C_{\Phi(\mathbf{X})} + \gamma I_{\mathcal{H}_K}), (C_{\Phi(\mathbf{Y})} + \mu I_{\mathcal{H}_K})] = d^{-1}[(C_{\Phi(\mathbf{Y})} + \mu I_{\mathcal{H}_K}), (C_{\Phi(\mathbf{X})} + \gamma I_{\mathcal{H}_K})].$$

Theorem 5.29   [75]. *Assume that* $\dim(\mathcal{H}_K) = \infty$. *The divergence* $d_{\text{logdet}}^{-1}[(C_{\Phi(\mathbf{X})} + \gamma I), (C_{\Phi(\mathbf{Y})} + \mu I)]$ *is given by*

$$
\begin{aligned}
d_{\text{logdet}}^{-1}[(C_{\Phi(\mathbf{X})} + \gamma I), (C_{\Phi(\mathbf{Y})} + \mu I)] &= \left(\frac{\mu}{\gamma} - 1 - \log\frac{\mu}{\gamma}\right) + \text{tr}\left[\frac{J_m K[\mathbf{Y}] J_m}{\gamma m}\right] \\
&\quad - \frac{\mu}{\gamma}\text{tr}\left[\left(\frac{J_m K[\mathbf{X}] J_m}{m} + \frac{J_m K[\mathbf{X}, \mathbf{Y}] J_m K[\mathbf{Y}, \mathbf{X}] J_m}{m^2 \mu}\right)\left(\gamma I_m + \frac{J_m K[\mathbf{X}] J_m}{m}\right)^{-1}\right] \\
&\quad + \frac{\mu}{\gamma}\log\det\left(\frac{J_m K[\mathbf{X}] J_m}{\gamma m} + I_m\right) - \frac{\mu}{\gamma}\log\det\left(\frac{J_m K[\mathbf{Y}] J_m}{\mu m} + I_m\right).
\end{aligned}
\tag{5.91}
$$

The corresponding finite-dimensional result is given by the following.

Theorem 5.30   [75]. *Assume that* $\dim(\mathcal{H}_K) < \infty$. *Then* $d_{\text{logdet}}^{-1}[(C_{\Phi(\mathbf{X})} + \gamma I_{\mathcal{H}_K}), (C_{\Phi(\mathbf{Y})} + \mu I_{\mathcal{H}_K})]$ *is given by*

$$
\begin{aligned}
&d_{\text{logdet}}^{-1}[(C_{\Phi(\mathbf{X})} + \gamma I_{\mathcal{H}_K}), (C_{\Phi(\mathbf{Y})} + \mu I_{\mathcal{H}_K})] \\
&= \left(\frac{\mu}{\gamma} - 1 - \log\frac{\mu}{\gamma}\right)\dim(\mathcal{H}_K) + \text{tr}\left[\frac{J_m K[\mathbf{Y}] J_m}{\gamma m}\right] \\
&\quad - \frac{\mu}{\gamma}\text{tr}\left[\left(\frac{J_m K[\mathbf{X}] J_m}{m} + \frac{J_m K[\mathbf{X}, \mathbf{Y}] J_m K[\mathbf{y}, \mathbf{x}] J_m}{m^2 \mu}\right)\left(\gamma I_m + \frac{J_m K[\mathbf{X}] J_m}{m}\right)^{-1}\right] \\
&\quad + \log\det\left(\frac{J_m K[\mathbf{X}] J_m}{\gamma m} + I_m\right) - \log\det\left(\frac{J_m K[\mathbf{Y}] J_m}{\mu m} + I_m\right).
\end{aligned}
\tag{5.92}
$$

Computational complexity. In both Theorems 5.26 and 5.27, the computation of the $d_{\text{logdet}}^{\alpha}$ divergences, for $-1 < \alpha < 1$, requires the Cholesky decompositions of a $2m \times 2m$ matrix and two $m \times m$ matrices. Thus the computational complexity required is $O(m^3)$. The computational complexity of d_{logdet}^{-1} (and hence d_{logdet}^{1}), as given in Theorems 5.29 and 5.30, is similarly $O(m^3)$. If we have a set of N data matrices $\{\mathbf{X}_j\}_{j=1}^N$, then the computational complexity required for computing all the pairwise divergences between the corresponding regularized covariance operators in $O(N^2 m^3)$.

Alpha-Beta Log-Determinant divergences between positive definite Hilbert-Schmidt operators. The Alpha Log-Determinant divergences on the cone of positive definite trace class operators presented in this section can be substantially generalized to the Alpha-Beta Log-Determinant divergences on the entire Hilbert manifold of positive definite Hilbert-Schmidt operators. These divergences generalize the Alpha-Beta Log-Determinant divergences on $\mathrm{Sym}^{++}(n)$, as presented in Section 2.7, and include the affine-invariant Riemannian distance in Section 5.2 as a special case. The generalization requires the concept of the *extended Hilbert-Carleman determinant* for extended Hilbert-Schmidt operators, in addition to the extended Fredholm determinant we presented here. The interested reader is referred to [79] and [80] for detail of the mathematical formulation.

5.4 SUMMARY

In this chapter, we presented several geometrical structures of positive trace class operators and positive Hilbert-Schmidt operators, along with the corresponding divergences, distances and inner products. We show in particular how they can be evaluated, via closed form expressions, in the case of RKHS covariance operators and/or their corresponding regularized versions. Specifically, the following were presented:

1. Hilbert-Schmidt distance and inner product;

2. affine-invariant Riemannian distance;

3. Log-Hilbert-Schmidt distance and inner product;

4. Alpha Log-Determinant divergences.

For the affine-invariant Riemannian distance, Log-Hilbert-Schmidt distance and inner product, and Alpha Log-Determinant divergences, the formulas in the infinite-dimensional case are generally *different* from the corresponding finite-dimensional versions, which generally *diverge* to infinity when the dimension goes to infinity. This can be seen by directly comparing Theorem 5.11 with Theorem 5.12, Theorem 5.15 with Theorem 5.17, and Theorem 5.26 with Theorem 5.27. These differences play a key role in the theoretical analysis of the finite-dimensional approximations of kernel methods on covariance operators, which we present next in Chapter 6.

CHAPTER 6

Kernel Methods on Covariance Operators

In Chapter 5, we presented explicit formulas, in terms of Gram matrices, for the Hilbert-Schmidt distance and inner product, affine-invariant Riemannian distance, and Log-Hilbert-Schmidt distance and inner product between RKHS covariance operators. In this chapter, we show how the Hilbert-Schmidt and Log-Hilbert-Schmidt distances and inner products can be used to define positive definite kernels, allowing us to apply kernel methods on top of covariance operators. This effectively creates a two-layer kernel machine, with the kernel in the first layer giving rise to covariance operators and the kernel in the second layer having those covariance operators as input for subsequent tasks such as regression and classification. We put emphasis in particular on the Log-Hilbert-Schmidt distance and inner product, which are intrinsic to the set of positive definite Hilbert-Schmidt operators. The kernel machine with the Log-Euclidean distance and inner product presented in Chapter 3 can be viewed as a special case of this framework, with the kernel in the first layer being the linear kernel. Along with kernels defined using the exact Log-Hilbert-Schmidt distance, we present kernels defined using finite-dimensional approximations of the infinite-dimensional Log-Hilbert-Schmidt distance, which incur considerably lower computational costs while largely preserving the capability of the exact formulation. The general theoretical framework is accompanied by a concrete numerical implementation along with experiments in image classification. Overall, the methods in this chapter can be viewed as the generalizations of the kernel methods on covariance matrices in Chapter 3 to the infinite-dimensional setting.

6.1 POSITIVE DEFINITE KERNELS ON COVARIANCE OPERATORS

In the following, we present positive definite kernels defined using the Hilbert-Schmidt metric and Log-Hilbert-Schmidt metric, which generalize the positive definite kernels defined using the Euclidean metric and Log-Euclidean metric in Section 3.2. A summary of the kernels defined via these metrics are given in Table 6.1. As of the time of writing, we are not aware of theoretical results on positive definite kernels defined using the infinite-dimensional symmetric Stein divergence in [75] (or the versions employed in [44, 135]) that are comparable to those in the finite-dimensional case, as proven in [110, 111] and described in Section 3.2.3.

Table 6.1: Common positive definite kernels on infinite-dimensional covariance operators. The explicit expressions of the Log-Hilbert-Schmidt inner product and Log-Hilbert-Schmidt distance in terms of Gram matrices are given in Section 5.2.2.

Kernels by Hilbert-Schmidt inner product and distance

$$K(C_{\Phi(X)}, C_{\Phi(Y)}) = (\langle C_{\Phi(X)}, C_{\Phi(Y)}\rangle_{\mathrm{HS}} + c)^d, c \geq 0, d \in \mathbb{N}$$
$$K(C_{\Phi(X)}, C_{\Phi(Y)}) = \exp(-\tfrac{1}{\sigma^2}||C_{\Phi(X)} - C_{\Phi(Y)}||_{\mathrm{HS}}^p), \sigma \neq 0, 0 < p \leq 2$$

Kernels by Log-Hilbert-Schmidt inner product and distance

$$K[(C_{\Phi(X)} + \gamma I), (C_{\Phi(Y)} + \mu I)] = (\langle \log(C_{\Phi(X)} + \gamma I), \log(C_{\Phi(Y)} + \mu I)\rangle_{\mathrm{eHS}} + c)^d,$$
$$\gamma > 0, \mu > 0, c \geq 0, d \in \mathbb{N}$$
$$K[(C_{\Phi(X)} + \gamma I), (C_{\Phi(Y)} + \mu I)] = \exp(-\tfrac{1}{\sigma^2}||\log(C_{\Phi(X)} + \gamma I) - \log(C_{\Phi(Y)} + \mu I)||_{\mathrm{eHS}}^p),$$
$$\gamma > 0, \mu > 0, \sigma \neq 0, 0 < p \leq 2$$

6.1.1 KERNELS DEFINED USING THE HILBERT-SCHMIDT METRIC

Since covariance operators are Hilbert-Schmidt operators, we can automatically apply to them any positive definite kernels that can be defined on Hilbert-Schmidt operators. Following the notation in Chapter 5, let $\mathcal{H}$ be a separable Hilbert space and $\mathrm{HS}(\mathcal{H})$ the Hilbert space of all Hilbert-Schmidt operators on $\mathcal{H}$. The following are some examples of positive definite kernels $K : \mathrm{HS}(\mathcal{H}) \times \mathrm{HS}(\mathcal{H}) \to \mathbb{R}$ that are defined either via the Hilbert-Schmidt inner product $\langle A, B\rangle_{\mathrm{HS}}$ or the Hilbert-Schmidt distance $||A - B||_{\mathrm{HS}}$.

1. Polynomial kernels

$$K(A, B) = [\langle A, B\rangle_{\mathrm{HS}} + c]^d = [\mathrm{tr}(A^*B) + c]^d, \quad c \geq 0, d \in \mathbb{N}. \tag{6.1}$$

2. Generalized Gaussian kernels

$$K(A, B) = \exp\left(-\frac{1}{\sigma^2}||A - B||_{\mathrm{HS}}^p\right), \quad \sigma \neq 0, 0 < p \leq 2. \tag{6.2}$$

For two RKHS covariance operators $C_{\Phi(X)}$ and $C_{\Phi(Y)}$, as we show in Section 5.1, both the Hilbert-Schmidt inner product $\langle C_{\Phi(X)}, C_{\Phi(Y)}\rangle_{\mathrm{HS}}$ and the Hilbert-Schmidt distance $||C_{\Phi(X)} - C_{\Phi(Y)}||_{\mathrm{HS}}$ admit closed form expressions via the corresponding Gram matrices. Thus, the corresponding kernel $K(C_{\Phi(X)}, C_{\Phi(Y)})$ also admits a closed form expression in terms of Gram matrices.

However, as in the finite-dimensional case, the Hilbert-Schmidt metric does not reflect the intrinsic geometry of the set of positive Hilbert-Schmidt operators. Thus, kernels defined in this metric are generally not optimal in practical applications.

6.1.2 KERNELS DEFINED USING THE LOG-HILBERT-SCHMIDT METRIC

We recall the Hilbert manifold $\Sigma(\mathcal{H}) = \{A + \gamma I > 0 \; : \; A \in \mathrm{HS}(\mathcal{H}), A^* = A, \gamma \in \mathbb{R}\}$ of positive definite operators on $\mathcal{H}$ which are Hilbert-Schmidt operators plus a multiple of the identity operator. As we discussed in Section 5.2.2,

$$(\Sigma(\mathcal{H}), \odot, \circledast, \langle \, , \, \rangle_{\mathrm{logHS}})$$

is a Hilbert space with the Log-Hilbert-Schmidt inner product

$$\langle (A + \gamma I), (B + \mu I) \rangle_{\mathrm{logHS}} = \langle \log(A + \gamma I), \log(B + \mu I) \rangle_{\mathrm{eHS}},$$

where $(A + \gamma I), (B + \mu I) \in \Sigma(\mathcal{H})$, along with the corresponding Log-Hilbert-Schmidt norm $||A + \gamma I||_{\mathrm{logHS}} = \sqrt{\langle (A + \gamma I), (A + \gamma I) \rangle_{\mathrm{logHS}}}$. The Log-Hilbert-Schmidt distance between $(A + \gamma I), (B + \mu I)$ is then the Hilbert distance

$$d_{\mathrm{logHS}}[(A + \gamma I), (B + \mu I)] = ||(A + \gamma I) \odot (B + \mu I)^{-1}||_{\mathrm{logHS}}$$
$$= || \log(A + \gamma I) - \log(B + \mu I)||_{\mathrm{eHS}}.$$

Consequently, we can define positive definite kernels on $\Sigma(\mathcal{H})$ using the inner product $\langle \, , \, \rangle_{\mathrm{logHS}}$ and the norm $|| \; ||_{\mathrm{logHS}}$. The following are the Log-Hilbert-Schmidt counterparts of the Hilbert-Schmidt kernels defined in Section 6.1.1 and the infinite-dimensional generalizations of the Log-Euclidean kernels defined in Section 3.2.2.

Theorem 6.1 [76]. *The following kernels* $K : \Sigma(\mathcal{H}) \times \Sigma(\mathcal{H}) \to \mathbb{R}$ *are positive definite*

$$K[(A + \gamma I), (B + \mu I)] = (\langle (A + \gamma I), (B + \mu I) \rangle_{\mathrm{logHS}} + c)^d, \quad c \geq 0, \; d \in \mathbb{N}$$
$$= (c + \langle \log(A + \gamma I), \log(B + \mu I) \rangle_{\mathrm{eHS}})^d, \qquad (6.3)$$

$$K[(A + \gamma I), (B + \mu I)] = \exp\left(-\frac{||(A + \gamma I) \odot (B + \mu I)^{-1}||_{\mathrm{logHS}}^p}{\sigma^2} \right)$$
$$= \exp\left(-\frac{|| \log(A + \gamma I) - \log(B + \mu I)||_{\mathrm{eHS}}^p}{\sigma^2} \right), \qquad (6.4)$$

for $\sigma \neq 0, 0 < p \leq 2$.

Theorem 6.1 thus generalizes Theorem 3.1 to the infinite-dimensional setting. In particular, for $\mathcal{H} = \mathbb{R}^n$, $\Sigma(\mathcal{H}) = \mathrm{Sym}^{++}(n)$, $\gamma = \mu = 0$, and $A, B \in \mathrm{Sym}^{++}(n)$, we recover Theorem 3.1.

For two RKHS covariance operators $C_{\Phi(\mathbf{X})}$ and $C_{\Phi(\mathbf{Y})}$, as we show in Section 5.2.2, for any $\gamma > 0$, $\mu > 0$, both the Log-Hilbert-Schmidt inner product $\langle (C_{\Phi(\mathbf{X})} + \gamma I), (C_{\Phi(\mathbf{Y})} + \mu I) \rangle_{\mathrm{logHS}}$, and the Log-Hilbert-Schmidt distance $d_{\mathrm{logHS}}[(C_{\Phi(\mathbf{X})} + \gamma I), (C_{\Phi(\mathbf{Y})} + \mu I)]$ admit closed form expressions in terms of the corresponding Gram matrices. Thus, it follows that the corresponding kernel $K[(C_{\Phi(\mathbf{X})} + \gamma I), (C_{\Phi(\mathbf{Y})} + \mu I)]$ also admits a closed form expression in terms of Gram matrices.

6.2 TWO-LAYER KERNEL MACHINES

We now combine the geometric framework of RKHS covariance operators in Chapter 5 with the analytic construction of positive definite kernels just described in Section 6.1. This gives us a two-layer kernel machine architecture, as presented in [76, 81, 83, 84], as follows.

1. In the first layer, let the input space $\mathcal{X}$ be any non-empty set. Let K be a positive definite kernel defined on $\mathcal{X} \times \mathcal{X}$, such as the Gaussian kernel. Then K defines, *implicitly*, a set of RKHS covariance operators, each of the form $C_{\Phi(\mathbf{X})}$, where $\mathbf{X}$ is a data matrix randomly sampled from $\mathcal{X}$ according to a probability distribution ρ. The corresponding set of regularized RKHS covariance operators $(C_{\Phi(\mathbf{X})} + \gamma I)$, $\gamma > 0$, forms a subset of the Hilbert manifold of positive definite Hilbert-Schmidt operators.

   In the context of image representation, $\mathcal{X} = \mathbb{R}^n$, for some $n \in \mathbb{N}$, and for each image one extracts a data matrix $\mathbf{X} = [x_1, \ldots, x_m]$ at m pixels, with each $x_i \in \mathbb{R}^n$ being the n-dimensional feature vector extracted at the ith pixel, $1 \leq i \leq m$. A positive definite kernel, such as the Gaussian kernel, defined on these feature vectors, then induces an *implicit* covariance operator representing the image.

   The Hilbert-Schmidt and Log-Hilbert-Schmidt distances (or inner products) between two covariance operators then represent the distances (or inner products) between the corresponding images.

2. In the second layer, using the pairwise Hilbert-Schmidt/Log-Hilbert-Schmidt distances (or inner products) obtained in the first layer, we define a new positive definite kernel, e.g., by Theorem 6.1. With this kernel, we can then apply any kernel method on top of the covariance operators defined in the first layer, such as least square regression or SVM classification.

This two-layer kernel machine is depicted graphically in Figure 6.1 and algorithmically in Algorithm 6.2. Numerical results on the task of image classification using this framework are presented in Section 6.4.

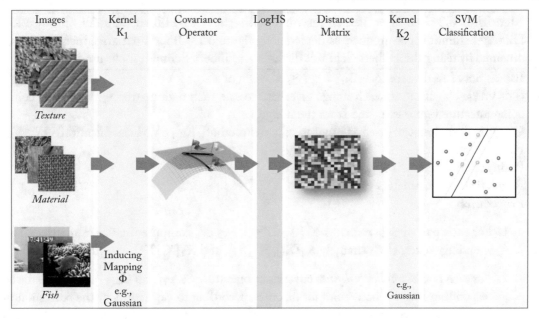

Figure 6.1: Two-layer kernel machine with the exact Log-Hilbert-Schmidt distance. Other alternative machines can be obtained by replacing the Log-Hilbert-Schmidt distance by the Log-Hilbert-Schmidt inner product, Hilbert-Schmidt distance, or Hilbert-Schmidt inner product.

Remark 6.2 The approach in [55, 72, 120], as presented in Section 3.3, which apply kernel methods on top of the Log-Euclidean distance and inner product, is a special case our framework with the Log-Hilbert-Schmidt distance and inner product, where the kernel in the first layer is linear (which is equivalent to *not* having the first layer).

6.3 APPROXIMATE METHODS

A key feature of kernel methods is their ability to capture nonlinear structures in data, which is achieved by implicitly mapping, via the corresponding feature maps, the original input data into a high-dimensional (and often infinite-dimensional) feature space and carrying out linear learning algorithms in the feature space. This is widely known as the *kernel trick* and has been employed extensively [102, 104]. However, this power to learn nonlinear structures in data also comes with a price in computational complexity. In exact kernel methods, the feature map Φ is often infinite-dimensional and, even if it is known explicitly (see [82] for explicit expressions of many feature maps), tends to be analytically complicated. Thus, Φ is only used *implicitly* and all computations are carried out using the corresponding Gram matrices. Therefore, on very large

---

Algorithm 6.2 Two-layer kernel machine with the Log-Hilbert-Schmidt distance/Log-Hilbert-Schmidt inner product, as depicted in Figure 6.1. Other alternative machines can be obtained by using the Hilbert-Schmidt distance or Hilbert-Schmidt inner product instead.

Input: Set of N data matrices $\mathbf{X}_i$, $1 \leq i \leq N$, each of size $n \times m$
(For image classification, each image gives rise to one such data matrix $\mathbf{X}_i$, with each column being a feature vector extracted from the image.)
Output: Kernel matrix (used as input to a kernel method, e.g., SVM classification)
Parameters:
Positive definite kernels K_1, K_2
Regularization parameters $\gamma_i > 0$, $1 \leq i \leq N$
Procedure:

1. For each pair of data matrices $\mathbf{X}_i$, $\mathbf{X}_j$, $1 \leq i, j \leq N$, compute the Gram matrices corresponding to kernel K_1, namely $K_1[\mathbf{X}_i]$, $K_1[\mathbf{X}_j]$, and $K_1[\mathbf{X}_i, \mathbf{X}_j]$, according to Eq. (5.9).

2. For each pair of *implicitly defined* covariance operators $C_{\Phi(\mathbf{X}_i)}$ and $C_{\Phi(\mathbf{X}_j)}$, compute the corresponding Log-Hilbert-Schmidt distance, according to Eq. (5.57), or the corresponding Log-Hilbert-Schmidt inner product, according to Eq. (5.58), using regularization parameters γ_i, γ_j, respectively.

3. Using kernel K_2, compute an $N \times N$ kernel matrix using the above Log-Hilbert-Schmidt distances, e.g., according to Eq. (6.4), or the above Log-Hilbert-Schmidt inner products, e.g., according to Eq. (6.3).

---

datasets, which result in very large Gram matrices, the required computational cost can be very high.

Motivated by the need to reduce the computational cost of exact kernel methods, a line of work has emerged recently, see e.g., [96, 124, 130], which proposes to work with *explicit approximations* of the high-dimensional feature map Φ. Specifically, given a kernel $K : \mathcal{X} \times \mathcal{X} \to \mathbb{R}$ and a corresponding feature map $\Phi : \mathcal{X} \to \mathcal{H}$, one computes an *explicit, low dimensional, approximate feature map*

$$\hat{\Phi}_D : \mathcal{X} \to \mathbb{R}^D, \quad \text{where } D \text{ is finite and } D << \dim(\mathcal{H}), \tag{6.5}$$

so that the corresponding kernel is approximately equal to the original kernel K, that is

$$\langle \hat{\Phi}_D(x), \hat{\Phi}_D(y) \rangle_{\mathbb{R}^D} = \hat{K}_D(x, y) \approx K(x, y) \quad \forall (x, y) \in \mathcal{X} \times \mathcal{X}, \tag{6.6}$$

and so that as the feature dimension $D \to \infty$, the approximate kernel $\hat{K}_D$ approaches the true kernel K, that is

$$\lim_{D \to \infty} \hat{K}_D(x, y) = K(x, y) \quad \forall (x, y) \in \mathcal{X} \times \mathcal{X}. \tag{6.7}$$

Having explicitly computed the approximate feature map $\hat{\Phi}_D$, we then use it directly as input in the learning algorithms, which no longer involve the computation and processing of large Gram matrices. We remark that the convergence stated in Eq. (6.7) can be either probabilistic, as in the case of the random Fourier feature map approach in [96], or deterministic, as in the case of the quasi-random Fourier feature map approach in [130]. It has been demonstrated, see e.g., [96, 124, 130], that this approximation approach can substantially reduce the computational cost of kernel methods, with relatively small loss in empirical performance.

We next show how to utilize the feature map approximation approach for reducing the computational complexity of the affine-invariant Riemannian and Log-Hilbert-Schmidt distances. In particular, the approximate Log-Hilbert-Schmidt distance gives rise to an approximate version of the two-layer kernel machine in Figure 6.1, which incurs considerably lower computational costs while largely preserving the capability of the exact formulation. On the other hand, we also show that the same approximation approach is generally *not* applicable to the Log-Hilbert-Schmidt inner product.

6.3.1   APPROXIMATE LOG-HILBERT-SCHMIDT DISTANCE AND APPROXIMATE AFFINE-INVARIANT RIEMANNIAN DISTANCE

In our current setting, we wish to reduce the computational cost of the exact infinite-dimensional affine-invariant Riemannian distance and the exact infinite-dimensional Log-Hilbert-Schmidt distance. As we saw in Section 5.2.2, to compute the exact Log-Hilbert-Schmidt distance between two infinite-dimensional covariance operators $C_{\Phi(\mathbf{X})}$ and $C_{\Phi(\mathbf{Y})}$, we need to compute the three corresponding $m \times m$ Gram matrices, namely $K[\mathbf{X}]$, $K[\mathbf{Y}]$, and $K[\mathbf{X}, \mathbf{Y}]$, and carry out the SVD of the first two matrices, with computational complexity $O(m^3)$. To reduce this computational cost, we employ *finite, low-dimensional covariance operators* to approximate the infinite-dimensional covariance operators $C_{\Phi(\mathbf{X})}$ and $C_{\Phi(\mathbf{Y})}$. The exact Log-Hilbert-Schmidt distance between $C_{\Phi(\mathbf{X})}$ and $C_{\Phi(\mathbf{Y})}$ is then approximated by the Log-Euclidean distance between the corresponding approximate covariance operators. This approach was first presented in [84] and is further extended upon in [83]. Similarly, the exact infinite-dimensional affine-invariant Riemannian distance between $C_{\Phi(\mathbf{X})}$ and $C_{\Phi(\mathbf{Y})}$ is approximated by the finite-dimensional affine-invariant Riemannian distance between the corresponding approximate covariance operators.

Approximate covariance operator. The low-dimensional, approximate covariance operator of $C_{\Phi(\mathbf{X})}$ can be computed via the approximate feature map $\hat{\Phi}_D$ in Eq. (6.5) as follows. Note that at the moment we are referring to an abstract, general feature map $\hat{\Phi}_D$. A concrete example of $\hat{\Phi}_D$, namely the Fourier feature map, along with its implementation, will be presented in detail later in Section 6.3.5. Applying the map $\hat{\Phi}_D$ to the original data matrix $\mathbf{X} = [x_1, \ldots, x_m]$, we obtain the corresponding feature matrix

$$\hat{\Phi}_D(\mathbf{X}) = [\hat{\Phi}_D(x_1), \ldots, \hat{\Phi}_D(x_m)] \tag{6.8}$$

of size $D \times m$, and the corresponding approximate covariance operator is given by

$$C_{\hat{\Phi}_D(\mathbf{X})} = \frac{1}{m}\hat{\Phi}_D(\mathbf{X})J_m\hat{\Phi}_D(\mathbf{X})^T : \mathbb{R}^D \to \mathbb{R}^D. \qquad (6.9)$$

This is a symmetric positive semi-definite matrix of size $D \times D$. By the assumption that $D << \mathcal{H}$, this matrix is much smaller than the potentially infinite matrix $C_{\Phi(\mathbf{X})}$ of size $\dim(\mathcal{H}) \times \dim(\mathcal{H})$.

Approximate Log-Hilbert-Schmidt distance. Given two covariance operators $C_{\Phi(\mathbf{X})}$ and $C_{\Phi(\mathbf{Y})}$ and their corresponding approximate covariance operators $C_{\hat{\Phi}_D(\mathbf{X})}$ and $C_{\hat{\Phi}_D(\mathbf{Y})}$, the Log-Euclidean distance between the approximate operators $C_{\hat{\Phi}_D(\mathbf{X})}$ and $C_{\hat{\Phi}_D(\mathbf{Y})}$ is then used as the approximate version of the Log-Hilbert-Schmidt distance between the infinite-dimensional covariance operators $C_{\Phi(\mathbf{X})}$ and $C_{\Phi(\mathbf{Y})}$. Specifically, the following is taken as an approximate version of the Log-Hilbert-Schmidt distance given in Eq. (5.51)

$$d_{\log E}[(C_{\hat{\Phi}_D(\mathbf{X})} + \gamma I_D), (C_{\hat{\Phi}_D(\mathbf{Y})} + \mu I_D)]$$
$$= \left\| \log(C_{\hat{\Phi}_D(\mathbf{X})} + \gamma I_D) - \log(C_{\hat{\Phi}_D(\mathbf{Y})} + \mu I_D) \right\|_F. \qquad (6.10)$$

Approximate affine-invariant Riemannian distance. Similarly, the finite-dimensional affine-invariant Riemannian distance between $C_{\hat{\Phi}_D(\mathbf{X})}$ and $C_{\hat{\Phi}_D(\mathbf{Y})}$ is used as the approximate version of the infinite-dimensional affine-invariant Riemannian distance between $C_{\Phi(\mathbf{X})}$ and $C_{\Phi(\mathbf{Y})}$. Specifically, the following is taken as an approximate version of the affine-invariant Riemannian distance in Eq. (5.38)

$$d_{\text{aiE}}[(C_{\hat{\Phi}_D(\mathbf{X})} + \gamma I_D), (C_{\hat{\Phi}_D(\mathbf{Y})} + \mu I_D)]$$
$$= ||\log[(C_{\hat{\Phi}_D(\mathbf{X})} + \gamma I_D)^{-1/2}(C_{\hat{\Phi}_D(\mathbf{Y})} + \mu I_D)(C_{\hat{\Phi}_D(\mathbf{X})} + \gamma I_D)^{-1/2}]||_F. \qquad (6.11)$$

Convergence of the approximations. We need to determine whether the Log-Euclidean distance in Eq. (6.10) is a *consistent* finite-dimensional approximation of the Log-Hilbert-Schmidt distance in Eq. (5.51), in the sense that

$$\lim_{D \to \infty} \left\| \log(C_{\hat{\Phi}_D(\mathbf{X})} + \gamma I_D) - \log(C_{\hat{\Phi}_D(\mathbf{Y})} + \mu I_D) \right\|_F$$
$$= ||\log(C_{\Phi(\mathbf{X})} + \gamma I_{\mathcal{H}}) - \log(C_{\Phi(\mathbf{Y})} + \mu I_{\mathcal{H}})||_{\text{eHS}}. \qquad (6.12)$$

Likewise, we need to determine whether the following convergence holds

$$\lim_{D \to \infty} || \log[(C_{\hat{\Phi}_D(\mathbf{X})} + \gamma I_D)^{-1/2}(C_{\hat{\Phi}_D(\mathbf{Y})} + \mu I_D)(C_{\hat{\Phi}_D(\mathbf{X})} + \gamma I_D)^{-1/2}]||_F$$
$$= || \log[(C_{\Phi(\mathbf{X})} + \gamma I_{\mathcal{H}})^{-1/2}(C_{\Phi(\mathbf{Y})} + \mu I_{\mathcal{H}})(C_{\Phi(\mathbf{X})} + \gamma I_{\mathcal{H}})^{-1/2}]||_{\text{eHS}}. \qquad (6.13)$$

It turns out that, *in general*, both of these convergences are *not* valid. This fact stands in sharp contrast to the assumption stated in Eq. (6.7) on the approximability of the exact kernel value $K(x, y)$ by the approximate kernel $\hat{K}_D(x, y)$, which is satisfied by many approximation schemes in practice, including the random Fourier feature approximation [96] and the quasi-random Fourier feature approximation [130]. This is because, as pointed out by [76], the infinite-dimensional Log-Hilbert-Schmidt distance is generally *not* obtainable as a limit of the finite-dimensional Log-Euclidean distance as the dimension approaches infinity, and the same is true regarding the infinite-dimensional and finite-dimensional affine-invariant Riemannian distances, as pointed out in [78].

Specifically, we have the following divergence result, first proved in [84].

Theorem 6.3 [84]. *Assume that $\gamma \neq \mu$, $\gamma > 0$, $\mu > 0$. Then, for the approximate Log–Hilbert–Schmidt distance,*

$$\lim_{D \to \infty} \left\| \log\left(C_{\hat{\Phi}_D(X)} + \gamma I_D \right) - \log\left(C_{\hat{\Phi}_D(Y)} + \mu I_D \right) \right\|_F = \infty. \tag{6.14}$$

The following is the corresponding divergence result for the approximate affine-invariant Riemannian distance.

Theorem 6.4 *Assume that $\gamma \neq \mu$, $\gamma > 0$, $\mu > 0$. Then, for the approximate affine-invariant Riemannian distance,*

$$\lim_{D \to \infty} \left\| \log[(C_{\hat{\Phi}_D(X)} + \gamma I_D)^{-1/2}(C_{\hat{\Phi}_D(Y)} + \mu I_D)(C_{\hat{\Phi}_D(X)} + \gamma I_D)^{-1/2}] \right\|_F = \infty. \tag{6.15}$$

Proof. See Appendix A.5.   □

The infinite limits in Theorems 6.3 and 6.4 show that in general, Eq. (6.7), which states the convergence of the approximate kernel value $\hat{K}_D(x, y)$ to the exact kernel value $K(x, y)$ as $D \to \infty$, is *not sufficient* to guarantee the convergence of the approximate Log-Hilbert-Schmidt distance to the exact Log-Hilbert-Schmidt distance, or the convergence of the approximate affine-invariant Riemannian distance to the exact infinite-dimensional version.

Both of these convergences are in fact non-trivial and are only valid in the following scenario. In the regularized covariance operators $(C_{\hat{\Phi}_D(X)} + \gamma I_D)$ and $(C_{\hat{\Phi}_D(Y)} + \mu I_D)$, we assume that the regularization parameters are the same, that is $\gamma = \mu$. This is a mild assumption that is also practically reasonable and realizable. In this setting, we obtain the desired convergence for the approximate Log-Hilbert-Schmidt distance, as stated in the following result.

Theorem 6.5 [84]. *Assume that $\gamma = \mu > 0$. Then, for the approximate Log–Hilbert–Schmidt distance,*

$$\lim_{D \to \infty} \left\| \log(C_{\hat{\Phi}_D(X)} + \gamma I_D) - \log(C_{\hat{\Phi}_D(Y)} + \gamma I_D) \right\|_F$$
$$= \| \log(C_{\Phi(X)} + \gamma I_{\mathcal{H}}) - \log(C_{\Phi(Y)} + \gamma I_{\mathcal{H}}) \|_{\text{eHS}}. \tag{6.16}$$

The following is the corresponding convergence result for the approximate affine-invariant Riemannian distance.

Theorem 6.6   *Assume that $\gamma = \mu > 0$. Then, for the approximate affine-invariant Riemannian distance,*

$$\lim_{D\to\infty} || \log[(C_{\hat{\Phi}_D(\mathbf{X})} + \gamma I_D)^{-1/2}(C_{\hat{\Phi}_D(\mathbf{Y})} + \gamma I_D)(C_{\hat{\Phi}_D(\mathbf{X})} + \gamma I_D)^{-1/2}]||_F$$
$$= || \log[(C_{\Phi(\mathbf{X})} + \gamma I_{\mathcal{H}})^{-1/2}(C_{\Phi(\mathbf{Y})} + \gamma I_{\mathcal{H}})(C_{\Phi(\mathbf{X})} + \gamma I_{\mathcal{H}})^{-1/2}]||_{\text{eHS}}. \qquad (6.17)$$

Proof. See Appendix A.5.   □

Mode of convergence. We remark that the mode of convergence in Theorems 6.3, 6.4, 6.5, and 6.6 is the same as that in Eq. (6.7) on the convergence of the approximate kernel $\hat{K}_D(x, y)$ to the exact kernel $K(x, y)$ as $D \to \infty$, which is either probabilistic, e.g., if the random Fourier feature map [96] is used in Eq. (6.7), or deterministic, e.g., if the quasi-random Fourier feature map [130] is used in Eq. (6.7).

Practical implication. With Theorems 6.3, 6.4, 6.5, and 6.6 as theoretical guidance, for *consistent* finite-dimensional approximations of the affine-invariant Riemannian distance and Log-Hilbert-Schmidt distance in practice, we need to use the same regularization parameter $\gamma > 0$ to compute the approximate affine-invariant Riemannian distances and approximate Log-Hilbert-Schmidt distances between all regularized approximate covariance operators $(C_{\hat{\Phi}_D(\mathbf{X})} + \gamma I_D)$.

Remark 6.7   In [33], the authors proposed two methods: (i) Nearest Neighbor using effectively the approximate affine-invariant Riemannian distance given in Eq. (6.19) with $\gamma = \mu = 0$ and (ii) the CDL algorithm in [127] using the representation $\log(C_{\hat{\Phi}_D(\mathbf{X})})$. Both of these methods require the assumption that $C_{\hat{\Phi}_D(\mathbf{X})}$ is positive definite. However, since $C_{\hat{\Phi}_D(\mathbf{X})}$ has rank at most $m - 1$ (see Section 1.1), when $D \geq m$, $C_{\hat{\Phi}_D(\mathbf{X})}$ is always rank-deficient and neither its inverse nor log can be computed. Thus, neither the CDL algorithm nor the approximate affine-invariant Riemannian distance *without regularization* can be used when $D \geq m$. In other words, these methods are *not* consistent.

6.3.2   COMPUTATIONAL COMPLEXITY

We now present the computational complexity analysis of the approximations of both the Log-Hilbert-Schmidt distance, as given in Eq. (6.10), and the affine-invariant Riemannian distance, as given in Eq. (6.11), along with the comparison on the scalability between the two approaches to large datasets.

Computational complexity of the approximation of the Log-Hilbert-Schmidt distance. Consider first the approximate Log-Hilbert-Schmidt distance, as given in Eq. (6.10), according to which we compute the following quantity

$$\left\| \log(C_{\hat{\Phi}_D(X)} + \gamma I_D) - \log(C_{\hat{\Phi}_D(Y)} + \mu I_D) \right\|_F . \tag{6.18}$$

The main computational cost in Eq. (6.18) is the SVD for $(C_{\hat{\Phi}_D(X)} + \gamma I_D)$ and $(C_{\hat{\Phi}_D(Y)} + \mu I_D)$, which takes time $O(D^3)$. Since the matrices $(C_{\hat{\Phi}_D(X)} + \gamma I_D)$ and $(C_{\hat{\Phi}_D(Y)} + \mu I_D)$ in Eq. (6.18) are *uncoupled*, if we have N data matrices $\{X_1, \ldots, X_N\}$, in order to compute their pairwise approximate Log-Hilbert-Schmidt distances using Eq. (6.18), we need to compute an SVD for each $(C_{\hat{\Phi}_D(X_i)} + \gamma I_D)$, which enables us to compute $\log(C_{\hat{\Phi}_D(X_i)} + \gamma I_D)$, then compute all the pairwise distances in the corresponding set of matrices $\{\log(C_{\hat{\Phi}_D(X_i)} + \gamma I_D)\}$, with total computational complexity $O(ND^3)$.

We recall that for N pairs of data matrices, the computational complexity of the exact Log-Hilbert-Schmidt formulation [76] and the RKHS Bregman divergences [44] is of order $O(N^2 m^3)$. Thus, for $D < m$ and N large, the approximate Log-Hilbert-Schmidt formulation will be much more efficient to compute than both the exact Log-Hilbert-Schmidt and the RKHS Bregman divergences (see [84] for the actual running time comparison between the approximate and exact Log-Hilbert-Schmidt formulations)

Computational complexity of the approximation of the affine-invariant Riemannian distance. Consider now the approximate affine-invariant Riemannian distance, as given in Eq. (6.11), according to which we compute the following quantity:

$$\left\| \log \left[(C_{\hat{\Phi}_D(X)} + \gamma I_D)^{-1/2} (C_{\hat{\Phi}_D(Y)} + \mu I_D)(C_{\hat{\Phi}_D(X)} + \gamma I_D)^{-1/2} \right] \right\|_F . \tag{6.19}$$

The main computational cost in Eq. (6.19), which consists of a matrix square root and inversion, two matrix multiplications and an SVD, is also $O(D^3)$. However, computationally, the key difference between Eq. (6.18) and Eq. (6.19) is that in Eq. (6.18), $(C_{\hat{\Phi}_D(X)} + \gamma I_D)$ and $(C_{\hat{\Phi}_D(Y)} + \mu I_D)$ are *uncoupled*, whereas in Eq. (6.19), they are *coupled*. Thus, if we have N data matrices $\{X_1, \ldots, X_N\}$, in order to compute all the pairwise approximate affine-invariant Riemannian distances using Eq. (6.19), we need to compute an SVD for each *pair* $(C_{\hat{\Phi}_D(X_i)} + \gamma I_D)$, $(C_{\hat{\Phi}_D(X_j)} + \gamma I_D)$, with computational complexity $O(N^2 D^3)$. Thus, on a set of N data matrices $\{X_1, \ldots, X_N\}$, the approximation of all the pairwise Log-Hilbert-Schmidt distances is $O(N)$ times faster than the approximation of all the pairwise affine-invariance Riemannian distances.

Comparison of scalability. The above analysis shows that for a large set of matrices, it is much faster to compute all the pairwise approximate Log-Hilbert-Schmidt distances than to compute all the pairwise affine-invariant Riemannian distances. Moreover, since the two terms $\log(C_{\hat{\Phi}_D(X)} + \gamma I_D)$ and $\log(C_{\hat{\Phi}_D(Y)} + \mu I_D)$ in Eq. (6.18) are uncoupled, they can be computed in *parallel*, further speeding up the computation of the Log-Hilbert-Schmidt distances. Thus, overall, in terms of computational complexity, the approximate Log-Hilbert-Schmidt distance is much more efficient than the approximate affine-invariant Riemannian distance, especially on large-scale datasets.

6.3.3   APPROXIMATE LOG-HILBERT-SCHMIDT INNER PRODUCT

We consider next the finite-dimensional approximation of the infinite-dimensional Log-Hilbert-Schmidt inner product between the covariance operators $C_{\Phi(X)}$ and $C_{\Phi(Y)}$, as defined by Eq. (5.58), namely

$$\langle (C_{\Phi(X)} + \gamma I_{\mathcal{H}}), (C_{\Phi(Y)} + \mu I_{\mathcal{H}}) \rangle_{\mathrm{logHS}} = \langle \log(C_{\Phi(X)} + \gamma I_{\mathcal{H}}), \log(C_{\Phi(Y)} + \mu I_{\mathcal{H}}) \rangle_{\mathrm{eHS}}. \quad (6.20)$$

As in the case of the approximate Log-Hilbert-Schmidt distance and approximate affine-invariant Riemannian distance in Section 6.3.1, we consider approximating the Log-Hilbert-Schmidt inner product $\langle \; \rangle_{\mathrm{logHS}}$ in Eq. (6.20) by the finite-dimensional Log-Euclidean inner product $\langle \; \rangle_{\mathrm{logE}}$, as defined by Eq. (2.70), between the approximate covariance operators $C_{\hat{\Phi}_D(X)}$ and $C_{\hat{\Phi}_D(Y)}$, namely

$$\langle (C_{\hat{\Phi}_D(X)} + \gamma I_D), (C_{\hat{\Phi}_D(Y)} + \mu I_D) \rangle_{\mathrm{logE}} = \langle \log(C_{\hat{\Phi}_D(X)} + \gamma I_D), \log(C_{\hat{\Phi}_D(Y)} + \mu I_D) \rangle_F. \quad (6.21)$$

Convergence of approximation. Assuming the approximation of the kernel K as given in Eq. (6.6) and Eq. (6.7), we need to determine whether the approximation of the Log-Hilbert-Schmidt inner product in Eq. (6.20) by the Log-Euclidean inner product in Eq. (6.21) is consistent, in the sense that

$$\lim_{D \to \infty} \left\langle \log(C_{\hat{\Phi}_D(X)} + \gamma I_D), \log(C_{\hat{\Phi}_D(Y)} + \mu I_D) \right\rangle_F$$
$$= \left\langle \log(C_{\Phi(X)} + \gamma I_{\mathcal{H}}), \log(C_{\Phi(Y)} + \mu I_{\mathcal{H}}) \right\rangle_{\mathrm{eHS}}. \quad (6.22)$$

It turns out that this is only true in the special case $\gamma = \mu = 1$. For all other values of $\gamma > 0, \mu > 0$, the left-hand side of Eq. (6.22) either approaches infinity or a finite limit that is *not* equal to the right-hand side.

Specifically, we have the following result, first presented in [83].

Theorem 6.8 [83].   *Assume that* $\dim(\mathcal{H}) = \infty$. *Let* $\gamma > 0$, $\mu > 0$. *There are four possible cases, as follows.*

1) If $\gamma = \mu = 1$, then

$$\lim_{D \to \infty} \left\langle \log(C_{\hat{\Phi}_D(X)} + I_D), \log(C_{\hat{\Phi}_D(Y)} + I_D) \right\rangle_F$$
$$= \left\langle \log(C_{\Phi(X)} + I_{\mathcal{H}}), \log(C_{\Phi(Y)} + I_{\mathcal{H}}) \right\rangle_{\mathrm{eHS}}. \tag{6.23}$$

2) If $\gamma = 1$, $\mu \neq 1$, then

$$\lim_{D \to \infty} \left\langle \log(C_{\hat{\Phi}_D(X)} + I_D), \log(C_{\hat{\Phi}_D(Y)} + \mu I_D) \right\rangle_F$$
$$= \left\langle \log(C_{\Phi(X)} + I_{\mathcal{H}}), \log(C_{\Phi(Y)} + \mu I_{\mathcal{H}}) \right\rangle_{\mathrm{eHS}}$$
$$+ (\log \mu) \mathrm{tr} \left[\log \left(\frac{1}{m} J_m K[\mathbf{X}] J_m + I_m \right) \right]. \tag{6.24}$$

3) If $\gamma \neq 1$, $\mu = 1$, then

$$\lim_{D \to \infty} \left\langle \log(C_{\hat{\Phi}_D(X)} + \gamma I_D), \log(C_{\hat{\Phi}_D(Y)} + I_D) \right\rangle_F$$
$$= \left\langle \log(C_{\Phi(X)} + \gamma I_{\mathcal{H}}), \log(C_{\Phi(Y)} + I_{\mathcal{H}}) \right\rangle_{\mathrm{eHS}}$$
$$+ (\log \gamma) \mathrm{tr} \left[\log \left(\frac{1}{m} J_m K[\mathbf{Y}] J_m + I_m \right) \right]. \tag{6.25}$$

4) If $\gamma \neq 1$, $\mu \neq 1$, then

$$\lim_{D \to \infty} \left\langle \log(C_{\hat{\Phi}_D(X)} + \gamma I_D), \log(C_{\hat{\Phi}_D(Y)} + \mu I_D) \right\rangle_F = \pm \infty. \tag{6.26}$$

The limiting value on the right-hand side of Eq. (6.26) depends on the sign of $(\log \gamma)(\log \mu)$. If $(\log \gamma)(\log \mu) > 0$, then this limit is $+\infty$. If $(\log \gamma)(\log \mu) < 0$, then this limit is $-\infty$.

Implications of Theorem 6.8 for the approximation of positive definite kernels defined using the Log-Hilbert-Schmidt inner product. The results stated in Theorem 6.8 mean that except in the special case $\gamma = \mu = 1$, it is *not* possible to approximate positive definite kernels which are functions of the infinite-dimensional Log-Hilbert-Schmidt inner product $\left\langle \log(C_{\Phi(X)} + \gamma I_{\mathcal{H}}), \log(C_{\Phi(Y)} + \mu I_{\mathcal{H}}) \right\rangle_{\mathrm{eHS}}$ by their natural corresponding finite-dimensional versions, which are functions of the Log-Euclidean inner product $\left\langle \log(C_{\hat{\Phi}_D(X)} + \gamma I_D), \log(C_{\hat{\Phi}_D(Y)} + \mu I_D) \right\rangle_F$. This is true in particular for the linear kernel, that is the Log-Hilbert-Schmidt inner product itself, and polynomial kernels, namely kernels of the form

$$\left(\langle \log(C_{\Phi(X)} + \gamma I_{\mathcal{H}}), \log(C_{\Phi(Y)} + \mu I_{\mathcal{H}}) \rangle_{\mathrm{eHS}} + c \right)^d, \quad c \geq 0, \ d \in \mathbb{N}.$$

In fact, for these kernels, in the case $\gamma \neq 1, \mu \neq 1, \gamma > 0, \mu > 0$, the corresponding finite-dimensional versions, namely kernels of the form

$$\left(\langle \log(C_{\hat{\Phi}_D(X)} + \gamma I_D), \log(C_{\hat{\Phi}_D(Y)} + \mu I_D) \rangle_F + c \right)^d, \quad c \geq 0, \ d \in \mathbb{N},$$

will approach $\pm\infty$ as $D \to \infty$.

6.3.4   TWO-LAYER KERNEL MACHINE WITH THE APPROXIMATE LOG-HILBERT-SCHMIDT DISTANCE

Having theoretically analyzed the finite-dimensional approximations of the Log-Hilbert-Schmidt distance, Log-Hilbert-Schmidt inner product, and affine-invariant Riemannian distance, along with their computational complexity, we now use this analysis as a guidance to construct a new two-layer kernel machine, depicted in Figure 6.2. This machine is built so that it mathematically approximates the exact two-layer kernel machine depicted in Figure 6.1, with considerably lower computational cost, while at the same time largely preserves the capability of the exact machine. It is based on the following steps.

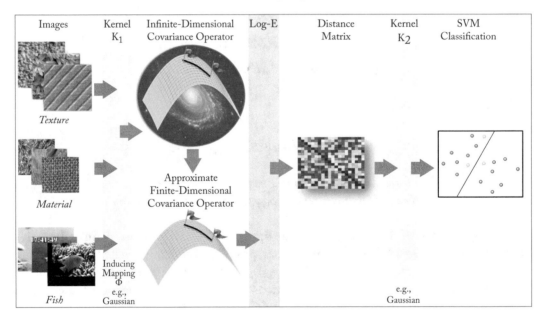

Figure 6.2: Two-layer kernel machine with the approximate Log-Hilbert-Schmidt distance.

1. The first step is defining a positive definite kernel K_1 in Figure 6.2, which induces an implicit feature map Φ from the original input space into an (infinite-dimensional) feature space. For each input data matrix X, the map Φ gives rise to the feature matrix $\Phi(X)$ and the corresponding covariance operator $C_{\Phi(X)}$.

For each input instance x, we compute the approximate feature map $\hat{\Phi}_D(x)$ (we describe two methods for computing the approximate feature map in Section 6.3.5). For each data matrix $\mathbf{X}$, we then obtain the approximate feature matrix $\hat{\Phi}_D(\mathbf{X})$, defined by Eq. (6.8) and the corresponding approximate covariance operator $C_{\hat{\Phi}_D(\mathbf{X})}$ of $C_{\Phi(\mathbf{X})}$, defined by Eq. (6.9).

2. Next, for two data matrices $\mathbf{X}$ and $\mathbf{Y}$, we compute the finite-dimensional Log-Euclidean distance

$$\| \log(C_{\hat{\Phi}_D(\mathbf{X})} + \gamma I_D) - \log(C_{\hat{\Phi}_D(\mathbf{Y})} + \mu I_D)\|_F.$$

By Theorems 6.3 and 6.5 in Section 6.3.1, this distance consistently approximates the infinite-dimensional Log-Hilbert-Schmidt distance $\| \log(C_{\Phi(\mathbf{X})} + \gamma I_\mathcal{H}) - \log(C_{\Phi(\mathbf{Y})} + \mu I_\mathcal{H})\|_{\mathrm{eHS}}$ if and only if $\gamma = \mu > 0$.

3. The previous step in turns implies that, for $\gamma = \mu > 0$, the generalized Gaussian kernel $\exp(-\| \log(C_{\Phi(\mathbf{X})} + \gamma I_\mathcal{H}) - \log(C_{\Phi(\mathbf{Y})} + \gamma I_\mathcal{H})\|_{\mathrm{eHS}}^p/\sigma^2)$, $0 < p \leq 2$, which is defined on the infinite-dimensional manifold $\Sigma(\mathcal{H})$, is consistently approximated by the corresponding kernel $\exp(-\| \log(C_{\hat{\Phi}_D(\mathbf{X})} + \gamma I_D) - \log(C_{\hat{\Phi}_D(\mathbf{Y})} + \gamma I_D)\|_F^p/\sigma^2)$, which is defined on the finite-dimensional manifold $\mathrm{Sym}^{++}(D)$.

Thus, as an example, we can choose as K_2 in Figure 6.2 the following positive definite kernel:

$$\exp(-\| \log(C_{\hat{\Phi}_D(\mathbf{X})} + \gamma I_D) - \log(C_{\hat{\Phi}_D(\mathbf{Y})} + \gamma I_D)\|_F^p/\sigma^2), \quad 0 < p \leq 2, \qquad (6.27)$$

with $p = 2$ giving the Gaussian kernel and $p = 1$ giving the Laplacian kernel.

The same line of reasoning is valid if the generalized Gaussian kernel is replaced by any continuous positive definite *shift-invariant kernels* defined on $\Sigma(\mathcal{H})$, under the assumption that all covariance operators share the same regularization parameter $\gamma > 0$.

4. Based on the results of Theorem 6.8 and its implications discussed in Section 6.3.3, when defining the kernel K_2 in Figure 6.2, we exclude kernels defined using the Log-Euclidean inner product of approximate covariance operators, since they generally do not converge to the corresponding kernels defined using the Log-Hilbert-Schmidt inner product of covariance operators and in fact often diverge to infinity.

5. Having defined the positive definite kernel K_2, we can then apply any kernel methods from machine learning using this kernel, such as SVM classification.

The approximate Log-Hilbert-Schmidt distance is chosen over the approximate affine-invariant Riemannian distance for the following reasons.

1. It is much more straightforward to define positive definite kernels using the approximate Log-Hilbert-Schmidt distance, by the discussion in Chapter 3.

2. For large-scale datasets, the approximate Log-Hilbert-Schmidt distance can be computed much more efficiently than the approximate affine-invariant Riemannian distance, by the complexity analysis in Section 6.3.2.

A concrete realization the two-layer kernel machine depicted in Figure 6.2 is presented in the next section.

6.3.5   CASE STUDY: APPROXIMATION BY FOURIER FEATURE MAPS

In the following, we assume that we have as input data matrices of the form $\mathbf{X} = [x_1, \dots, x_m]$ of size $n \times m$, with each matrix representing one input instance. A concrete implementation of the kernel machine in Figure 6.2 involves a choice of the kernel K_1, along with an approximate feature map $\hat{\Phi}_D$, and a choice of the kernel K_2.

For the kernel K_2, as discussed in Section 6.3.4, we choose a shift-invariant kernel, e.g., the one defined in Eq. (6.27).

The choice of the kernel K_1 is more flexible. If we choose K_1 to be shift-invariant, then two general methods for computing the approximate feature map $\hat{\Phi}_D$ are Random Fourier features [96] and Quasi-random Fourier features [130], which we now describe (see the discussion below for other choices of kernels and feature maps).

Random Fourier feature maps. This is the approach first proposed in [96] for computing approximate feature maps $\hat{\Phi}_D$ of shift-invariant kernels. Let $K : \mathbb{R}^n \times \mathbb{R}^n \to \mathbb{R}$ be a continuous positive definite kernel of the form $K(x, y) = k(x - y)$, for some continuous positive definite function $k : \mathbb{R}^n \to \mathbb{R}$. A fundamental result for such a function is Bochner's Theorem, see e.g., [97], which states that k is positive definite if and only if it is the Fourier transform of a finite positive measure ρ on $\mathbb{R}^n$, that is if and only if

$$k(x) = \int_{\mathbb{R}^n} e^{-i\langle \omega, x \rangle} d\rho(\omega), \tag{6.28}$$

so that

$$K(x, y) = k(x - y) = \int_{\mathbb{R}^n} e^{-i\langle \omega, x-y \rangle} d\rho(\omega) \tag{6.29}$$

$$= \int_{\mathbb{R}^n} \phi_\omega(x)\overline{\phi_\omega(y)} d\rho(\omega), \text{ where } \phi_\omega(x) = e^{-i\langle \omega, x \rangle}.$$

Without loss of generality, we can assume that ρ is a probability measure on $\mathbb{R}^n$, so that

$$K(x, y) = \mathbb{E}_{\omega \sim \rho}[\phi_\omega(x)\overline{\phi_\omega(y)}]. \tag{6.30}$$

By symmetry, $K(x, y) = \frac{1}{2}[K(x, y) + K(y, x)]$, so that by the relation $\frac{1}{2}[e^{-i\langle \omega, x-y \rangle} + e^{i\langle \omega, x-y \rangle}] = \cos(\langle \omega, x - y \rangle)$ we have

$$K(x, y) = \int_{\mathbb{R}^n} \cos(\langle \omega, x - y \rangle) d\rho(\omega) = \mathbb{E}_{\omega \sim \rho}[\cos(\langle \omega, x - y \rangle)]. \tag{6.31}$$

Motivated by the expectation interpretation of $K(x, y)$, in order to approximate $K(x, y)$, we can randomly sample D points $\{\omega_j\}_{j=1}^D$ independently from the distribution ρ and compute the empirical version

$$\hat{K}_D(x, y) = \frac{1}{D} \sum_{j=1}^D \cos(\langle \omega_j, x - y \rangle). \tag{6.32}$$

By the law of large numbers, Eq. (6.7) is satisfied, namely

$$\lim_{D \to \infty} \hat{K}_D(x, y) = K(x, y),$$

where the convergence is almost surely for each fixed pair $(x, y) \in \mathbb{R}^n \times \mathbb{R}^n$ (see [96] for the original convergence analysis, and [112, 114] for improved, optimal convergence rates).

Let $W = (\omega_1, \ldots, \omega_D)$ be a matrix of size $n \times D$, with each column $\omega_j \in \mathbb{R}^n$ randomly sampled according to ρ. Motivated by the cosine addition formula, $\cos(\langle \omega_j, x - y \rangle) = \cos\langle \omega_j, x \rangle \cos\langle \omega_j, y \rangle + \sin\langle \omega_j, x \rangle \sin\langle \omega_j, y \rangle$, we define

$$\cos(W^T x) = (\cos\langle \omega_j, x \rangle)_{j=1}^D \in \mathbb{R}^D, \tag{6.33}$$
$$\sin(W^T x) = (\sin\langle \omega_j, x \rangle)_{j=1}^D \in \mathbb{R}^D. \tag{6.34}$$

The desired approximate feature map is the concatenation of these two vectors, that is

$$\hat{\Phi}_D(x) = \frac{1}{\sqrt{D}} \begin{pmatrix} \cos(W^T x) \\ \sin(W^T x) \end{pmatrix} \in \mathbb{R}^{2D}, \tag{6.35}$$

which obviously satisfies

$$\langle \hat{\Phi}_D(x), \hat{\Phi}_D(y) \rangle = \hat{K}_D(x, y),$$

which is the assumption stated in Eq. (6.6).

For computational purposes, we assume further that the probability distribution ρ has a density, which we also denote by ρ. If the function $k : \mathbb{R}^n \to \mathbb{R}$ is integrable, then the density ρ is uniquely determined as the inverse Fourier transform of k, that is

$$\rho(\omega) = \frac{1}{(2\pi)^n} \int_{\mathbb{R}^n} k(x) e^{i\langle \omega, x \rangle} dx. \tag{6.36}$$

In the case of the Gaussian kernel $K(x, y) = e^{-\frac{\|x-y\|^2}{\sigma^2}}$, which is used in the experiments in Section 6.4 below, ρ is a multivariate Gaussian probability distribution with mean zero and density function given by

$$\rho(\omega) = \frac{(\sigma\sqrt{\pi})^n}{(2\pi)^n} e^{-\frac{\sigma^2\|\omega\|^2}{4}} \sim \mathcal{N}\left(0, \frac{2}{\sigma^2}\right). \tag{6.37}$$

Quasi-random Fourier feature maps. The Random Fourier feature maps presented above arise from the Monte-Carlo approximation of the kernel K expressed as the integral in Eq. (6.29), using a *random* set of points ω_j's sampled according to the distribution ρ. An alternative approach, first proposed in [130], employs the methodology of Quasi-Monte Carlo integration [26], in which the ω_j's are *deterministic* points arising from a *low-discrepancy* sequence in $[0, 1]^n$. Having generated the ω_j's, $1 \leq j \leq D$, the approximate feature map $\hat{\Phi}_D$ is then constructed in the same way as in the case of random Fourier features, namely by Eq. (6.35). We describe this approach in detail in Appendix A.4.

Algorithm 6.3 Two-layer kernel machine with the approximate Log-Hilbert-Schmidt distance, as depicted in Figure 6.2. In the algorithm, steps 2 and 3 are fixed, whereas step 1 depends on the choice of kernel K_1 and feature map $\hat{\Phi}_D$, and step 4 depends on the choice of kernel K_2.

Input: Set of N data matrices $\mathbf{X}_i$, $1 \leq i \leq N$, each of size $n \times m$

(For image classification, each image gives rise to one such data matrix $\mathbf{X}_i$, with each column being a feature vector extracted from the image.)

Output: Kernel matrix (used as input to a kernel method, e.g., SVM classification)

Parameters:

Positive definite kernels K_1, K_2, where K_2 is shift-invariant

Regularization parameter $\gamma > 0$

Approximate feature dimension D

Procedure:

1. For each data matrix $\mathbf{X}_i = [x_{i1}, \dots, x_{im}]$, compute the feature matrix $\hat{\Phi}_D(\mathbf{X}_i) = [\hat{\Phi}_D(x_{i1}), \dots, \hat{\Phi}_D(x_{im})]$ where $\hat{\Phi}_D(x_{ij})$, $1 \leq i \leq m$, is the approximate feature of x_{ij} induced by the kernel K_1, computed according to, e.g., Eq. (6.35).

2. With the feature matrix $\hat{\Phi}_D(\mathbf{X}_i)$, compute the corresponding approximate covariance operator $C_{\hat{\Phi}_D(\mathbf{X}_i)}$, according to Eq. (6.9).

3. For each pair of approximate covariance operators $C_{\hat{\Phi}_D(\mathbf{X}_i)}$ and $C_{\hat{\Phi}_D(\mathbf{X}_j)}$, compute the corresponding approximate Log-Hilbert-Schmidt distance, according to Eq. (6.10), using the same regularization parameter $\gamma > 0$.

4. Using kernel K_2, compute a kernel matrix using the above approximate Log-Hilbert-Schmidt distances, e.g., according to Eq. (6.27).

Other choices of kernels and feature maps. The random Fourier and quasi-random Fourier feature maps are two general methods for computing approximate feature maps of shift-invariant kernels. In the literature on kernel approximation, other feature maps have been studied and can be readily employed in the current framework. Examples include the feature maps for additive homogeneous kernels proposed in [124] and the random feature maps for inner product kernels proposed in [59].

Complete implementation pipeline. Having defined the kernels K_1, K_2, and computed the approximate feature map $\hat{\Phi}_D$ corresponding to kernel K_1, the two-layer kernel machine in Figure 6.2 can be readily implemented and applied to a practical application. The complete pipeline for this framework is summarized in Algorithm 6.3. Actual numerical results obtained using this algorithm are presented in Section 6.4 below.

6.4   EXPERIMENTS IN IMAGE CLASSIFICATION

In this section, we present several numerical experiments to illustrate the two-layer kernel machines in Figures 6.1 and 6.2. These experiments were reported in [76, 83, 84].

Fish recognition. We apply the framework described here to the task of Fish recognition, using the Fish Recognition dataset [12]. Samples from this dataset are displayed in Figure 6.3. The fish data are acquired from a live video dataset resulting in 27,370 verified fish images. The whole dataset is divided into 23 classes. The number of images per class ranges from 21–12,112, with a medium resolution of roughly 150×120 pixels. The challenges in the recognition task are due to the significant variations in color, pose, and illumination inside each class.

Two experiments were carried out. In the first experiment, we resized each image to 128×128 and sampled from $m = 1,024$ pixels using a coarse 4×4 grid, that is every 4 pixels in the horizontal and vertical directions. At the pixel location (x, y), the following 3-dimensional feature vector of the color channels Red, Green, and Blue was extracted

$$\mathbf{f}(x, y) = [R(x, y), G(x, y), B(x, y)]. \tag{6.38}$$

We randomly selected 5 images from each class for training and 15 for testing, repeating the entire procedure 10 times. The classification was carried using Gaussian SVM (except with *Stein*), with the Euclidean distance, Log-Euclidean distance, Hilbert-Schmidt distance, exact Log-Hilbert-Schmidt distance, and approximate Log-Hilbert-Schmidt distance. For the last three distances, the kernel K_1 in the first layer is the Gaussian kernel. The approximate Log-Hilbert-Schmidt distance was implemented using both the random and quasi-random Fourier feature approaches, with the feature dimension $D = 200$. All parameters were chosen by cross-validation. For the experiments using the symmetric Stein divergence (*Stein*), the Nearest Neighbor approach was used.

In the second experiment, the CNN features from [47] were used. We randomly selected 5 images from each class for training and used the rest of the images for testing. The two approximate Log-Hibert-Schmidt distance methods were tested using the same protocol as in the previous experiment.

The classification accuracies are reported in Table 6.2.

Further experiments with the KTH-TIPS2b and ETH-80 datasets. Table 6.3, on the other hand, is an extension of Table 3.2 in Section 3.4. In this table, we report results on the task

Figure 6.3: Samples from each of the 23 classes of the Fish Recognition dataset [12].

of image classification using the KTH-TIPS2b and ETH-80 datasets, obtained using Gaussian SVM, with the Hilbert-Schmidt distance and approximate Log-Hilbert-Schmidt distance. In both cases, the kernel K_1 in the first layer is the Gaussian kernel. The approximate Log-Hilbert-Schmidt distance was implemented using both the random and quasi-random Fourier

Table 6.2: Experimental results obtained on the task of image classification on the Fish recognition dataset. The classification was carried out by SVM classification with the Gaussian kernels, defined using the Euclidean distance (*E*), Log-Euclidean distance (*Log-E*), Hilbert-Schmidt distance (*HS*), approximate Log-Hilbert-Schmidt distance with quasi-random Fourier features (*QApprox-LogHS*), approximate Log-Hilbert-Schmidt distance with random Fourier features (*Approx-LogHS*), and exact Log-Hilbert-Schmidt distance (*Log-HS*). By comparison, the experiments *Stein*, using the symmetric Stein divergence, were carried out using the Nearest Neighbor approach. The two entries *Approx-LogHS (CNN)* and *QApprox-LogHS (CNN)* were experiments tested with CNN features.

Method	Accuracy
E	26.9% (±3.5%)
Stein	43.9% (±3.5%)
Log-E	42.7% (±3.4%)
HS	50.2% (±2.2%)
Q Approx-LogHS	54.3% (±3.4%)
Approx-LogHS	53.9% (±4.3%)
Log-HS	56.7% (±2.9%)
Q Approx-LogHS (CNN)	74.6% (±3.6%)
Approx-LogHS (CNN)	75.3% (±3.5%)

feature approaches, with the feature dimension $D = 200$. All parameters were chosen by cross-validation.

Running time in comparison with the exact Log-Hilbert-Schmidt distance. We carried out a comparison of running time in the first experiment with the Fish data set. This shows that both *Approx LogHS* and *QApprox LogHS* incur much smaller computation costs compared to the exact Log-Hilbert-Schmidt distance. Using a MATLAB implementation on an Intel Xeon E5-2650, 2.60 GHz PC, we obtained a speed up of 30 times with *QApprox LogHS* (Train: 6.7 sec. Test: 18 sec.) and more than 50 times with *Approx LogHS* (Train: 3.6 sec. Test: 9.9 sec.) with respect to the baseline Log-Hilbert-Schmidt (Train: 175.7 sec. Test: 565.1 sec.).

Results. As can be seen in both Tables 6.2 and 6.3, there are generally strong improvements when one moves from the Euclidean to the Log-Euclidean and the Hilbert-Schmidt to the Log-Hilbert-Schmidt framework. More importantly, there are generally substantial improvements when one moves from the finite-dimensional setting (Euclidean and Log-Euclidean) to the infinite-dimensional setting (Hilbert-Schmidt and Log-Hilbert-Schmidt). The improvement of the Log-Hilbert-Schmidt distance, both exact and approximate, framework over the Euclidean distance framework is particularly remarkable, which clearly demon-

Table 6.3: Experimental results obtained on the task of image classification on the KTH-TIPS2b and ETH-80 datasets. The classification was carried out by SVM classification with the Gaussian kernels, defined using the Euclidean distance (*E*), Log-Euclidean distance (*Log-E*), Hilbert-Schmidt distance (*HS*), approximate Log-Hilbert-Schmidt distance with quasi-random Fourier features (*QApprox-LogHS*), and approximate Log-Hilbert-Schmidt distance with random Fourier features (*Approx-LogHS*). By comparison, the experiments *Stein*, using the symmetric Stein divergence, were carried out using the Nearest Neighbor approach.

Method	KTH-TIPS2b	ETH-80
E	55.3% (±7.6%)	64.4% (±0.9%)
Stein	73.1% (±8.0%)	67.5% (±0.4%)
Log-E	74.1% (±7.4%)	71.1% (±1.0%)
HS	79.3% (±8.2%)	93.1% (±0.4%)
Q Approx-LogHS	83.4% (±5.6%)	94.9% (±0.6%)
Approx-LogHS	83.6% (±5.4%)	95.0% (±0.5%)

strates the power of the infinite-dimensional covariance operator approach. We also observe that the use of the approximate Log-Hilbert-Schmidt distance, which is much faster to compute than the exact Log-Hilbert-Schmidt distance, results in relatively small loss in practical performance. Lastly, the CNN features from [47] can be seen to be much more descriptive than the three color features R, G, and B.

6.5   SUMMARY

In this chapter, we presented the following concepts.

1. A two-layer kernel machine using the Hilbert-Schmidt distance/inner product and the Log-Hilbert-Schmidt distance/inner product, with particular attention paid to the Log-Hilbert-Schmidt distance/inner product, which are intrinsic to positive definite operators.

2. A two-layer kernel machine with the finite-dimensional approximate Log-Hilbert-Schmidt distance, which is more computationally efficient than the exact Log-Hilbert-Schmidt distance while largely preserving its capability. We also show that this approximation approach is *not* applicable to the exact Log-Hilbert-Schmidt inner product.

3. We also show that, on large datasets, it is much more efficient to compute the approximate Log-Hilbert-Schmidt distance than the approximate affine-invariant Riemannian distance. The mathematical analysis is accompanied by a concrete implementation using the random and quasi-random Fourier feature maps.

4. The theoretical framework is accompanied by numerical experiments in image classification, which demonstrate substantial improvements of the infinite-dimensional covariance operator setting over the finite-dimensional covariance matrix framework in Chapter 3.

CHAPTER 7

Conclusion and Future Outlook

We presented a methodical survey of the data representation framework using covariance matrices and its generalization to infinite-dimensional covariance operators. Mathematically, we focused in particular on the geometry of covariance matrices and covariance operators and discussed the distances and divergences that arise by viewing them as Riemannian manifolds and convex cones. Computationally, we focused on kernel methods on covariance matrices and covariance operators and illustrated them with applications in computer vision. We showed that infinite-dimensional covariance operators, which model *nonlinear correlations* in the input data, can substantially outperform finite-dimensional covariance matrices, which only model *linear correlations* in the input. This performance gain comes at higher computational costs and we showed how to substantially decrease these costs via approximation methods.

We believe that the study of covariance matrices and covariance operators and their applications is a fruitful area of research. Some potential directions for future research include the following.

Applications of covariance operators. In this book, we focused on the applications of covariance operators in computer vision. However, given the numerous applications of covariance matrices in various domains, including statistics, machine learning, image and signal processing, to name just a few, we expect that the current mathematical framework for covariance operators will find many more applications beyond those we have presented here.

Covariance matrices and covariance operators in deep learning. So far in the literature, most authors have considered handcrafted features of images in building covariance descriptors. Recently, covariance matrices of convolutional neural network (CNN) features have been employed as part of deep networks with end-to-end-learning [53, 131]. In our ongoing work [83], we applied the covariance operator framework to CNN features, with significantly better results than the same framework applied on handcrafted features. In [126], which was carried out concurrently with our work in [84], the authors also reported empirical results on covariance operators of CNN features that are substantially better than methods using handcrafted features. Given the success of deep learning methods, this direction is certainly worth exploring, both theoretically and computationally.

Connection between the geometry of positive definite operators and the geometry of infinite-dimensional Gaussian measures. As we have shown, in the finite-dimensional setting, there is a close connection between the affine-invariant Riemannian metric on the manifold of $n \times n$ SPD matrices and the Fisher-Rao metric on the statistical manifold of Gaussian measures with zero mean in $\mathbb{R}^n$. Similarly, there is a close connection between the Alpha Log-Determinant divergences on the convex cone of SPD matrices and the Rényi divergences between Gaussian measures with zero mean. Thus, it would be of interest to explore this connection in the infinite-dimensional setting. We will present initial results in this direction in an upcoming work.

APPENDIX A

Supplementary Technical Information

A.1 MEAN SQUARED ERRORS FOR EMPIRICAL COVARIANCE MATRICES

We briefly review here the concepts of *mean squared error (MSE)*, *bias*, *variance*, and *bias-variance tradeoff* from the theory of statistical estimation (see, e.g., [15] for further detail). For an estimator $\hat{\theta}$ of a real-valued parameter θ, its MSE with respect to θ is defined to be

$$\text{MSE}(\hat{\theta}) = \mathbb{E}_\theta(\hat{\theta} - \theta)^2. \tag{A.1}$$

The MSE decomposes into two components

$$\text{MSE}(\hat{\theta}) = [\mathbb{E}_\theta(\hat{\theta}) - \theta]^2 + \mathbb{E}_\theta[\hat{\theta} - \mathbb{E}_\theta(\hat{\theta})]^2 = [\text{bias}_\theta(\hat{\theta})]^2 + \text{var}_\theta(\hat{\theta}), \tag{A.2}$$

with the bias, defined by $\text{bias}_\theta(\hat{\theta}) = \mathbb{E}_\theta(\hat{\theta}) - \theta$, measuring the accuracy of the estimation and the variance, defined by $\text{var}_\theta(\hat{\theta}) = \mathbb{E}_\theta[\hat{\theta} - \mathbb{E}_\theta(\hat{\theta})]^2$, measuring the precision of the estimation.

In the more general case where $\theta, \hat{\theta}$ are matrix-valued, with $\theta, \hat{\theta} \in \mathbb{R}^{n \times m}$, for some $m, n \in \mathbb{N}$, the MSE is defined in terms of the Frobenius norm by

$$\text{MSE}(\hat{\theta}) = \mathbb{E}||\hat{\theta} - \theta||_F^2 = \mathbb{E}\text{tr}[(\hat{\theta} - \theta)^T(\hat{\theta} - \theta)], \tag{A.3}$$

which decomposes into

$$\text{MSE}(\hat{\theta}) = ||\mathbb{E}_\theta(\hat{\theta}) - \theta||_F^2 + \mathbb{E}_\theta||\hat{\theta} - \mathbb{E}_\theta(\hat{\theta})||_F^2 = [\text{bias}_\theta(\hat{\theta})]^2 + \text{var}_\theta(\hat{\theta}), \tag{A.4}$$

with the bias of $\hat{\theta}$ defined to be $\text{bias}_\theta(\hat{\theta}) = ||\mathbb{E}_\theta(\hat{\theta}) - \theta||_F$ and the variance of $\hat{\theta}$ defined to be $\text{var}_\theta(\hat{\theta}) = \mathbb{E}_\theta||\hat{\theta} - \mathbb{E}_\theta(\hat{\theta})||_F^2$.

An estimator with low MSE must have both small bias and small variance. It can happen that a small increase in bias may lead to a larger decrease in variance, or vice versa, leading to an improvement in the MSE. This phenomenon is called the *bias-variance tradeoff*. This happens under the Gaussian distribution, where the biased MLE estimate C_X has smaller overall MSE than the unbiased estimate $\tilde{C}_X$, since it has smaller variance.

In the following, we assume that in the data matrix $\mathbf{X} = [x_1, \ldots, x_m]$, the columns x_i's are sampled IID from a Gaussian distribution $\mathcal{N}(\mu, C)$ on $\mathbb{R}^n$, with $\mu \in \mathbb{R}^n$ and C being an $n \times n$ SPD matrix.

Lemma A.1   *Assume that $m \in \mathbb{N}$, $m \geq 2$. Then for $C_{\mathbf{X}} = \frac{1}{m} \sum_{i=1}^{m}(x_i - \mu_{\mathbf{X}})(x_i - \mu_{\mathbf{X}})^T$ and $\tilde{C}_{\mathbf{X}} = \frac{1}{m-1} \sum_{i=1}^{m}(x_i - \mu_{\mathbf{X}})(x_i - \mu_{\mathbf{X}})^T$, the MSEs are given by*

$$\mathbb{E}||C_{\mathbf{X}} - C||_F^2 = \frac{m-1}{m^2}[\text{tr}(C)]^2 + \frac{1}{m}\text{tr}(C^2) < \mathbb{E}||\tilde{C}_{\mathbf{X}} - C||_F^2 = \frac{1}{m-1}\{[\text{tr}(C)]^2 + \text{tr}(C^2)\},$$
(A.5)

with the variances given by

$$\text{var}(C_{\mathbf{X}}) = \frac{(m-1)}{m^2}\{[\text{tr}(C)]^2 + \text{tr}(C^2)\} < \text{var}(\tilde{C}_{\mathbf{X}}) = \frac{1}{m-1}\{[\text{tr}(C)]^2 + \text{tr}(C^2)\}.\quad \text{(A.6)}$$

More generally, for the empirical covariance matrix of the form $\hat{C}_{c,\mathbf{X}} = c \sum_{i=1}^{m}(x_i - \mu_{\mathbf{X}})(x_i - \mu_{\mathbf{X}})^T$, $c \in \mathbb{R}$, its MSE is given by

$$\mathbb{E}||\hat{C}_{c,\mathbf{X}} - C||_F^2 = c^2(m-1)[\text{tr}(C)]^2 + [c^2m(m-1) - 2c(m-1) + 1]\text{tr}(C^2)$$
$$= [\text{bias}(\hat{C}_{c,\mathbf{X}})]^2 + \text{var}(\hat{C}_{c,\mathbf{X}}),\quad \text{(A.7)}$$

where the bias and variance of $\hat{C}_{c,\mathbf{X}}$ are given by

$$[\text{bias}(\hat{C}_{c,\mathbf{X}})]^2 = [1 - c(m-1)]^2\text{tr}(C^2), \quad \text{var}(\hat{C}_{c,\mathbf{X}}) = c^2(m-1)\{[\text{tr}(C)]^2 + \text{tr}(C^2)\}.\quad \text{(A.8)}$$

The MSE of $\hat{C}_{c,\mathbf{X}}$ has global minimum value at the point c^* given by

$$\frac{1}{m+n} \leq c^* = \frac{\text{tr}(C^2)}{[\text{tr}(C)]^2 + m\text{tr}(C^2)]} \leq \frac{1}{m+1},\quad \text{(A.9)}$$

with equality on the right-hand side if and only if $[\text{tr}(C)]^2 = \text{tr}(C^2)$ and equality on the left-hand side if and only if C is a multiple of the identity matrix I.

For the degenerate case $m = 1$, Eq. (A.7) gives $\mathbb{E}||\hat{C}_{c,\mathbf{X}} - C||_F^2 = \text{tr}(C^2) = ||C||_F^2 \ \forall c \in \mathbb{R}$, which is obviously true, since $\hat{C}_{c,\mathbf{X}} = 0_{n \times n}$, the zero $n \times n$ matrix. Thus, Eq. (A.7) is also valid for the case $m = 1$. We see immediately that $\hat{C}_{c,\mathbf{X}}$ is unbiased if and only if $c = \frac{1}{m-1}$, in which case the bias term vanishes. In the univariate case, i.e., $n = 1$, we have $[\text{tr}(C)]^2 = \text{tr}(C^2)$, so that the global minimum of the MSE is $c^* = \frac{1}{m+1}$. In general, since C is unknown, the exact value of c^* is also unknown, but the inequalities $\frac{1}{m+n} \leq c^* \leq \frac{1}{m+1}$ are always valid and tight.

Proof of Lemma A.1. Let $\mathcal{W}_n(d, \Sigma)$ denote the Wishart probability distribution on the cone of $n \times n$ SPD matrices, with d degrees of freedom and associated matrix Σ (see e.g., [30, 54]). As shown in [54], the MLE estimates $\mu_{\mathbf{X}}$ and $C_{\mathbf{X}}$ satisfy

$$\mu_{\mathbf{X}} \sim \mathcal{N}\left(\mu, \frac{1}{m}C\right), \quad mC_{\mathbf{X}} \sim \mathcal{W}_n(m-1, C).\quad \text{(A.10)}$$

By Formula (3.130) in [54],

$$\mathbb{E}(mC_X) = (m-1)C \Rightarrow \mathbb{E}(C_X) = \frac{m-1}{m}C.$$

From [71] (Theorem 4 and the subsequent discussion), we have for $U \sim \mathcal{W}_n(m, \Sigma)$,

$$\mathbb{E}(U^2) = m\Sigma\text{tr}(\Sigma) + m(m+1)\Sigma^2. \tag{A.11}$$

Thus with $mC_X \sim \mathcal{W}_n(m-1, C)$, we have

$$\mathbb{E}(m^2 C_X^2) = (m-1)C\text{tr}(C) + (m-1)mC^2$$
$$\Rightarrow \mathbb{E}(C_X^2) = \frac{m-1}{m^2}C\text{tr}(C) + \frac{m-1}{m}C^2. \tag{A.12}$$

It thus follows by the linearity of the trace operation that

$$\mathbb{E}||C_X - C||_F^2 = \mathbb{E}\text{tr}(C_X - C)^2 = \mathbb{E}[\text{tr}(C_X^2 - 2C_XC + C^2)]$$
$$= \text{tr}[\mathbb{E}(C_X^2 - 2C_XC + C^2)] = \frac{m-1}{m^2}[\text{tr}(C)]^2 + \frac{1}{m}\text{tr}(C^2),$$

giving us the first part of Eq. (A.5). The variance of C_X is

$$\text{var}(C_X) = \mathbb{E}||C_X - \mathbb{E}(C_X)||_F^2 = \mathbb{E}||C_X - \frac{m-1}{m}C||_F^2 = \frac{m-1}{m^2}[\text{tr}(C)]^2 + \frac{m-1}{m^2}\text{tr}(C^2).$$

Similarly,

$$\mathbb{E}||\tilde{C}_X - C||_F^2 = \mathbb{E}\left\|\frac{m}{m-1}C_X - C\right\|_F^2 = \mathbb{E}\left[\text{tr}\left(\frac{m^2}{(m-1)^2}C_X^2 - \frac{2m}{m-1}C_XC + C^2\right)\right]$$
$$= \frac{1}{m-1}[\text{tr}(C)]^2 + \frac{1}{m-1}\text{tr}(C^2) = \text{var}(\tilde{C}_X),$$

giving us the second part of Eq. (A.5).

In general, for $\hat{C}_{c,X} = c\sum_{i=1}^{m}(x_i - \mu_X)(x_i - \mu_X)^T = cmC_X$, with $c \in \mathbb{R}$, we have

$$f(c) = \mathbb{E}||\hat{C}_{c,X} - C||_F^2 = \mathbb{E}||cmC_X - C||_F^2 = \mathbb{E}\text{tr}[c^2m^2C_X^2 - 2cmC_XC + C^2]$$
$$= c^2(m-1)[\text{tr}(C)]^2 + [c^2m(m-1) - 2c(m-1) + 1]\text{tr}(C^2)$$
$$= [\text{bias}(\hat{C}_{c,X})]^2 + \text{var}(\hat{C}_{c,X}),$$

where the bias and variance of $\hat{C}_{c,X}$ are given by

$$[\text{bias}(\hat{C}_{c,X})]^2 = ||C - \mathbb{E}(\hat{C}_{c,X})||_F^2 = ||C - c(m-1)C||_F^2 = [1 - c(m-1)]^2\text{tr}(C^2),$$
$$\text{var}(\hat{C}_{c,X}) = \mathbb{E}||\hat{C}_{c,X} - \mathbb{E}(\hat{C}_{c,X})||_F^2 = \mathbb{E}||cmC_X - c(m-1)C||_F^2$$
$$= c^2(m-1)[\text{tr}(C)]^2 + c^2(m-1)\text{tr}(C^2).$$

For $m \geq 2$, by differentiating $f(c)$, which is quadratic in c, we have

$$f'(c) = 2c[(m-1)(\text{tr}(C))^2 + m(m-1)\text{tr}(C^2)] - 2(m-1)\text{tr}(C^2)$$

and it is straightforward to see that f is minimum at $c^* = \frac{\text{tr}(C^2)}{[\text{tr}(C)]^2 + m\text{tr}(C^2)]}$. Let $\{\lambda_k\}_{k=1}^n$ be the eigenvalues of C, which are all non-negative, then we have

$$\text{tr}(C^2) = \sum_{k=1}^n \lambda_k^2 \leq \left(\sum_{k=1}^n \lambda_k\right)^2 = [\text{tr}(C)]^2.$$

Thus, it follows that

$$c^* = \frac{\text{tr}(C^2)}{[\text{tr}(C)]^2 + m\text{tr}(C^2)]} \leq \frac{1}{m+1},$$

with equality if and only $[\text{tr}(C)]^2 = \text{tr}(C^2)$. Furthermore, by the Cauchy-Schwarz inequality, we have

$$[\text{tr}(C)]^2 = \left(\sum_{k=1}^n \lambda_k\right)^2 \leq n\left(\sum_{k=1}^n \lambda_k^2\right) = n\text{tr}(C^2),$$

with equality if and only if $\lambda_1 = \cdots = \lambda_n$, which happens if and only if C is a multiple of the identity matrix I. It thus follows that

$$c^* = \frac{\text{tr}(C^2)}{[\text{tr}(C)]^2 + m\text{tr}(C^2)]} \geq \frac{1}{m+n}.$$

This completes the proof. □

A.2   MATRIX EXPONENTIAL AND PRINCIPAL LOGARITHM

In Eqs. (2.36), (2.37), (2.38), and subsequently, $\exp(A)$ refers to the matrix exponential map, which is well-defined for any matrix $A \in \mathbb{C}^{n \times n}$ and is given by

$$\exp : \mathbb{C}^{n \times n} \to \mathbb{C}^{n \times n}, \quad \exp(A) = \sum_{k=0}^\infty \frac{A^k}{k!}.$$

In Eq. (2.39) and subsequently in all the mathematical expressions in the rest of Chapter 2, $\log(A)$ refers to the *principal matrix logarithm* of A, which is an inverse function of $\exp$ and is defined as follows (see e.g., [49]). For any $A \in \mathbb{C}^{n \times n}$, any matrix $B \in \mathbb{C}^{n \times n}$ such that $\exp(B) = A$ is called a logarithm of A. This matrix logarithm does not always exist, and when it does exist, may not be unique. However, if A has no real negative eigenvalues, then there exists a unique logarithm B of A with all eigenvalues of B lying in the horizontal strip $\{z : -\pi < \text{Im}(z) < \pi\}$ on the complex plane $\mathbb{C}$. This is called the principal logarithm of A and we write $B = \log(A)$.

For $A \in \text{Sym}^{++}(n)$, its principal logarithm $\log(A)$ has a particularly simple form. Let $\{\lambda_k\}_{k=1}^n$ denote its eigenvalues, which are all positive, arranged in decreasing order, with corresponding orthonormal eigenvectors $\{\mathbf{u}_k\}_{k=1}^n$. Then A admits the spectral decomposition

$$A = \sum_{k=1}^n \lambda_k \mathbf{u}_k \mathbf{u}_k^T = U \Lambda U^T,$$

where $\Lambda = \text{diag}(\lambda_1, \ldots, \lambda_n)$ and $U = [\mathbf{u}_1, \ldots, \mathbf{u}_k]$. The principal logarithm of A is then given by

$$\log(A) = \sum_{k=1}^n \log(\lambda_k) \mathbf{u}_k \mathbf{u}_k^T = U \log(\Lambda) U^T, \tag{A.13}$$

where $\log(\Lambda) = \text{diag}(\log(\lambda_1), \ldots, \log(\lambda_n))$.

A.3   FRÉCHET DERIVATIVE

For completeness, we present the definition of the Fréchet derivative here, with particular attention on the derivatives $D \exp$ of the matrix exponential map $\exp$ and $D \log$ of the principal matrix logarithm $\log$. The derivative $D \log$, in particular, is part of the definition of the Log-Euclidean Riemannian metric, as given in Eq. (2.62).

Let X and Y be two finite-dimensional normed spaces, with norms $\| \|_X$ and $\| \|_Y$, respectively (for the infinite-dimensional treatment, see e.g., [57]). Let $\Omega \subset X$ be an open subset and $x_0 \in \Omega$. Then f is said to be Fréchet differentiable at x_0 if there is a continuous linear map $Df(x_0) : X \to Y$ such that

$$\lim_{h \to 0} \frac{\|f(x_0 + h) - f(x_0) - Df(x_0)(h)\|_Y}{\|h\|_X} = 0. \tag{A.14}$$

Such a linear map $Df(x_0)$, if it exists, is unique and is called the Fréchet derivative of f at x_0. The simplest scenario is when $X = Y = \mathbb{R}$, in which case for a function f which is differentiable at x_0, its derivative is given by $f'(x_0) = Df(x_0)(1)$.

Let $X = \mathbb{R}^{n \times n}$, the space of all real $n \times n$ matrices, under the Frobenius norm. Then for the function $f : \mathbb{R}^{n \times n} \to \mathbb{R}^{n \times n}$ defined by $f(A) = A^k$, $k \in \mathbb{N}$, it can be verified that for any fixed $A_0 \in \mathbb{R}^{n \times n}$, the Fréchet derivative of f at A_0 is given by

$$Df(A_0)(A) = A_0^{k-1} A + A_0^{k-2} A A_0 + \cdots + A A_0^{k-1}, \quad A \in \mathbb{R}^{n \times n} \tag{A.15}$$

In particular, for $f(A) = A$, we have

$$Df(A_0)(A) = A \iff Df(A_0) = \text{id} \; \forall A_0 \in \mathbb{R}^{n \times n},$$

where id on the right-hand side denotes the identity operator mapping $\mathbb{R}^{n \times n}$ to $\mathbb{R}^{n \times n}$.

For the exponential map $\exp(A) = \sum_{k=0}^{\infty} \frac{A^k}{k!}$, the Fréchet derivative is given by

$$D \exp(A_0)(A) = \sum_{k=1}^{\infty} \frac{A_0^{k-1} A + A_0^{k-2} A A_0 + \cdots + A A_0^{k-1}}{k!}, \quad A \in \mathbb{R}^{n \times n}. \tag{A.16}$$

Thus, $D \exp(A_0)$ has an analytical expression, which is generally complicated. In the special case $A_0 = 0$, the zero matrix, it simplifies to

$$D \exp(0)(A) = A \iff D \exp(0) = \mathrm{id}.$$

On the open set $\mathrm{Sym}^{++}(n)$ of $\mathbb{R}^{n \times n}$, the principal matrix logarithm $\log : \mathrm{Sym}^{++}(n) \to \mathrm{Sym}(n)$ is well-defined as presented in Section A.2. Since $\exp(\log(A)) = A \; \forall A \in \mathrm{Sym}^{++}(n)$, by the chain rule, we have $\forall A_0 \in \mathrm{Sym}^{++}(n)$,

$$\mathrm{id} = D(\exp \circ \log)(A_0)) = D \exp(\log(A_0)) \circ D \log(A_0).$$

Similarly from $\log(\exp(B)) = B$ and the chain rule, we have $\forall B \in \mathrm{Sym}(n)$,

$$\mathrm{id} = D(\log \circ \exp)(B_0) = D \log(\exp(B_0)) \circ D \exp(B_0).$$

Since each $B_0 \in \mathrm{Sym}(n)$ corresponds to a unique $A_0 \in \mathrm{Sym}^{++}(n)$ by $B_0 = \log(A_0)$, one has $\forall A_0 \in \mathrm{Sym}^{++}(n)$,

$$\mathrm{id} = D \log(A_0) \circ D \exp(\log(A_0)).$$

It thus follows that $\forall A_0 \in \mathrm{Sym}^{++}(n)$,

$$[D \exp(\log(A_0))][D \log(A_0)] = [D \log(A_0)][D \exp(\log(A_0))] = \mathrm{id}.$$

which is equivalent to

$$D \log(A_0) = [D \exp(\log(A_0))]^{-1}, \tag{A.17}$$

where the linear operator $D \exp(A_0)$ is defined by Eq. (A.16). Thus $D \log(A_0)$ also admits an analytical expression, which is complicated in general. This is the expression that appears in the definition of the Log-Euclidean Riemannian metric, as stated in Eq. (2.62). In the special case $A_0 = I$, it simplifies to

$$D \log(I) = [D \exp(0)]^{-1} = \mathrm{id}. \tag{A.18}$$

A.4   THE QUASI-RANDOM FOURIER FEATURES

In this section, we describe in more detail the Quasi-random Fourier feature approach for constructing approximate kernel feature maps, as discussed in Section 6.3.5. This approach was first proposed in [130].

Let $K : \mathbb{R}^n \times \mathbb{R}^n \to \mathbb{R}$ be a continuous positive definite kernel of the form $K(x, y) = k(x - y)$, where $k : \mathbb{R}^n \to \mathbb{R}$ is a positive definite function, that is K is shift-invariant. We recall that by Bochner's theorem, there is a unique finite, positive measure ρ, which we assume to be a probability distribution, such that

$$K(x, y) = k(x - y) = \int_{\mathbb{R}^n} e^{-i\langle \omega, x-y \rangle} d\rho(\omega) \tag{A.19}$$

$$= \int_{\mathbb{R}^n} \phi_\omega(x) \overline{\phi_\omega(y)} d\rho(\omega), \text{ where } \phi_\omega(x) = e^{-i\langle \omega, x \rangle}.$$

The Random Fourier feature maps arise from the Monte-Carlo approximation of the integral in Eq. (A.19), using a *random* set of points ω_j's sampled according to the distribution ρ.

In the methodology of Quasi-Monte Carlo integration, see e.g., [26], the ω_j's are *deterministic* points arising from a *low-discrepancy* sequence in $[0, 1]^n$ (see below for further detail). This approach gives rise to a different method for constructing the Fourier features described in Section 6.3.5, as follows.

We assume that the probability distribution ρ in Eq. (A.19) has a density function, which we also denote by ρ. Assume that the density function ρ has the product form

$$\rho(\omega) = \prod_{j=1}^{n} \rho_j(\omega_j),$$

with each ρ_j, $1 \le j \le n$, being a one-dimensional density function. Assume further that each component cumulative distribution function

$$\psi_j(x_j) = \int_{-\infty}^{x_j} \rho_j(z_j) dz_j$$

is strictly increasing, so that the inverse functions $\psi_j^{-1} : [0, 1] \to \mathbb{R}$ are all well-defined. Let $\psi : \mathbb{R}^n \to [0, 1]^n$ be defined by

$$\psi(x) = \psi(x_1, \ldots, x_n) = (\psi_1(x_1), \ldots, \psi_n(x_n)).$$

Then its inverse function $\psi^{-1} : [0, 1]^n \to \mathbb{R}^n$ is well-defined and is given component-wise by

$$\psi^{-1}(z) = \psi^{-1}(z_1, \ldots, z_n) = (\psi_1^{-1}(z_1), \ldots, \psi_n^{-1}(z_n)). \tag{A.20}$$

With the change of variable $\omega = \psi^{-1}(t)$, the integral in Eq. (A.19) becomes

$$\int_{\mathbb{R}^n} e^{-i\langle \omega, x-y \rangle} \rho(\omega) d\omega = \int_{[0,1]^n} e^{-i\langle \psi^{-1}(t), x-y \rangle} dt. \tag{A.21}$$

Instead of approximating the left-hand side of Eq. (A.21) using a random set of points $\{\omega_j\}_{j=1}^D$ in $\mathbb{R}^n$ sampled according to ρ, in the Quasi-Monte Carlo approach, one approximates the right-hand side using a deterministic, low-discrepancy sequence of points $\{t_j\}_{j=1}^D$ in $[0,1]^n$. This sequence gives rise to a deterministic sequence ω_j's, which are given by

$$\omega_j = \psi^{-1}(t_j), \quad 1 \leq j \leq D. \tag{A.22}$$

Having generated the sequence $\{\omega_j\}_{j=1}^D$, we then construct the Fourier feature map as described by Eqs. (A.23), (A.24), and (A.25),

$$\cos\left(W^T x\right) = (\cos(\langle \omega_1, x \rangle), \ldots, \cos(\langle \omega_D, x \rangle))^T \in \mathbb{R}^D, \tag{A.23}$$

$$\sin\left(W^T x\right) = (\sin(\langle \omega_1, x \rangle), \ldots, \sin(\langle \omega_D, x \rangle))^T \in \mathbb{R}^D. \tag{A.24}$$

$$\hat{\Phi}_D(x) = \frac{1}{\sqrt{D}} \begin{pmatrix} \cos(W^T x) \\ \sin(W^T x) \end{pmatrix} \in \mathbb{R}^{2D}, \tag{A.25}$$

just as in the case of random Fourier features.

A.4.1   LOW-DISCREPANCY SEQUENCES

In this section, we briefly review the concept of *low-discrepancy sequences* in Quasi-Monte Carlo methods. For a comprehensive treatment, we refer to [88]. Let $n \in \mathbb{N}$ be fixed. Let $I^n = [0,1)^n$ and denote its closure by $\overline{I}^n = [0,1]^n$. For an integrable function f in $\overline{I}^n$, we consider the approximation

$$\int_{\overline{I}^n} f(u)du \approx \frac{1}{N} \sum_{j=1}^N f(x_j) \tag{A.26}$$

using a deterministic set of points $P = (x_1, \ldots, x_N)$, which are part of an infinite sequence $(x_j)_{j\in\mathbb{N}}$ in $\overline{I}^n$, such that the integration error satisfies

$$\lim_{N\to\infty} \left| \frac{1}{N} \sum_{j=1}^N f(x_j) - \int_{\overline{I}^n} f(u)du \right| = 0. \tag{A.27}$$

This convergence can be measured via the concept of *discrepancy* as follows. Let N be fixed. For an arbitrary set $B \subset \overline{I}^n$, define the counting function

$$A(B; P) = \sum_{j=1}^N \chi_B(x_j), \tag{A.28}$$

where χ_B denotes the characteristic function for B. Thus, $A(B; P)$ denotes the number of points in P that lie in the set B.

Let $\mathcal{B}$ be a non-empty family of Lebesgue-measurable subsets of $\overline{I}^n$. The discrepancy of the set P with respect to $\mathcal{B}$ is then defined by

$$D_N(\mathcal{B}; P) = \sup_{B \in \mathcal{B}} \left| \frac{A(B; P)}{N} - \text{vol}(B) \right|, \tag{A.29}$$

with $\text{vol}(B)$ denoting the volume of B with respect to the Lebesgue measure.

The *star discrepancy* $D_N^*(P)$ is defined by

$$D_N^*(P) = D_N(\mathcal{J}^*; P), \tag{A.30}$$

where $\mathcal{J}^*$ denotes the family of all subintervals of I^n of the form $\prod_{j=1}^n [0, x_j)$. The star discrepancy and the integration error are related via the Koksma- Hlawka inequality, as follows. Define

$$V(f) = \sum_{k=1}^n \sum_{1 \le i_1 \le \cdots \le i_k \le n} \int_0^1 \cdots \int_0^1 \left| \frac{\partial^k f}{\partial u_{i_1} \dots \partial u_{i_k}} \right| du_{i_1} \dots du_{i_k}, \tag{A.31}$$

which is called the *variation of f on $\overline{I}^n$ in the sense of Hardy-Krause*.

Theorem A.2 Koksma-Hlawka inequality. *If f has bounded variation $V(f)$ on $\overline{I}^n$ in the sense of Hardy-Krause, then for any set $(x_1, \dots, x_N)$ in I^n,*

$$\left| \frac{1}{N} \sum_{j=1}^N f(x_j) - \int_{\overline{I}^n} f(u) du \right| \le V(f) D_N^*(x_1, \dots, x_N). \tag{A.32}$$

By Theorem A.2, to achieve a small integration error, we need a sequence $(x_j)_{j \in \mathbb{N}}$ with *low discrepancy* $D_N^*(x_1, \dots, x_N) \to 0$ as $N \to \infty$. Some examples of low-discrepancy sequences are Halton and Sobol sequences (we refer to [26, 88] for the detailed constructions of these and other sequences). The Halton sequence in particular satisfies $D_N^*(x_1, \dots, x_N) = C(n) \frac{(\log N)^n}{N}$ for $N \ge 2$. We remark that the implementations for the Halton and Sobol sequences are readily available in MATLAB.[1]

A.4.2 THE GAUSSIAN CASE

In this section, we give the explicit expression for the functions ψ and ψ^{-1}, as defined above, in the case of the Gaussian kernel. It suffices for us to consider the one-dimensional setting here, since the multivariate case is defined component wise using the one-dimensional

[1]http://www.mathworks.com/help/stats/generating-quasi-random-numbers.html

case. For the one-dimensional Gaussian kernel $K(x, y) = e^{-\frac{(x-y)^2}{\sigma^2}}$, the corresponding probability density function is $\rho(z) = \frac{\sigma}{2\sqrt{\pi}} e^{-\frac{\sigma^2 z^2}{4}}$. We recall the Gaussian error function erf defined by $\mathrm{erf}(x) = \frac{2}{\sqrt{\pi}} \int_0^x e^{-z^2} dz$ and the complementary Gaussian error function erfc defined by $\mathrm{erfc}(x) = \frac{2}{\sqrt{\pi}} \int_x^\infty e^{-z^2} dz = 1 - \mathrm{erf}(x)$. By definition, the cumulative distribution function ψ for ρ is given by

$$\psi(x) = \int_{-\infty}^x \rho(z)dz = 1 - \int_x^\infty \rho(z)dz = 1 - \frac{\sigma}{2\sqrt{\pi}} \int_x^\infty e^{-\frac{\sigma^2 z^2}{4}} dz = 1 - \frac{1}{\sqrt{\pi}} \int_{\frac{x\sigma}{2}}^\infty e^{-u^2} du$$

$$= 1 - \frac{1}{2} \mathrm{erfc}\left(\frac{x\sigma}{2}\right).$$

It follows that the inverse function ψ^{-1} is given by

$$x = \psi^{-1}(t) = \frac{2}{\sigma} \mathrm{erfc}^{-1}(2 - 2t) = \frac{2}{\sigma} \mathrm{erf}^{-1}(2t - 1). \tag{A.33}$$

This is the one-dimensional component of the expression that is used in Eq. (A.22) for generating the sequence ω_j's in $\mathbb{R}^n$, given a sequence t_j's in $[0, 1]^n$.

A.5   PROOFS OF SEVERAL MATHEMATICAL RESULTS

In this section, we prove Theorems 4.1, 6.4, and 6.6. For clarity, we restate all the results that we wish to prove here.

Assume that ρ is a Borel probability distribution on $\mathcal{X}$, with

$$\int_{\mathcal{X}} ||\Phi(x)||_{\mathcal{H}_K}^2 d\rho(x) = \int_{\mathcal{X}} K(x, x) d\rho(x) < \infty. \tag{A.34}$$

The covariance operator $C_\Phi : \mathcal{H}_K \to \mathcal{H}_K$ is defined to be

$$C_\Phi = \int_{\mathcal{X}} (\Phi(x) - \mu_\Phi) \otimes (\Phi(x) - \mu_\Phi) d\rho(x) = \int_{\mathcal{X}} \Phi(x) \otimes \Phi(x) d\rho(x) - \mu_\Phi \otimes \mu_\Phi. \tag{A.35}$$

The following is Theorem 4.1, restated as Theorem A.3.

Theorem A.3   *Let $\mathcal{X}$ be a complete, separable metric space and $K : \mathcal{X} \times \mathcal{X} \to \mathbb{R}$ be a continuous, positive definite kernel. Let ρ be a Borel probability measure on $\mathcal{X}$. Assume that Eq. (A.34) is satisfied. Then the covariance operator $C_\Phi : \mathcal{H}_K \to \mathcal{H}_K$, as defined in Eq. (A.35), is a positive trace class operator. In other words, C_Φ possesses a countable set of eigenvalues $\{\lambda_k\}_{k=1}^\infty$, $\lambda_k \geq 0\ \forall k \in \mathbb{N}$, and*

$$\sum_{k=1}^\infty \lambda_k < \infty. \tag{A.36}$$

Proof. We make use of the following result from Chapter III in [25], which defines the following operator $L_K : L^2_\rho(\mathcal{X}) \to L^2_\rho(\mathcal{X})$, given by

$$(L_K f)(x) = \int_{\mathcal{X}} K(x, y) f(y) d\rho(y), \quad f \in L^2_\rho(\mathcal{X}).$$

This is a self-adjoint, positive, trace class operator on $L^2_\rho(\mathcal{X})$, with eigenvalues $\{\mu_k\}_{k=1}^\infty$ satisfying

$$\sum_{k=1}^\infty \mu_k = \int_{\mathcal{X}} K(x, x) d\rho(x) < \infty$$

by the assumption stated in Eq. (A.34) (we note that by assuming that ρ is a probability measure, the assumption that $\mathcal{X}$ is compact in [25] can be relaxed to requiring that $\mathcal{X}$ be a complete, separable metric space). Since $L_K^{1/2} : L^2_\rho(\mathcal{X}) \to \mathcal{H}_K$, when restricted to $\mathcal{H}_K$, the operator $L_K : \mathcal{H}_K \to \mathcal{H}_K$ is also self-adjoint, positive, trace class, with the same eigenvalues and eigenvectors.

Let now $f \in \mathcal{H}_K$. We have from the reproducing property $\langle \Phi(y), f \rangle_{\mathcal{H}_K} = \langle K_y, f \rangle_{\mathcal{H}_K} = f(y)$ that

$$\left(\left[\int_{\mathcal{X}} \Phi(y) \otimes \Phi(y) d\rho(y) \right] f \right)(x) = \left[\int_{\mathcal{X}} \Phi(y) f(y) d\rho(y) \right](x) = \int_{\mathcal{X}} K(x, y) f(y) d\rho(y)$$
$$= (L_K f)(x) \quad \forall x \in \mathcal{X}.$$

Thus, it follows that

$$C_\Phi = L_K - \mu_\Phi \otimes \mu_\Phi.$$

Since the operator $\mu_\Phi \otimes \mu_\Phi$ is self-adjoint and of rank one, it follows that C_Φ is also a self-adjoint, trace class operator. C_Φ is also positive, since $\forall f \in \mathcal{H}_K$,

$$\langle f, C_\Phi f \rangle_{\mathcal{H}_K} = \mathbb{E}_\rho(f^2) - (\mathbb{E}_\rho f)^2 = \mathbb{E}_\rho[f - \mathbb{E}_\rho f]^2 \geq 0.$$

This completes the proof. $\qquad\qquad\qquad\qquad\qquad\qquad\qquad\qquad\qquad\qquad\qquad\qquad\qquad\qquad$ $\square$

The following is Theorem 6.4, restated as Theorem A.4.

Theorem A.4   *Assume that $\gamma \neq \mu$, $\gamma > 0$, $\mu > 0$. Then, for the approximate affine-invariant Riemannian distance,*

$$\lim_{D \to \infty} \| \log[(C_{\hat{\Phi}_D(\mathbf{X})} + \gamma I_D)^{-1/2} (C_{\hat{\Phi}_D(\mathbf{Y})} + \mu I_D)(C_{\hat{\Phi}_D(\mathbf{X})} + \gamma I_D)^{-1/2}] \|_F = \infty. \quad \text{(A.37)}$$

The following is Theorem 6.6, restated as Theorem A.5.

Theorem A.5   *Assume that $\gamma = \mu > 0$. Then, for the approximate affine-invariant Riemannian distance,*

$$\lim_{D \to \infty} \| \log[(C_{\hat{\Phi}_D(\mathbf{X})} + \gamma I_D)^{-1/2} (C_{\hat{\Phi}_D(\mathbf{Y})} + \gamma I_D)(C_{\hat{\Phi}_D(\mathbf{X})} + \gamma I_D)^{-1/2}] \|_F$$
$$= \| \log[(C_{\Phi(\mathbf{X})} + \gamma I_{\mathcal{H}})^{-1/2} (C_{\Phi(\mathbf{Y})} + \gamma I_{\mathcal{H}})(C_{\Phi(\mathbf{X})} + \gamma I_{\mathcal{H}})^{-1/2}] \|_{\text{eHS}}. \quad \text{(A.38)}$$

To prove Theorems A.4 and A.5, in the following, let $\hat{K}_D[\mathbf{X}]$, $\hat{K}_D[\mathbf{Y}]$, $\hat{K}_D[\mathbf{X}, \mathbf{Y}]$, $\hat{K}_D[\mathbf{Y}, \mathbf{X}]$ be the $m \times m$ Gram matrices defined by

$$
\begin{aligned}
(\hat{K}_D[\mathbf{X}])_{ij} &= \hat{K}_D(x_i, x_j) = \langle \hat{\Phi}_D(x_i), \hat{\Phi}_D(x_j) \rangle, \quad 1 \le i, j \le m, & \text{(A.39)} \\
(\hat{K}_D[\mathbf{Y}])_{ij} &= \hat{K}_D(y_i, y_j) = \langle \hat{\Phi}_D(y_i), \hat{\Phi}_D(y_j) \rangle, \quad 1 \le i, j \le m, & \text{(A.40)} \\
(\hat{K}_D[\mathbf{X}, \mathbf{Y}])_{ij} &= \hat{K}_D(x_i, y_j) = \langle \hat{\Phi}_D(x_i), \hat{\Phi}_D(y_j) \rangle, \quad 1 \le i, j \le m, & \text{(A.41)} \\
(\hat{K}_D[\mathbf{Y}, \mathbf{X}])_{ij} &= \hat{K}_D(y_i, x_j) = \langle \hat{\Phi}_D(y_i), \hat{\Phi}_D(x_j) \rangle, \quad 1 \le i, j \le m. & \text{(A.42)}
\end{aligned}
$$

For $m \in \mathbb{N}$ fixed, since the Gram matrices are all finite $m \times m$ matrices, by assumption, as $D \to \infty$, we have

$$
\begin{aligned}
&\lim_{D \to \infty} ||\hat{K}_D[\mathbf{X}] - K[\mathbf{X}]||_F = 0, \quad \lim_{D \to \infty} ||\hat{K}_D[\mathbf{Y}] - K[\mathbf{Y}]||_F = 0, \\
&\lim_{D \to \infty} ||\hat{K}_D[\mathbf{X}, \mathbf{Y}] - K[\mathbf{X}, \mathbf{Y}]||_F = 0, \quad \lim_{D \to \infty} ||\hat{K}_D[\mathbf{Y}, \mathbf{X}] - K[\mathbf{Y}, \mathbf{X}]||_F = 0. \quad \text{(A.43)}
\end{aligned}
$$

Proof of Theorems A.4 and A.5. We recall that by Theorem 5.11, when $\dim(\mathcal{H}_K) = \infty$, we have

$$
d^2_{\text{aiHS}}[(C_{\Phi(\mathbf{X})} + \gamma I_{\mathcal{H}_K}), (C_{\Phi(\mathbf{Y})} + \mu I_{\mathcal{H}_K})] = \text{tr} \left\{ \log \left[\begin{pmatrix} C_{11} & C_{12} & C_{13} \\ C_{21} & C_{22} & C_{23} \\ C_{11} & C_{12} & C_{13} \end{pmatrix} + I_{3m} \right] \right\}^2
$$
$$
+ \left(\log \frac{\gamma}{\mu} \right)^2,
$$

where the $m \times m$ matrices C_{ij}, $i = 1, 2$, $j = 1, 2, 3$, are given by

$$
C_{11} = \frac{1}{\mu m} J_m K[\mathbf{Y}] J_m,
$$
$$
C_{12} = -\frac{1}{\sqrt{\gamma\mu}m} J_m K[\mathbf{Y}, \mathbf{X}] J_m \left(I_m + \frac{1}{\gamma m} J_m K[\mathbf{X}] J_m \right)^{-1},
$$
$$
C_{13} = -\frac{1}{\gamma\mu m^2} J_m K[\mathbf{Y}, \mathbf{X}] J_m \left(I_m + \frac{1}{\gamma m} J_m K[\mathbf{X}] J_m \right)^{-1} J_m K[\mathbf{X}, \mathbf{Y}] J_m,
$$
$$
C_{21} = \frac{1}{\sqrt{\gamma\mu}m} J_m K[\mathbf{X}, \mathbf{Y}] J_m,
$$
$$
C_{22} = -\frac{1}{\gamma m} J_m K[\mathbf{X}] J_m \left(I_m + \frac{1}{\gamma m} J_m K[\mathbf{X}] J_m \right)^{-1},
$$
$$
C_{23} = -\frac{1}{\gamma m} J_m K[\mathbf{X}] J_m \left(I_m + \frac{1}{\gamma m} J_m K[\mathbf{X}] J_m \right)^{-1} \frac{1}{\sqrt{\gamma\mu}m} J_m K[\mathbf{X}, \mathbf{Y}] J_m.
$$

By Theorem 5.12, we have

$$d^2_{\text{aiHS}}[(C_{\hat{\Phi}_D(\mathbf{X})} + \gamma I_D), (C_{\hat{\Phi}_D(\mathbf{Y})} + \mu I_D)] = \text{tr}\left\{\log\left[\begin{pmatrix} \hat{C}_{D,11} & \hat{C}_{D,12} & \hat{C}_{D,13} \\ \hat{C}_{D,21} & \hat{C}_{D,22} & \hat{C}_{D,23} \\ \hat{C}_{D,11} & \hat{C}_{D,12} & \hat{C}_{D,13} \end{pmatrix} + I_{3m}\right]\right\}^2$$

$$- 2\left(\log\frac{\gamma}{\mu}\right)\text{tr}\left\{\log\left[\begin{pmatrix} \hat{C}_{D,11} & \hat{C}_{D,12} & \hat{C}_{D,13} \\ \hat{C}_{D,21} & \hat{C}_{D,22} & \hat{C}_{D,23} \\ \hat{C}_{D,11} & \hat{C}_{D,12} & \hat{C}_{D,13} \end{pmatrix} + I_{3m}\right]\right\} + \left(\log\frac{\gamma}{\mu}\right)^2 D,$$

where the $m \times m$ matrices $\hat{C}_{D,ij}$, $i = 1, 2, j = 1, 2, 3$, are given by

$$\hat{C}_{D,11} = \frac{1}{\mu m} J_m \hat{K}_D[\mathbf{Y}] J_m,$$

$$\hat{C}_{D,12} = -\frac{1}{\sqrt{\gamma\mu}m} J_m \hat{K}_D[\mathbf{Y}, \mathbf{X}] J_m \left(I_m + \frac{1}{\gamma m} J_m \hat{K}_D[\mathbf{X}] J_m\right)^{-1},$$

$$\hat{C}_{D,13} = -\frac{1}{\gamma\mu m^2} J_m \hat{K}_D[\mathbf{Y}, \mathbf{X}] J_m \left(I_m + \frac{1}{\gamma m} J_m \hat{K}_D[\mathbf{X}] J_m\right)^{-1} J_m \hat{K}_D[\mathbf{X}, \mathbf{Y}] J_m,$$

$$\hat{C}_{D,21} = \frac{1}{\sqrt{\gamma\mu}m} J_m \hat{K}_D[\mathbf{X}, \mathbf{Y}] J_m,$$

$$\hat{C}_{D,22} = -\frac{1}{\gamma m} J_m \hat{K}_D[\mathbf{X}] J_m \left(I_m + \frac{1}{\gamma m} J_m \hat{K}_D[\mathbf{X}] J_m\right)^{-1},$$

$$\hat{C}_{D,23} = -\frac{1}{\gamma m} J_m \hat{K}_D[\mathbf{X}] J_m \left(I_m + \frac{1}{\gamma m} J_m \hat{K}_D[\mathbf{X}] J_m\right)^{-1} \frac{1}{\sqrt{\gamma\mu}m} J_m \hat{K}_D[\mathbf{X}, \mathbf{Y}] J_m.$$

Since the Gram matrices are all finite $m \times m$ matrices, for $\gamma \neq \mu$, we clearly have

$$\lim_{D\to\infty} d^2_{\text{aiHS}}[(C_{\hat{\Phi}_D(\mathbf{X})} + \gamma I_D), (C_{\hat{\Phi}_D(\mathbf{Y})} + \mu I_D)] = \infty.$$

For $\gamma = \mu$, by the limits in Eq. (A.43), we have

$$\lim_{D\to\infty} d^2_{\text{aiHS}}[(C_{\hat{\Phi}_D(\mathbf{X})} + \gamma I_D), (C_{\hat{\Phi}_D(\mathbf{Y})} + \gamma I_D)]$$

$$= \lim_{D\to\infty} \text{tr}\left\{\log\left[\begin{pmatrix} \hat{C}_{D,11} & \hat{C}_{D,12} & \hat{C}_{D,13} \\ \hat{C}_{D,21} & \hat{C}_{D,22} & \hat{C}_{D,23} \\ \hat{C}_{D,11} & \hat{C}_{D,12} & \hat{C}_{D,13} \end{pmatrix} + I_{3m}\right]\right\}^2$$

$$= \text{tr}\left\{\log\left[\begin{pmatrix} C_{11} & C_{12} & C_{13} \\ C_{21} & C_{22} & C_{23} \\ C_{11} & C_{12} & C_{13} \end{pmatrix} + I_{3m}\right]\right\}^2$$

$$= d^2_{\text{aiHS}}[(C_{\Phi(\mathbf{X})} + \gamma I_{\mathcal{H}_K}), (C_{\Phi(\mathbf{Y})} + \gamma I_{\mathcal{H}_K})].$$

This completes the proof. $\qquad\qquad\qquad\qquad\qquad\qquad\qquad\qquad\qquad\qquad\square$

Bibliography

[1] S. Amari and H. Nagaoka. *Methods of Information Geometry*. American Mathematical Society, 2000. 36

[2] S. Anand, S. Mittal, O. Tuzel, and P. Meer. Semi-supervised Kernel mean shift clustering. *IEEE Transactions on Pattern Analysis and Machine Intelligence*, 36(6):1201–1215, 2014. DOI: 10.1109/tpami.2013.190. 1

[3] M. Arnaudon, F. Barbaresco, and L. Yang. Riemannian medians and means with applications to radar signal processing. *IEEE Journal of Selected Topics in Signal Processing*, 7(4):595–604, 2013. DOI: 10.1109/jstsp.2013.2261798. 1

[4] N. Aronszajn. Theory of reproducing Kernels. *Transactions of the American Mathematical Society*, 68:337–404, 1950. DOI: 10.2307/1990404. 55

[5] V. Arsigny, P. Fillard, X. Pennec, and N. Ayache. Fast and simple calculus on tensors in the Log-Euclidean framework. In *Medical Image Computing and Computer-assisted Intervention (MICCAI)*, pages 115–122, Springer, 2005. DOI: 10.1007/11566465_15. 1, 2

[6] V. Arsigny, P. Fillard, X. Pennec, and N. Ayache. Geometric means in a novel vector space structure on symmetric positive-definite matrices. *SIAM Journal on Matrix Analysis and Applications*, 29(1):328–347, 2007. DOI: 10.1137/050637996. 2, 19, 38, 39, 41, 42, 43, 90

[7] A. Barachant, S. Bonnet, M. Congedo, and C. Jutten. Multiclass brain-computer interface classification by Riemannian geometry. *IEEE Transactions on Biomedical Engineering*, 59(4):920–928, 2012. DOI: 10.1109/tbme.2011.2172210. 1

[8] A. Barachant, S. Bonnet, M. Congedo, and C. Jutten. Classification of covariance matrices using a Riemannian-based Kernel for BCI applications. *Neurocomputing*, 112:172–178, 2013. DOI: 10.1016/j.neucom.2012.12.039. 1

[9] F. Barbaresco. Information geometry of covariance matrix: Cartan-Siegel homogeneous bounded domains, Mostow/Berger fibration and Frechet median. In *Matrix Information Geometry*, pages 199–255, Springer, 2013. DOI: 10.1007/978-3-642-30232-9_9. 1

[10] R. Bhatia. *Positive Definite Matrices*. Princeton University Press, 2007. DOI: 10.1515/9781400827787. 1, 32

[11] D. A. Bini and B. Iannazzo. Computing the Karcher mean of symmetric positive definite matrices. *Linear Algebra and its Applications*, 438(4):1700–1710, 2013. DOI: 10.1016/j.laa.2011.08.052. 1, 32

[12] B. J. Boom, J. He, S. Palazzo, P. X. Huang, C. Beyan, H.-M. Chou, F.-P. Lin, C. Spampinato, and R. B. Fisher. A research tool for long-term and continuous analysis of fish assemblage in coral-reefs using underwater camera footage. *Ecological Informatics*, 23:83–97, 2014. DOI: 10.1016/j.ecoinf.2013.10.006. 121, 122

[13] L. M. Bregman. The relaxation method of finding the common point of convex sets and its application to the solution of problems in convex programming. *USSR Computational Mathematics and Mathematical Physics*, 7(3):200–217, 1967. DOI: 10.1016/0041-5553(67)90040-7. 45

[14] B. Caputo, E. Hayman, and P. Mallikarjuna. Class-specific material categorisation. In *IEEE International Conference on Computer Vision (ICCV)*, 2005. DOI: 10.1109/iccv.2005.54. 61, 62

[15] G. Casella and R. Berger. *Statistical Inference*. Duxbury, 2002. DOI: 10.2307/2532634. 13, 14, 129

[16] J. Cavazza, A. Zunino, M. San-Biagio, and V. Murino. Kernelized covariance for action recognition. In *23rd International Conference on Pattern Recognition, ICPR*, pages 408–413, Cancún, Mexico, December 4–8, 2016. DOI: 10.1109/icpr.2016.7899668. 68

[17] C.-C. Chang and C. Lin. LIBSVM: A library for support vector machines. *ACM Transactions on Intelligent Systems and Technology*, 2(3):27:1–27:27, May 2011. DOI: 10.1145/1961189.1961199. 63

[18] Z. Chebbi and M. Moakher. Means of Hermitian positive-definite matrices based on the log-determinant α-divergence function. *Linear Algebra and its Applications*, 436(7):1872–1889, 2012. 2, 45, 46, 47

[19] A. Cherian and S. Sra. Positive definite matrices: Data representation and applications to computer vision. In *Algorithmic Advances in Riemannian Geometry and Applications: For Machine Learning, Computer Vision, Statistics, and Optimization*, page 93, Springer, 2016. DOI: 10.1007/978-3-319-45026-1_4. 1, 13, 64

[20] A. Cherian and S. Sra. Riemannian dictionary learning and sparse coding for positive definite matrices. *IEEE Transactions on Neural Networks and Learning Systems*, 2016. DOI: 10.1109/tnnls.2016.2601307. 1, 64

[21] A. Cherian, S. Sra, A. Banerjee, and N. Papanikolopoulos. Jensen-Bregman LogDet divergence with application to efficient similarity search for covariance matrices. *IEEE*

Transactions on Pattern Analysis and Machine Intelligence, 35(9):2161–2174, 2013. DOI: 10.1109/tpami.2012.259. 1, 2, 45, 47

[22] A. Cichocki, S. Cruces, and S. Amari. Log-Determinant divergences revisited: Alpha-Beta and Gamma Log-Det divergences. *Entropy*, 17(5):2988–3034, 2015. DOI: 10.3390/e17052988. 49, 50

[23] P. Cirujeda, X. Mateo, Y. Dicente, and X. Binefa. MCOV: A covariance descriptor for fusion of texture and shape features in 3D point clouds. In *3D Vision (3DV), 2nd International Conference on*, volume 1, pages 551–558, IEEE, 2014. DOI: 10.1109/3dv.2014.11. 1, 10

[24] M. Congedo, A. Barachant, and R. Bhatia. Riemannian geometry for EEG-based brain-computer interfaces; a primer and a review. *Brain-computer Interfaces*, pages 1–20, 2017. DOI: 10.1080/2326263x.2017.1297192. 1

[25] F. Cucker and S. Smale. On the mathematical foundations of learning. *Bulletin of the American Mathematical Society*, 39(1):1–49, January 2002. DOI: 10.1090/s0273-0979-01-00923-5. 70, 139

[26] J. Dick, F. Kuo, and I. Sloan. High-dimensional integration: The quasi-Monte Carlo way. *Acta Numerica*, 22:133–288, 2013. DOI: 10.1017/s0962492913000044. 120, 135, 137

[27] M. do Carmo. *Differential Geometry of Curves and Surfaces*. Prentice Hall, 1976. DOI: 10.1007/978-3-642-57951-6_5. 23, 24, 29

[28] M. P. do Carmo. *Riemannian Geometry*. Mathematics: Theory & Applications. Birkhäuser, 2013. DOI: 10.1007/978-1-4757-2201-7. 23, 24, 26, 28, 29, 30, 31, 33, 42

[29] I. Dryden, A. Koloydenko, and D. Zhou. Non-Euclidean statistics for covariance matrices, with applications to diffusion tensor imaging. *Annals of Applied Statistics*, 3:1102–1123, 2009. DOI: 10.1214/09-aoas249. 1, 50

[30] M. L. Eaton. *Multivariate Statistics: A Vector Space Approach*. Institute of Mathematical Statistics Lecture Notes—Monograph Series, 2007. 130

[31] H. Engl, M. Hanke, and A. Neubauer. *Regularization of Inverse Problems*, volume 375 of *Mathematics and its Applications*. Springer, 1996. 51

[32] K. Fan. On a theorem of Weyl concerning eigenvalues of linear transformations: II. *Proc. of the National Academy of Sciences of the United States of America*, 36(1):31, 1950. DOI: 10.1073/pnas.36.1.31. 46

[33] M. Faraki, M. Harandi, and F. Porikli. Approximate infinite-dimensional region covariance descriptors for image classification. In *IEEE International Conference on Acoustics, Speech, and Signal Processing (ICASSP)*, 2015. DOI: 10.1109/icassp.2015.7178193. 112

[34] M. Faraki, M. T. Harandi, and F. Porikli. Image set classification by symmetric positive semi-definite matrices. In *Applications of Computer Vision (WACV), Winter Conference on*, pages 1–8, IEEE, 2016. DOI: 10.1109/wacv.2016.7477621. 1

[35] D. Fehr, A. Cherian, R. Sivalingam, S. Nickolay, V. Morellas, and N. Papanikolopoulos. Compact covariance descriptors in 3D point clouds for object recognition. In *Robotics and Automation (ICRA), International Conference on*, pages 1793–1798, IEEE, 2012. DOI: 10.1109/icra.2012.6224740. 1, 10, 13

[36] D. Fehr, W. J. Beksi, D. Zermas, and N. Papanikolopoulos. RGB-D object classification using covariance descriptors. In *Robotics and Automation (ICRA), International Conference on*, pages 5467–5472, IEEE, 2014. DOI: 10.1109/icra.2014.6907663. 1, 10

[37] D. Felice, M. Hà Quang, and S. Mancini. The volume of Gaussian states by information geometry. *Journal of Mathematical Physics*, 58(1):012201, 2017. DOI: 10.1063/1.4973507. 37

[38] A. Feragen, F. Lauze, and S. Hauberg. Geodesic exponential Kernels: When curvature and linearity conflict. In *Proc. of the IEEE Conference on Computer Vision and Pattern Recognition*, pages 3032–3042, 2015. DOI: 10.1109/cvpr.2015.7298922. 59

[39] T. J. Fisher and X. Sun. Improved Stein-type shrinkage estimators for the high-dimensional multivariate normal covariance matrix. *Computational Statistics and Data Analysis*, 55(5):1909–1918, 2011. DOI: 10.1016/j.csda.2010.12.006. 15

[40] P. Formont, J.-P. Ovarlez, and F. Pascal. On the use of matrix information geometry for polarimetric SAR image classification. In *Matrix Information Geometry*, pages 257–276, Springer, 2013. DOI: 10.1007/978-3-642-30232-9_10. 1

[41] K. Guo, P. Ishwar, and J. Konrad. Action recognition using sparse representation on covariance manifolds of optical flow. In *Advanced Video and Signal Based Surveillance (AVSS), 7th International Conference on*, pages 188–195, IEEE, 2010. DOI: 10.1109/avss.2010.71. 1, 10

[42] B. Hall. *Lie Groups, Lie Algebras, and Representations: An Elementary Introduction*. Graduate Texts in Mathematics 222, Springer, 2003. DOI: 10.1007/978-0-387-21554-9. 39

[43] G. Hämmerlin and K.-H. Hoffmann. *Numerical Mathematics*. Springer-Verlag, 1991. DOI: 10.1007/978-1-4612-4442-4. 48

[44] M. Harandi, M. Salzmann, and F. Porikli. Bregman divergences for infinite dimensional covariance matrices. In *IEEE Conference on Computer Vision and Pattern Recognition (CVPR)*, pages 1003–1010, 2014. DOI: 10.1109/cvpr.2014.132. 2, 62, 68, 74, 94, 103, 113

[45] M. Harandi, M. Salzmann, and R. Hartley. Dimensionality reduction on SPD manifolds: The emergence of geometry-aware methods. *IEEE Transactions on Pattern Analysis and Machine Intelligence*, 2017. DOI: 10.1109/tpami.2017.2655048. 64

[46] M. T. Harandi, R. Hartley, B. Lovell, and C. Sanderson. Sparse coding on symmetric positive definite manifolds using Bregman divergences. *IEEE Transactions on Neural Networks and Learning Systems*, 27(6):1294–1306, 2016. DOI: 10.1109/tnnls.2014.2387383. 1, 64

[47] B. Hariharan, P. Arbeláez, R. Girshick, and J. Malik. Hypercolumns for object segmentation and fine-grained localization. In *Proc. of the IEEE Conference on Computer Vision and Pattern Recognition*, pages 447–456, 2015. DOI: 10.1109/cvpr.2015.7298642. 121, 124

[48] W. Hariri, H. Tabia, N. Farah, A. Benouareth, and D. Declercq. 3D face recognition using covariance based descriptors. *Pattern Recognition Letters*, 78:1–7, 2016. DOI: 10.1016/j.patrec.2016.03.028. 1, 10, 13

[49] N. J. Higham. *Functions of Matrices: Theory and Computation*. SIAM, 2008. DOI: 10.1137/1.9780898717778. 132

[50] W. Hu, X. Li, W. Luo, X. Zhang, S. Maybank, and Z. Zhang. Single and multiple object tracking using Log-Euclidean Riemannian subspace and block-division appearance model. *IEEE Transactions on Pattern Analysis and Machine Intelligence*, 34(12):2420–2440, 2012. DOI: 10.1109/tpami.2012.42. 1

[51] Z. Huang, R. Wang, S. Shan, and X. Chen. Hybrid Euclidean-and-Riemannian metric learning for image set classification. In *Computer Vision (ACCV): 12th Asian Conference on Computer Vision, Revised Selected Papers, Part III*, pages 562–577, Springer International Publishing, Cham, 2014. DOI: 10.1007/978-3-319-16811-1_37. 1

[52] Z. Huang, R. Wang, S. Shan, X. Li, and X. Chen. Log-Euclidean metric learning on symmetric positive definite manifold with application to image set classification. In *International Conference on Machine Learning (ICML)*, 2015. 1, 64

[53] C. Ionescu, O. Vantzos, and C. Sminchisescu. Matrix backpropagation for deep networks with structured layers. In *ICCV*, pages 2965–2973, 2015. DOI: 10.1109/iccv.2015.339. 1, 127

[54] A. J. Izenman. *Modern Multivariate Statistical Techniques*. Springer, 2008. DOI: 10.1007/978-0-387-78189-1. 12, 130, 131

[55] S. Jayasumana, R. Hartley, M. Salzmann, H. Li, and M. Harandi. Kernel methods on the Riemannian manifold of symmetric positive definite matrices. In *IEEE Conference on Computer Vision and Pattern Recognition (CVPR)*, pages 73–80, 2013. DOI: 10.1109/cvpr.2013.17. 2, 58, 60, 63, 107

[56] S. Jayasumana, R. Hartley, M. Salzmann, H. Li, and M. Harandi. Kernel methods on Riemannian manifolds with Gaussian RBF Kernels. *IEEE Transactions on Pattern Analysis and Machine Intelligence*, 37(12):2464–2477, 2015. DOI: 10.1109/tpami.2015.2414422. 58, 60, 63

[57] J. Jost. *Postmodern Analysis*. Springer, 1998. DOI: 10.1007/978-3-662-05306-5. 133

[58] J. Jost. *Riemannian Geometry and Geometric Analysis*. Springer Science & Business Media, 2008. DOI: 10.1007/978-3-662-22385-7. 23, 26, 28, 31

[59] P. Kar and H. Karnick. Random feature maps for dot product Kernels. In *International Conference on Artificial Intelligence and Statistics*, pages 583–591, 2012. 121

[60] B. Kulis, M. A. Sustik, and I. S. Dhillon. Low-rank Kernel learning with Bregman matrix divergences. *The Journal of Machine Learning Research*, 10:341–376, 2009. 1, 2, 45, 47

[61] S. Kullback and R. A. Leibler. On information and sufficiency. *Annals of Mathematical Statistics*, 22(1):79–86, March 1951. DOI: 10.1214/aoms/1177729694. 49

[62] S. Lang. *Fundamentals of Differential Geometry*, volume 191. Springer Science & Business Media, 1999. DOI: 10.1007/978-1-4612-0541-8. 31, 33, 86

[63] G. Larotonda. *Geodesic Convexity, Symmetric Spaces and Hilbert–Schmidt Operators*. Ph.D. thesis, Universidad Nacional de General Sarmiento, Buenos Aires, Argentina, 2005. 80, 85, 86

[64] G. Larotonda. Nonpositive curvature: A geometrical approach to Hilbert-Schmidt operators. *Differential Geometry and its Applications*, 25:679–700, 2007. DOI: 10.1016/j.difgeo.2007.06.016. 2, 74, 80, 85, 86, 87

[65] J. D. Lawson and Y. Lim. The geometric mean, matrices, metrics, and more. *The American Mathematical Monthly*, 108(9):797–812, 2001. DOI: 10.2307/2695553. 1, 32

[66] D. Le Bihan, J.-F. Mangin, C. Poupon, C. A. Clark, S. Pappata, N. Molko, and H. Chabriat. Diffusion tensor imaging: Concepts and applications. *Journal of Magnetic Resonance Imaging*, 13(4):534–546, 2001. DOI: 10.1002/jmri.1076. 1

[67] O. Ledoit and M. Wolf. A well-conditioned estimator for large-dimensional covariance matrices. *Journal of Multivariate Analysis*, 88(2):365–411, 2004. DOI: 10.1016/s0047-259x(03)00096-4. 15

[68] J. M. Lee. Introduction to smooth manifolds. *Graduate Texts in Mathematics*, 2012. DOI: 10.1007/978-0-387-21752-9. 24, 26

[69] B. Leibe and B. Schiele. Analyzing appearance and contour based methods for object categorization. In *CVPR*, pages II–409–15, June 2003. DOI: 10.1109/cvpr.2003.1211497. 62

[70] C. Lenglet, M. Rousson, R. Deriche, and O. Faugeras. Statistics on the manifold of multivariate normal distributions: Theory and application to diffusion tensor MRI processing. *Journal of Mathematical Imaging and Vision*, 25(3):423–444, 2006. DOI: 10.1007/s10851-006-6897-z. 37, 38

[71] G. Letac and H. Massam. All invariant moments of the Wishart distribution. *Scandinavian Journal of Statistics*, 31(2):295–318, 2004. DOI: 10.1111/j.1467-9469.2004.01-043.x. 131

[72] P. Li, Q. Wang, W. Zuo, and L. Zhang. Log-Euclidean Kernels for sparse representation and dictionary learning. In *International Conference on Computer Vision (ICCV)*, pages 1601–1608, 2013. DOI: 10.1109/iccv.2013.202. 1, 2, 44, 58, 60, 64, 107

[73] B. Ma, Y. Su, and F. Jurie. Covariance descriptor based on bio-inspired features for person re-identification and face verification. *Image and Vision Computing*, 32(6):379–390, 2014. DOI: 10.1016/j.imavis.2014.04.002. 1

[74] T. Matsuzawa, R. Relator, J. Sese, and T. Kato. Stochastic Dykstra algorithms for metric learning with positive definite covariance descriptors. In *European Conference on Computer Vision*, pages 786–799, Springer, 2016. DOI: 10.1007/978-3-319-46466-4_47. 64

[75] H. Minh. Infinite-dimensional Log-Determinant divergences between positive definite trace class operators. *Linear Algebra and its Applications*, 528:331–383, 2017. DOI: 10.1016/j.laa.2016.09.018. 2, 14, 68, 74, 75, 77, 94, 96, 97, 98, 99, 100, 103

[76] H. Minh, M. San Biagio, and V. Murino. Log-Hilbert-Schmidt metric between positive definite operators on Hilbert spaces. In *Advances in Neural Information Processing Systems (NIPS)*, pages 388–396, 2014. 2, 14, 61, 68, 74, 80, 83, 85, 90, 91, 92, 93, 105, 106, 111, 113, 121

[77] H. Q. Minh. Some properties of Gaussian reproducing Kernel Hilbert spaces and their implications for function approximation and learning theory. *Constructive Approximation*, 32:307–338, 2010. DOI: 10.1007/s00365-009-9080-0. 68

[78] H. Q. Minh. Affine-invariant Riemannian distance between infinite-dimensional co-variance operators. In *Geometric Science of Information (GSI)*, pages 30–38, 2015. DOI: 10.1007/978-3-319-25040-3_4. 2, 74, 80, 83, 85, 88, 89, 111

[79] H. Q. Minh. Infinite-dimensional Log-Determinant divergences II: Alpha-Beta divergences. *arXiv preprint arXiv:1610.08087*, 2016. 2, 77, 101

[80] H. Q. Minh. Log-Determinant divergences between positive definite Hilbert-Schmidt operators. In *Geometric Science of Information (GSI)*, page in press, 2017. DOI: 10.1007/978-3-319-68445-1_59. 2, 77, 101

[81] H. Q. Minh and V. Murino. *From Covariance Matrices to Covariance Operators: Data Representation from Finite to Infinite-dimensional Settings*, pages 115–143, Springer International Publishing, Cham, 2016. DOI: 10.1007/978-3-319-45026-1_5. 58, 68, 74, 80, 83, 85, 88, 90, 106

[82] H. Q. Minh, P. Niyogi, and Y. Yao. Mercer's theorem, feature maps, and smoothing. In *Learning Theory*, pages 154–168, Springer, 2006. DOI: 10.1007/11776420_14. 68, 107

[83] H. Q. Minh, M. S. Biagio, L. Bazzani, and V. Murino. Kernel methods on approximate infinite-dimensional covariance operators for image classification. *arXiv preprint arXiv:1609.09251*, 2016. 61, 106, 109, 114, 121, 127

[84] H. Q. Minh, M. San Biagio, L. Bazzani, and V. Murino. Approximate Log-Hilbert-Schmidt distances between covariance operators for image classification. In *Proc. of the IEEE Conference on Computer Vision and Pattern Recognition*, pages 5195–5203, 2016. DOI: 10.1109/cvpr.2016.561. 3, 14, 61, 106, 109, 111, 113, 121, 127

[85] M. Moakher and M. Zéraï. The Riemannian geometry of the space of positive-definite matrices and its application to the regularization of positive-definite matrix-valued data. *Journal of Mathematical Imaging and Vision*, 40(2):171–187, 2011. DOI: 10.1007/s10851-010-0255-x. 34

[86] G. Mostow. Some new decomposition theorems for semi-simple groups. *Memoirs of the American Mathematical Society*, 14:31–54, 1955. 1, 32

[87] W. K. Nicholson. *Linear Algebra with Applications*, 3rd ed., PWS Publishing Company, 1995. 33

[88] H. Niederreiter. *Random Number Generation and Quasi-Monte Carlo Methods*. SIAM, 1992. DOI: 10.1137/1.9781611970081. 136, 137

[89] V. Y. Pan and Z. Q. Chen. The complexity of the matrix Eigen problem. In *Proc. of the 31st Annual ACM Symposium on Theory of Computing*, pages 507–516, ACM, 1999. DOI: 10.1145/301250.301389. 36

[90] Y. Pang, Y. Yuan, and X. Li. Gabor-based region covariance matrices for face recognition. *IEEE Transactions on Circuits and Systems for Video Technology*, 18(7):989–993, 2008. DOI: 10.1109/tcsvt.2008.924108. 1

[91] L. Pardo. *Statistical Inference Based on Divergence Measures*. CRC Press, 2005. DOI: 10.1201/9781420034813. 49

[92] X. Pennec, P. Fillard, and N. Ayache. A Riemannian framework for tensor computing. *International Journal of Computer Vision*, 66(1):41–66, 2006. DOI: 10.1007/s11263-005-3222-z. 1, 21, 27, 29, 32

[93] W. Petryshyn. Direct and iterative methods for the solution of linear operator equations in Hilbert spaces. *Transactions of the American Mathematical Society*, 105:136–175, 1962. DOI: 10.2307/1993925. 83

[94] F. Porikli, O. Tuzel, and P. Meer. Covariance tracking using model update based on Lie algebra. In *Conference on Computer Vision and Pattern Recognition (CVPR)*, volume 1, pages 728–735, 2006. DOI: 10.1109/cvpr.2006.94. 1, 7, 13

[95] A. Qiu, A. Lee, M. Tan, and M. K. Chung. Manifold learning on brain functional networks in aging. *Medical Image Analysis*, 20(1):52–60, 2015. DOI: 10.1016/j.media.2014.10.006. 1

[96] A. Rahimi and B. Recht. Random features for large-scale Kernel machines. In *Advances in Neural Information Processing Systems*, 2007. 108, 109, 110, 112, 118, 119

[97] M. Reed and B. Simon. *Methods of Modern Mathematical Physics: Fourier analysis, Self-adjointness*. Academic Press, 1975. 118

[98] M. Reed and B. Simon. *Methods of Modern Mathematical Physics: Functional Analysis*. Academic Press, 1980. 77

[99] A. Rényi. On measures of entropy and information. In *Proc. of the 4th Berkeley Symposium on Mathematical Statistics and Probability, Volume 1: Contributions to the Theory of Statistics*, pages 547–561, University of California Press, Berkeley, CA, 1961. 49

[100] K. Sadatnejad and S. S. Ghidary. Kernel learning over the manifold of symmetric positive definite matrices for dimensionality reduction in a BCI application. *Neurocomputing*, 179:152–160, 2016. DOI: 10.1016/j.neucom.2015.11.065. 1

[101] A. Sanin, C. Sanderson, M. T. Harandi, and B. C. Lovell. Spatio-temporal covariance descriptors for action and gesture recognition. In *Applications of Computer Vision (WACV), Workshop on*, pages 103–110, IEEE, 2013. DOI: 10.1109/wacv.2013.6475006. 1, 10

[102] B. Schölkopf and A. Smola. *Learning with Kernels: Support Vector Machines, Regularization, Optimization, and Beyond*. The MIT Press, Cambridge, 2002. 55, 107

[103] B. Schölkopf, A. Smola, and K.-R. Müller. Nonlinear component analysis as a Kernel eigenvalue problem. *Neural Computing*, 10(5), July 1998. DOI: 10.1162/089976698300017467. 2, 55

[104] J. Shawe-Taylor and N. Cristianini. *Kernel Methods for Pattern Analysis*. Cambridge University Press, 2004. DOI: 10.1017/cbo9780511809682. 2, 55, 107

[105] C. L. Siegel. Symplectic geometry. *American Journal of Mathematics*, 65(1):1–86, 1943. DOI: 10.2307/2371774. 32

[106] B. Simon. Notes on infinite determinants of Hilbert space operators. *Advances in Mathematics*, 24:244–273, 1977. DOI: 10.1016/0001-8708(77)90057-3. 95

[107] B. Simon. *Trace Ideals and their Applications*. London Mathematical Society Lecture Note Series 35. Cambridge University Press, 1979. DOI: 10.1090/surv/120. 77

[108] R. Sivalingam, D. Boley, V. Morellas, and N. Papanikolopoulos. Tensor sparse coding for positive definite matrices. *IEEE Transactions on Pattern Analysis and Machine Intelligence*, 36(3):592–605, 2014. DOI: 10.1109/tpami.2013.143. 1, 64

[109] L. T. Skovgaard. A Riemannian geometry of the multivariate normal model. *Scandinavian Journal of Statistics*, pages 211–223, 1984. 37, 38

[110] S. Sra. A new metric on the manifold of Kernel matrices with application to matrix geometric means. In *Advances in Neural Information Processing Systems (NIPS)*, pages 144–152, 2012. 2, 45, 47, 59, 103

[111] S. Sra. Positive definite matrices and the S-divergence. *Proc. of the American Mathematical Society*, 144(7):2787–2797, 2016. DOI: 10.1090/proc/12953. 45, 47, 59, 103

[112] B. Sriperumbudur and Z. Szabó. Optimal rates for random Fourier features. In *NIPS*, pages 1144–1152, 2015. 119

[113] I. Steinwart and A. Christmann. *Support Vector Machines*. Springer Science & Business Media, 2008. 70

[114] D. J. Sutherland and J. Schneider. On the error of random Fourier features. In *UAI*, pages 862–871, 2015. 119

[115] H. Tabia and H. Laga. Covariance-based descriptors for efficient 3D shape matching, retrieval, and classification. *IEEE Transactions on Multimedia*, 17(9):1591–1603, 2015. DOI: 10.1109/tmm.2015.2457676. 1, 10

[116] H. Tabia, H. Laga, D. Picard, and P.-H. Gosselin. Covariance descriptors for 3D shape matching and retrieval. In *Proc. of the IEEE Conference on Computer Vision and Pattern Recognition*, pages 4185–4192, 2014. DOI: 10.1109/cvpr.2014.533. 1, 10, 13

[117] A. Terras. *Harmonic Analysis on Symmetric Spaces and Applications II*. Springer-Verlag, 1988. DOI: 10.1007/978-1-4612-3820-1. 32

[118] A. Tikhonov and V. Arsenin. *Solutions of Ill-posed Problems*. Winston, 1977. 51

[119] D. Tosato, M. Farenzena, M. Spera, V. Murino, and M. Cristani. Multi-class classification on Riemannian manifolds for video surveillance. *European Conference on Computer Vision (ECCV)*, pages 378–391, 2010. DOI: 10.1007/978-3-642-15552-9_28. 1

[120] D. Tosato, M. Spera, M. Cristani, and V. Murino. Characterizing humans on Riemannian manifolds. *IEEE Transactions on Pattern Analysis and Machine Intelligence*, 35(8):1972–1984, August 2013. DOI: 10.1109/tpami.2012.263. 1, 2, 33, 41, 60, 107

[121] A. Touloumis. Nonparametric Stein-type shrinkage covariance matrix estimators in high-dimensional settings. *Computational Statistics & Data Analysis*, 83:251–261, 2015. DOI: 10.1016/j.csda.2014.10.018. 15

[122] O. Tuzel, F. Porikli, and P. Meer. Region covariance: A fast descriptor for detection and classification. In *European Conference on Computer Vision (ECCV)*, pages 589–600, 2006. DOI: 10.1007/11744047_45. 1, 7, 13

[123] O. Tuzel, F. Porikli, and P. Meer. Pedestrian detection via classification on Riemannian manifolds. *IEEE Transactions on Pattern Analysis and Machine Intelligence*, 30(10):1713–1727, 2008. DOI: 10.1109/tpami.2008.75. 1, 13, 64

[124] A. Vedaldi and A. Zisserman. Efficient additive Kernels via explicit feature maps. *IEEE Transactions on Pattern Analysis and Machine Intelligence*, 34(3):480–492, 2012. DOI: 10.1109/tpami.2011.153. 108, 109, 121

[125] R. Vemulapalli, J. K. Pillai, and R. Chellappa. Kernel learning for extrinsic classification of manifold features. In *Proc. of the IEEE Conference on Computer Vision and Pattern Recognition (CVPR)*, pages 1782–1789, 2013. DOI: 10.1109/cvpr.2013.233. 1

[126] Q. Wang, P. Li, W. Zuo, and L. Zhang. RAID-G: Robust estimation of approximate infinite dimensional Gaussian with application to material recognition. In *CVPR*, pages 4433–4441, 2016. DOI: 10.1109/cvpr.2016.480. 1, 127

[127] R. Wang, H. Guo, L. S. Davis, and Q. Dai. Covariance discriminative learning: A natural and efficient approach to image set classification. In *IEEE Conference on Computer Vision and Pattern Recognition (CVPR)*, pages 2496–2503, 2012. DOI: 10.1109/cvpr.2012.6247965. 1, 60, 112

[128] Y. Wang, O. Camps, M. Sznaier, and B. R. Solvas. Jensen Bregman LogDet divergence optimal filtering in the manifold of positive definite matrices. In *Computer Vision (ECCV): 14th European Conference Proceedings, Part VII*, pages 221–235, Springer International Publishing, Cham, 2016. DOI: 10.1007/978-3-319-46478-7_14. 2

[129] Y. Wu, Y. Jia, P. Li, J. Zhang, and J. Yuan. Manifold Kernel sparse representation of symmetric positive-definite matrices and its applications. *IEEE Transactions on Image Processing*, 24(11):3729–3741, 2015. DOI: 10.1109/tip.2015.2451953. 64

[130] J. Yang, V. Sindhwani, H. Avron, and M. Mahoney. Quasi-Monte Carlo feature maps for shift-invariant Kernels. In *International Conference on Machine Learning (ICML)*, pages 485–493, 2014. 108, 109, 111, 112, 118, 120, 135

[131] K. Yu and M. Salzmann. Second-order convolutional neural networks. *arXiv preprint arXiv:1703.06817*, 2017. 1, 127

[132] J. Zhang. Divergence function, duality, and convex analysis. *Neural Computation*, 16(1):159–195, 2004. DOI: 10.1162/08997660460734047. 46

[133] X. Zhang, Y. Wang, M. Gou, M. Sznaier, and O. Camps. Efficient temporal sequence comparison and classification using Gram matrix embeddings on a Riemannian manifold. In *The IEEE Conference on Computer Vision and Pattern Recognition (CVPR)*, June 2016. DOI: 10.1109/cvpr.2016.487. 1

[134] W. Zheng, H. Tang, Z. Lin, and T. Huang. Emotion recognition from arbitrary view facial images. *European Conference on Computer Vision (ECCV)*, pages 490–503, 2010. DOI: 10.1007/978-3-642-15567-3_36. 1

[135] S. K. Zhou and R. Chellappa. From sample similarity to ensemble similarity: Probabilistic distance measures in reproducing kernel Hilbert space. *IEEE Transactions on Pattern Analysis and Machine Intelligence*, 28(6):917–929, 2006. DOI: 10.1109/tpami.2006.120. 2, 68, 74, 103

Authors' Biographies

HÀ QUANG MINH

Hà Quang Minh received his Ph.D. in mathematics from Brown University, Providence, RI, in May 2006, under the supervision of Steve Smale. He is currently a Researcher in the Department of Pattern Analysis and Computer Vision (PAVIS) with the Istituto Italiano di Tecnologia (IIT), Genova, Italy. Prior to joining IIT, he held research positions at the University of Chicago, the University of Vienna, Austria, and Humboldt University of Berlin, Germany. He was also a Junior Research Fellow at the Erwin Schrodinger International Institute for Mathematical Physics in Vienna and a Fellow at the Institute for Pure and Applied Mathematics (IPAM) at the University of California, Los Angeles (UCLA). His current research interests include applied and computational functional analysis, applied and computational differential geometry, machine learning, computer vision, and image and signal processing. His recent research contributions include the infinite-dimensional Log-Hilbert-Schmidt metric and Log-Determinant divergences between positive definite operators, along with their applications in machine learning and computer vision in the setting of kernel methods. He received the Microsoft Best Paper Award at the Conference on Uncertainty in Artificial Intelligence (UAI) in 2013 and the IBM Pat Goldberg Memorial Best Paper Award in Computer Science, Electrical Engineering, and Mathematics in 2013.

VITTORIO MURINO

Vittorio Murino is a full professor and head of the Pattern Analysis and Computer Vision (PAVIS) department at the Istituto Italiano di Tecnologia (IIT), Genoa, Italy. He received his Ph.D. in electronic engineering and computer science in 1993 at the University of Genoa, Italy. Then, he was first at the University of Udine and, since 1998, at the University of Verona where he was chairman of the Department of Computer Science from 2001 to 2007. Since 2009, he is leading the PAVIS department in IIT, which is involved in computer vision, pattern recognition and machine learning activities. His specific research interests are focused on statistical and probabilistic techniques for image and video processing, with application on (human) behavior analysis and related applications, such as video surveillance, biomedical imaging, and bioinformatics. Prof. Murino is co-author of more than 400 papers published in refereed journals and international conferences, member of the technical committees of important conferences (CVPR, ICCV, ECCV, ICPR, ICIP, etc.), and guest co-editor of special issues in relevant scientific journals. He is currently a member of the editorial board of *Computer Vision and Image Understanding*, *Pattern Analysis and Applications*, and *Machine Vision & Applications* journals. Finally, he is a Senior Member of the IEEE and Fellow of the IAPR.

Printed in the United States
by Baker & Taylor Publisher Services